Test Construction

Test Construction

A Bibliography of Selected Resources

Compiled by
Nancy Patricia O'Brien

Greenwood Press
New York • Westport, Connecticut • London

Library of Congress Cataloging-in-Publication Data

O'Brien, Nancy P.
  Test construction.

  Includes index.
  1. Examinations—Design and construction—
Bibliography. I. Title.
Z5814.E9018   1988   016.3712'61   87-25119
[LB3060.65]
ISBN 0-313-23435-3 (lib. bdg. : alk. paper)

British Library Cataloguing in Publication Data is available.

Library of Congress Catalog Card Number: 87-25119
ISBN: 0-313-23435-3

First published in 1988

Greenwood Press, Inc.
88 Post Road West, Westport, Connecticut 06881

Printed in the United States of America

The paper used in this book complies with the
Permanent Paper Standard issued by the National
Information Standards Organization (Z39.48-1984)

10 9 8 7 6 5 4 3 2 1

For Nicole Pamela O'Brien whose patience and understanding made it possible to undertake this project.

Contents

Acknowledgments

As with any work, acknowledgment must be made to those who provided assistance: Barton M. Clark for administrative support; Romy Borooah, Vera Luner, and Claudia Wheeler for assistance in filing, verifying, and editing entries; and special thanks and recognition to my ever-patient typist, Kay Bainter.

Introduction

This bibliography was compiled in order to supply information about test construction and design in one source and make it available to scholars, researchers, educators, and practitioners. Materials from the early 1900s through 1986 are included. While there is a vast body of literature about test construction, there are few bibliographies that deal specifically with the subject and those that are available are outdated. This bibliography duplicates only a few significant entries contained in those works. Of particular note is the fact that this work does not deal with questionnaires or surveys. It addresses the issue of test construction and design and the related area of item construction. While references in the subject index may be found on test bias, validity, and reliability, there was no attempt to include citations to works on those topics or any others unless related specifically to test construction. The great deal of information on test bias, test validity, and test reliability is more appropriately sought elsewhere--particularly in journal indexes. The topic of test construction is of sufficient magnitude to warrant a volume solely devoted to it.

PURPOSE

While this work does not claim to be exhaustive, it does include materials about test construction from a wide range of areas. It provides a listing of materials on how to construct tests, the rationale for test construction, and the pitfalls involved in test construction. Not only does this work include citations to works about general test construction and design, but it also includes information about the development, design, and construction of specific tests, such as the Minnesota Multiphasic Personality Inventory. Modifications such as short forms of specific tests have also been included as potentially helpful items. Consequently, a practitioner seeking a modified version of the Wechsler Adult Intelligence Scale (WAIS) could turn to the Subject Index to determine if a modified, revised, or adapted form has been included. Should the same practitioner prefer an intelligence test, not necessarily the WAIS, a perusal of the category for intelligence tests might be sufficient.

This bibliography can be used to find materials on developing categories of tests such as classroom tests, specific types of tests such as algebra tests, or to locate information on the construction of a specific test. This last aspect can be of immense value to an individual seeking information about the development and construction of a particular measure, whether to verify the usefulness for a specific testing situation or to use the construction techniques to develop a similar test. Information about implementation of a particular test or testing program only was included if it also related to the design and development of the test. This standard applies to other topics as well; they were included insofar as they relate to test construction. However works dealing solely with topics other than test construction were not included. And though the major contributions made by Mental Measurement Yearbook (MMY) in identifying and listing tests is acknowledged, this bibliography moves beyond MMY in providing a much needed listing of works that examine how and why tests are constructed. And while MMY provides a description and review of standardized tests, this bibliography provides information about the development of tests, whether standardized or not. This volume, therefore, can be used independently or to supplement MMY.

SCOPE

This bibliography contains 2,759 citations. And although because of the large number of citations, annotations were not provided, access to the literature of test construction is provided through entries in the Subject Index.

Included in this bibliography are citations for books, reports, journal articles, dissertations, and ERIC documents. ERIC (Educational Resources Information Center) is a federally funded source of "fugitive" literature as well as journal articles and commercially produced publications. Fugitive materials are items that are not easily accessible, such as conference proceedings, school district reports, papers, and some government publications. Most ERIC documents are available in microfiche format.

Entries for this bibliography were selected from published material, such as books, as well as from online database searches of Psychological Abstracts, Dissertation Abstracts International, and the ERIC system (Current Index to Journals in Education and Resources in Education). Social Science Citation Index, Science Citation Index and Sociological Abstracts were also searched online. Entries were also selected from the Education Index. Terms used in seeking information on the literature of test construction included tests, measures, inventories, and construction, design, and development. Specific terms for types of tests such as personality measures or achievement measures were also used when appropriate. Criteria used in the compilation of entries for this bibliography were lack of inclusion elsewhere, historical research value, and need for additional information on the subject.

ORGANIZATION

This work follows the scheme used in the early Mental Measurements Yearbooks. Tests have been classified following the subject scheme used in MMY. All entries are arranged in numerical sequence. The contents provides an easy-to-use listing of the subject headings and subdivisions used in this work. A general section on test construction precedes the topical sections on specific categories of tests.

In addition to those categories listed in the contents, an addendum was added and includes materials that were published from 1983 to 1986. The same categories used in the bibliography were used in the addendum, though not all categories were mentioned because of a lack of additionally published materials in that area. Consequently, a reader wishing to locate information about the construction of intelligence tests should browse through both the initial chapter on intelligence tests as well as the section on intelligence tests in the addendum. If recent materials only are desired, the addendum alone may be consulted. Within each category, entries are listed alphabetically by author.

INDEXES

Author and Subject Indexes have been provided to aid the reader. The Author Index is an alphabetical listing of authors in both the main section and addendum. The Subject Index provides topical access to the entries listed in the main section and addendum also. Subject terms were listed for each entry as appropriate. In many instances several subject terms were listed for a single entry. For example, item number 1979, "Development of an Instrument Measuring Attitudes Toward Reading in Primary Pupils," is listed in the chapter on reading tests. In addition to access under the chapter topic, this entry can also be located by consulting the Subject Index under the following terms: "Reading Attitudes" and the test title, "Primary Pupil Reading Attitude Inventory." The Subject Index is of major importance in locating information about a particular topic. When an entry deals with multiple subjects, such as vocational guidance for handicapped individuals, the entry is listed in the chapter for the predominant subject. Additional references are made in the Subject Index as warranted. Another major use of the Subject Index is to locate tests by titles, acronyms, or abbreviations. A large number of both commercially published and unpublished tests are listed by title in the Subject Index. Whenever known, the abbreviation or variant popular form of the test title are also listed. This increases the likelihood of locating a test through either its proper name or a well-known form, such as CTBS (Comprehensive Tests of Basic Skills).

ENTRIES

Each entry (or citation) in this bibliography contains the following elements: author (if available), title, publisher and place of publication (if a book), year of publication, and source (if a journal article or dissertation). Following are examples of citations and their elements.

2378.   (item number)
Remer, Rory and William Sease.   (authors)
"The Development of a Criterion Instrument for Counselor
   Selection."   (title)

<u>Measurement and Evaluation in Guidance</u>   (source)
7(3): 181-7 (1974).   (volume and year)

1447.   (item number)
Brook, Mona Stephanie.   (author)
"Competency Test Construction: Learning Disabilities
    Instructional Personnel."   (title)
Ed.D. diss., University of Kansas, 1976. (supplementary data)
<u>Dissertation Abstracts International</u>   (source)
37(8-A): 5030 (1976).   (volume and year)

785.   (item number)
Travers, R.M.W.   (author)
<u>How to Make Achievement Tests.</u>   (title)
(New York: (place of publication)
Odyssey Press,   (publisher)
1950).   (year)

    In addition, since many entries were culled from the ERIC
system, reference may be made to ERIC document numbers. ERIC
document numbers have a prefix of the letters ED followed by six
digits (e.g., ED 000 000). Most of these documents are available
in microfiche format. Locations of agencies and institutions can
be found in the <u>Directory of ERIC Information Service Providers</u>
(1). In some instances, an entry with an ERIC document number
may also be available in published paper format. In those cases,
the entry will list the ERIC document number as well as a
specific publisher other than ERIC. The following examples
provide information on both types of entries.

297.   (item number)
Haladyna, Thomas Michael   (author)
<u>Measuring Performance: Teacher-made Tests.</u>   (title)
ED 143 688   (ERIC document no.)
(Arlington, VA: (place of publication)
ERIC,   (publisher)
1977).   (year)

1840.   (item number)
Henerson, Marlene E. and others.   (authors)
<u>How to Measure Attitudes. Program Evaluation Kit, 5.</u>   (title)
ED 175 894   (ERIC document no.)
(Beverly Hills, CA: (place of publication)
Sage,   (publisher)
1978).   (year)

AVAILABILITY OF RESOURCES

    Entries in this bibliography can be located in libraries,
particularly college or university libraries. Journal articles,
government documents, books, and dissertations are available in
most major libraries. Libraries that do not have these materials
can usually obtain them through interlibrary loan procedures.
The <u>Directory of ERIC Information Service Providers</u> will
identify collections of ERIC documents on microfiche available
in different geographic locations. Further inquiries about
obtaining any of the entries listed in this bibliography can be
directed to the nearest library.

ADDITIONAL RESOURCES

Many different sources that discuss test construction were included in this bibliography, though resources that discuss survey and questionnaire design were intentionally excluded. Although rather outdated, the following sources may be of benefit to anyone seeking information about questionnaire or survey construction.

Berdie, Douglas R. and John F. Anderson. Questionnaires: Design and Use (Metuchen, NJ: Scarecrow, 1974).

Daniel, Wayne W. Questionnaire Design: A Selected Bibliography for the Survey Researcher. Public Administration Series: Bibliography, P-307. (Monticello, IL: Vance Bibliographies, 1979).

Oppenheim, A.N. Questionnaire Design and Attitude Measurement (New York: Basic Books, 1966).

Potter, Dale R., Kathryn M. Sharpe, John C. Hendee and Roger N. Clark. Questionnaires for Research: An Annotated Bibliography on Design, Construction and Use. USDA Forest Service Research Paper PNW-140. (Portland, OR: Pacific Northwest Forest and Range Experiment Station, 1972).

SUMMARY

Test construction is an extremely critical issue in our current society. An editorial appearing in Change: The Magazine of Higher Learning on the permanence of the assessment movement stated that "assessment has behind it a sponsorship and public policy logic that was never there" for other movements (2). There is an increasing pressure to assess, evaluate, and measure. In order to undertake any sort of assessment, a measure or test must first be constructed. The initial step in test construction is to determine the content of what is to be measured. Once this decision has been made, items (questions) must be developed for inclusion in the test. Items should be edited, verified, screened, and evaluated for content, bias, and correctness. Only items that meet the needs of the assessment should be included. Items should be tested and revisions made as necessary. Test construction can be a lengthy process as well as a frustrating one. Specialists should be involved in the test construction process, particularly when validity and reliability are considered (3). While an instructor may not feel that such extensive steps are necessary in developing a classroom test, the same principles apply to the development of a measure of mathematics achievement as to the construction of a battery of intelligence tests. Standards should be applied in both situations (4).

The entries in this bibliography will be of value to the instructor seeking a model for a simple classroom test or an actual test that may be reproduced; to the researcher seeking detailed information about the construction of a particular test; and to the novice seeking general information about test construction practices. Extensive entries in the Subject Index under "computer assisted tests" clearly indicate that not only traditional methods of test construction are listed, but also innovative practices utilizing new technologies.

   This bibliography will provide extensive information about test design and construction in a single volume. It should prove an invaluable tool to identify resources addressing the issue of construction of assessment tools.

NOTES

1. Directory of ERIC Information Service Providers. (Washington, D.C.: U.S. Government Printing Office, 1986).

2. Marchese, Ted. "Assessment: Fact or Fad?" Change: The Magazine of Higher Learning 19(1): 4 (1987).

3. Green, Bert F. "A Primer of Testing." American Psychologist 36(10): 1001-11 (1981).

4. Standards for Educational and Psychological Testing. (Washington, D.C.: American Psychological Association, 1985).

BIBLIOGRAPHY

Test Construction

1. Abeles, Harold F. "A Facet-factorial Approach to the Construction of Rating Scales to Measure Complex Behavior." Journal of Educational Measurement 10(2): 145-51 (1973).

2. Abramson, Theodore, and Steven Grass. Instructional Support System -- Occupational Education II. ISSOE Teacher Assessment Guidelines. ED 167 589 (Arlington, VA: ERIC, 1978).

3. Adkins, Arthur. "Testing: Alternative to Grading; Students Write and Score Tests." Educational Leadership 32(4): 271-3 (1975).

4. Ahmann, J.S. and M.D. Glock. Evaluating Student Progress, 6th ed. (Boston: Allyn and Bacon, 1981).

5. Aiken, Lewis R. "Writing Multiple-choice Items to Measure Higher-Order Educational Objectives." Educational and Psychological Measurement 42(3): 803-6 (Fall 1982).

6. Aikenhead, Glen S. "Course Evaluation: The Construction and Interpretation of Tests." Saskatchewan Journal of Educational Research and Development 4(1): 45-53 (1973).

7. _____. "Course Evaluation. I: A New Methodology for Test Construction." Journal of Research in Science Teaching 11(1): 17-22 (1974).

8. _____. "Course Evaluation. II: Interpretation of Student Performance on Evaluative Tests." Journal of Research in Science Teaching 11(1): 23-30 (1974).

9. _____. The Measurement of Knowledge About Science and Scientists: An Investigation Into the Development of Instruments for Formative Evaluation. ED 068 307 (Ann Arbor, MI: University Microfilms, 1972).

10. _____. A New Methodology for Test Construction in Course Evaluation. Paper presented at the annual meeting of the National Association for Research in Science

Teaching, 1973. ED 080 312 (Arlington, VA: ERIC, 1973).

11.   Albrecht, James E. and Duwayne Carnes. "Guidelines for
       Developing, Administering the Essay Test." NASSP Bulletin
       66(457): 47-53 (1982).

12.   Aleamoni, Lawrence M. "Development and Factorial
       Validation of the Arizona Course/Instructor Evaluation
       Questionnaire." Educational and Psychological Measurement
       38(4): 1063-67 (1978).

13.   Aleamoni, Lawrence M. and R.E. Spencer. "Illinois Course
       Evaluation Questionnaire: A Description of Its
       Development and a Report of Some of Its Results."
       Educational and Psychological Measurement 33: 669-84
       (Autumn 1973).

14.   Allen, Dwight W. and others. An Introduction to
       Longitudinal Testing Using Item Sampling Techniques:
       Comprehensive Achievement Monitoring. From "Designing
       Instructional Systems with Longitudinal Testing Using
       Item Sampling Techniques." Annual meeting of the American
       Educational Research Association, 1970. ED 041 934
       (Arlington, VA: ERIC, 1970).

15.   Allen, Dwight W. and William P. Gorth. The Development of
       Randomized Achievement Monitoring. Third Annual Report,
       Charles F. Kettering Foundation. ED 042 795 (Arlington,
       VA: ERIC, 1969).

16.   Allison, Howard K. Rating Scale Format As It Affects
       Ratings in Student Teaching. Paper presented at the
       annual meeting of the American Educational Research
       Association, 1978. ED 152 857 (Arlington, VA: ERIC,
       1978).

17.   Alvir, Howard P. (The Evolution of a Program Evaluation
       Form: With Samples of: Criteria, Procedures, Examples. A
       Step-by-step Approach Designed for Replication). ED 154
       030 (Arlington, VA: ERIC, 1978).

18.   _____. The Evolution of an Evaluation Form. ED 120 222
       (Arlington, VA: ERIC, 1976).

19.   _____. Nine Performance Procedure Competencies with Which
       to Analyze, Organize, and Develop Hands-on
       Performance Evaluation. ED 117 171 (Arlington, VA: ERIC,
       1974).

20.   Amend, J. R. "Alternate Approach to Multiple Choice
       Examinations." Journal of College Science Teaching 7(2):
       104 (November 1977).

21.   American Psychological Association Committee. "Technical
       Recommendations for Psychological Test and Diagnostic
       Techniques." Psychological Bulletin Supplement 51(2),
       Part 2: 1-38 (1954).

22.   Anastasi, Anne. "Focus on Test Construction."
       Contemporary Psychology: A Journal of Reviews 16(11):
       694-5. (1971).

23. Anastasio, Ernest J. and others. Computer-assisted Item Writing-II. (Sentence Completion Items). Paper presented at the National Council on Measurement in Education, 1969. ED 032 776 (Arlington, VA: ERIC, 1969).

24. Anderson, Norman H. "Functional Measurement of Social Desirability." Sociometry 36(1): 89-98 (1973).

25. Anderson, Scarvia B. "Take this Crash Course on Test Design." American School Board Journal 168(7): 28-30 (1981).

26. Andrich, David. "Relationships Between the Thurstone and Rasch Approaches to Item Scaling." Applied Psychological Measurement 2(3): 451-62 (1978).

27. _____. "Scaling Attitude Items Constructed and Scored in the Likert Tradition." Educational and Psychological Measurement 38(3): 665-80 (1978).

28. Ansfield, Paul J. "A User Oriented Computing Procedure for Compiling and Generating Examinations." Educational Technology 13(3): 12-13 (1973).

29. Archambault, Francis X. Jr. and others. The Classroom Activities Log: A Personalized Record of a Child's School Day as Recorded by His/Her Teacher. Paper presented at annual meeting of the National Council on Measurement in Education, 1979. ED 178 609 (Arlington, VA: ERIC, 1979).

30. Armstrong, David G. Behavioral Objectives, Major Concepts, a Topic Organization Matrix, and a Developmental Version of a 50-item Test for a Secondary School Course in Free Enterprise. ED 144 993 (Arlington, VA: ERIC, 1977).

31. Arndt, Stephan. New Developments in the Analysis and Measurement of Change. ED 219 411 (Arlington, VA: ERIC, 1981).

32. Arter, J.A. and L. Clinton. "Time and Error Consequences of Irrelevant Data and Question Placement in Arithmetic Word Problems II: Fourth Graders." Journal of Educational Research 68: 28-31 (1974).

33. Atkinson, Bill. "Shell Games." Journal of Learning Disabilities 15(6): 373 (1982).

34. Atkinson, George F. and Edward Doadt. "Matrexam: A New Form of Computer Graded Examination." Assessment in Higher Education 5(2): 112-21 (1980).

35. Atwood, Beth S. Assessing Communication Skills with Non-threatening Tools. A Connecticut ABE Staff Development Project Resource Unit. ED 226 348 (Arlington, VA: ERIC, 1977).

36. Ault, Leslie H. Multiple-choice Versus Created-response Test Items. ED 091 426 (Arlington, VA: ERIC, 1972).

37. Australian Item Bank Program: Handbook for Science Item

Bank. ED 161 912. Available from Australian Council for Educational Research, P. O. Box 210, Hawthorne, Victoria, Australia. (1976).

38.   Australian Item Bank Program: Handbook for Social Science Item Bank. ED 161 908. Available from Australian Council for Educational Research, P. O. Box 210, Hawthorne, Victoria, Australia. (1978).

39.   Australian Item Bank Program: Mathematics Item Bank. Book 1: Arthmetic, Algebra. ED 161 904. Available from Australian Council for Educational Research, P. O. Box 210, Hawthorne, Victoria, Australia. (1978).

40.   Australian Item Bank Program: Mathematics Item Bank. Book 2: Abstract Algebra, Relations and Functions, Analysis, Geometry, Trigonometry, Applied Mathematics, Statistics and Probability. ED 161 905. Available from Australian Council for Educational Research, P. O. Box 210, Hawthorne, Victoria, Australia. (1978).

41.   Australian Item Bank Program: Social Science Item Bank. ED 161 907. Available from Australian Council for Educational Research, P. O. Box 210, Hawthorne, Victoria, Australia. (1978).

42.   Ayre, Elizabeth L. Amendment to Quality Control Project for Intensive Development for the Evaluation Components of Computer Based Resource Units. ED 073 685 (Arlington, VA: ERIC, 1972).

43.   Backman, Margaret E. The Effectiveness of Relevant Item Content in Reducing Test Bias. Paper presented at the annual conference of the National Rehabilitation Association, 1974. ED 152 833 (Arlington, VA: ERIC, 1974).

44.   Bailey, Gerald D. "The Use of Criterion-referenced Items in Student-feedback Instruments." Educational Technology 20(3): 56-58 (1980).

45.   Baillargeon, Jarvis H. "Chopping Through the Testing Jungle." School Shop 36(7): 44-45 (1977).

46.   Baker, Eva L. "Beyond Objectives: Domain-referenced Tests for Evaluation and Instructional Improvement." Educational Technology 14(6): 10-16 (1974).

47.   _____. "Cooperation and the State of the World in Criterion-referenced Tests." Educational Horizons 52(4): 193-96 (1974).

48.   _____. "The Effects of Manipulated Item Writing Constraints on the Homogeneity of Test Items." Journal of Educational Measurement 8(4): 305-309 (1971).

49.   _____. The Effects of Manipulated Item Writing Constraints on the Homogeneity of Test Items. Center for the Study of Evaluation Reprint Series No. 11. Paper presented at the National Council for Measurement in Education Conference, 1970. ED 036 870 (Arlington VA:

ERIC, 1970).

50.   _____. Regional Conferences on Testing and Instruction.
       Final Report. ED 223 721 (Arlington, VA: ERIC, 1980).

51.   _____. Using Measurement to Improve Instruction. Paper
       presented at the annual meeting of the American
       Psychological Association, 1972. ED 069 762 (Arlington,
       VA: ERIC, 1972).

52.   Baker, Eva L. and Linda Polin. Ongoing Studies in
       Domain-referenced Content Validity: First Look at the
       "Judgment" Issue. ED 212 656 (Arlington, VA: ERIC, 1978).

53.   Baker, Eva L. and W. James Popham. Expanding Dimensions
       of Instructional Objectives. ED 076 037 (Englewood
       Cliffs, NJ: Prentice-Hall, 1973).

54.   Baker, Frank B. "An Interactive Approach to Test
       Construction." Educational Technology 13(3): 13-15
       (1973).

55.   Baldauf, Richard B. Jr. Evaluation Models and
       Instrumentation: Problems for Title I in America's
       Pacific Possessions. Paper presented at the Trust
       Territory Title I Conference, 1978. ED 156 691
       (Arlington, VA: ERIC, 1978).

56.   Baldauf, Richard B. Jr. and Peter Dunn-Rankin. A Progress
       Report on a Plan for Curriculum Assessment in American
       Samoa. ED 074 200 (Arlington, VA: ERIC, 1972).

57.   Bannatyne, A. "Establishment of a National Research
       Institute for the Construction and Standardization of
       Tests." Journal of Learning Disabilities 2: 659-60
       (1969).

58.   Barcikowski, Robert S. "A Monte Carlo Study of Item
       Sampling (Versus Traditional Sampling) for Norm
       Construction." Journal of Educational Measurement 9(3):
       209-14 (1972).

59.   Barcikowski, Robert S. and Henry Olsen. "Test Item
       Arrangement and Adaptation Level." Journal of Psychology
       90: 87-93 (1975).

60.   Barcikowski, Robert S. and Jerry L. Patterson. "A
       Computer Program for Randomly Selecting Test Items From
       an Item Population." Educational and Psychological
       Measurement 32(3): 795-8 (1972).

61.   Bargmann, Rolf E. Representative Ordering and Selection
       of Variables, Volumes A and B -- Statistical Models for
       the Evaluation and Interpretation of Educational
       Criteria, Part 3. ED 003 044 (Arlington, VA: ERIC, 1962).

62.   Barickman, Joan Estes. "Evaluation Procedures: False and
       True." English Journal 67(7): 24-29 (1978).

63.   Baril, G. L. and C. Thomas Skaggs. "Selecting Items for a
       College Course Evaluation Form." College Student Journal

10(2): 183-87 (1976).

64. Barker, Douglas and Robert L. Ebel. "A Comparison of Difficulty and Discrimination Values of Selected True-false Item Types." Contemporary Educational Psychology 7(1): 35-40 (1982).

65. Barnett, Samuel B. Inner City Schools in Crisis -- Can We Meet the Challenge? or Do We Want to Meet the Challenge. Paper presented at Conference of Black Educators, 1977. ED 185 175 (Arlington, VA: ERIC, 1977).

66. Bart, William M. "Test Validity and Reliability from an Ordering-theoretic Framework." Educational Technology 14(1): 62-63 (1974).

67. Bean, Kenneth L. Construction of Educational and Personnel Tests. (New York: McGraw-Hill, 1953).

68. Beatty, Brondon and Herbert W. Marsh. Students' Evaluations of Instructional Effectiveness: Research and a Survey Instrument. ED 141 413 (Arlington, VA: ERIC, 1977).

69. Bedard, R. "Partly Tailored Examinations." Alberta Journal of Educational Research 20(1): 15-23 (1974).

70. Behr, M. J. and P. M. Eastman. "Development and Validation of Two Cognitive Preference Scales" Journal of Experimental Education 46: 28-34 (Spring 1978).

71. Bell, John A. "Stability of the Factor Structure of a Short Form of the Minnesota Teacher Attitude Inventory." Psychology in the Schools 14(2): 169-71 (1977).

72. Belson, William A. "Research into Question Design." Business Review 7: 14-19 (1964).

73. Belson, William A. and Judith A. Duncan. "A Comparison of the Check-list and the Open Response Questioning Systems." Applied Statistics 11: 120-32 (1962).

74. Benbasat Izak, and others. "A Database System for Course Administration." Computers and Education 6(4): 333-39 (1982).

75. Benson, Jeri. A Comparion of the One-and Three-parameter Logistic Models on Measures of Test Efficiency. Paper presented at the annual meeting of the National Council on Measurement in Education, 1979. ED 178 556 (Arlington, VA: ERIC, 1979).

76. _____. "A Redefinition of Content Validity." Educational and Psychological Measurement 41(3): 793-802 (1981).

77. Benson, Jeri and Linda Crocker. "The Effects of Item Format and Reading Ability on Objective Test Performance: A Question of Validity." Educational and Psychological Measurement 39(2): 381-87 (1979).

78. Benson, Jeri and others. A Comparison of Three Types of

Item Analysis in Test Development Using Classical and Latent Trait Methods. Paper presented at the annual meeting of the National Council on Measurement in Education, 1978. ED 163 039 (Arlington, VA: ERIC, 1978).

79.   Bentler, P. M. and Arthur J. Woodward. "Inequalities Among Lower Bounds to Reliability -- with Applications to Test-construction and Factor-analysis." Psychometrika 45(2): 249-67 (1980).

80.   Benton, Sidney E. "Instruments for Students' Assessment." CEDR Quarterly 12(4): 13-15, 22 (1979).

81.   Berdie, Frances S. "What Test Questions are Likely to Offend the General Public." Journal of Educational Measurement 8(2): 87-93 (1971).

82.   Berger, Philip K. and James E. Sullivan. "Instructional Set, Interview Context, and the Incidence of 'Don't Know' Responses." Journal of Applied Psychology 54(5): 414-16 (1970).

83.   Berk, Ronald A. "Comparison of Six Content Domain Specification Strategies for Criterion-referenced Tests." Educational Technology 20: 49-52 (1980).

84.   _____. "Construction of Rating Instruments for Faculty Evaluation; a Review of Methodological Issues." Journal of Higher Education 50: 650-69 (1979).

85.   _____. A Consumers' Guide to Criterion-referenced Test Item Statistics. Paper presented at the annual meeting of the National Council on Measurement in Education, 1978. ED 159 214 (Arlington, VA: ERIC, 1978).

86.   _____. Criterion-referenced Measurement: The State of the Art. John Hopkins University National Symposium on Educational Research, 1st, 1978. (Baltimore: John Hopkins University Press, 1980).

87.   _____. A Critical Review of Content Domain Specification/Item Generation Strategies for Criterion-referenced Tests. Paper presented at the annual meeting of the Educational Research Association, 1979. ED 170 382 (Arlington, VA: ERIC, 1979).

88.   _____. Domain-referenced Versus Mastery Conceptualization of Criterion-referenced Measurement: A Clarification. Paper presented at the annual meeting of the National Council on Measurement in Education, 1980. ED 189 114 Arlington, VA: ERIC, 1980).

89.   _____. Guide to Criterion-referenced Test Construction. (Baltimore, MD: John Hopkins University Press, 1984).

90.   _____. "Practical Guidelines for Determining the Length of Objectives-based, Criterion-referenced Tests." Educational Technology 20(11): 36-41 (1980).

91.   _____. Some Guidelines for Determining the Length of Objectives-based Criterion-referenced Tests. Paper

presented at the annual meeting of the National Council on Measurement in Education, 1979. ED 170 381 (Arlington, VA: ERIC, 1979).

92. Bernal, Ernest M. Jr. Adapting Assessment Procedures to Specific Population Characteristics: The Chicano Child. Paper presented at the annual convention of the American Psychological Association, 1977. ED 145 943 (Arlington, VA: ERIC, 1977).

93. Bernknopf, Stanley and W. L. Bashaw. An Investigation of Criterion-referenced Tests Under Different Conditions of Sample Variability and Item Homogeneity. Paper presented at the annual meeting of the American Educational Research Association, 1976. ED 120 205 (Arlington, VA: ERIC, 1976).

94. Berry, Gene A. and others. "The Effects of Audio-visual Test Presentation." College Student Journal 7(2): 76-78 (1973).

95. Besel, Ronald. Using Group Performance to Interpret Individual Responses to Criterion-referenced Tests. Professional Paper 25. ED 129 910 (Arlington, VA: ERIC, 1973).

96. Bethune, Paul P. "A Comparison of the Ability to Read a Standardized Science Test and a Revised Standardized Science Test with the Test Results as Interpreted Through Practice in the Schools." Ed.D. diss., University of Southern Mississippi, 1972. (Available from University Microfilms, Ann Arbor, MI).

97. Betz, Nancy E. and David J. Weiss. Empirical and Simulation Studies of Flexilevel Ability Testing. Research Report No. 75-3. ED 111 861 (Arlington,VA: ERIC, 1975).

98. _____. Simulation Studies of Two-stage Ability Testing. Research Report 74-4. ED 103 466 (Arlington, VA: ERIC, 1974).

99. Biggers, Julian L. "An A Priori Approach for Developing Short-forms of Tests and Inventories." Journal of Experimental Education 44(3): 8-10 (1976).

100. Biggs, John and Pran Chopra. "Pupil Evaluation of Teachers." Australian Journal of Education 23(1): 45-57 (1979).

101. Blair, Ed, Seymour Sudman, Norman M. Bradburn, and Carol Stocking. "How to Ask Questions About Drinking and Sex: Response Effects in Measuring Consumer Behavior." Journal of Marketing Research 14: 316-21 (1977).

102. Blaney, Paul H. and Charles L. Cox. "The Activity Preference Questionnaire: Is the Forced Choice Format Necessary." Journal of Personality Assessment 39(6): 630-3 (1975).

103. Blankenship, Albert B. "The Choice of Words in Poll

Questions." <u>Sociology and Social Research</u> 25: 12-18 (1940).

104. Bloom, Benjamin S. and others. <u>Handbook on Formative and Summative Evaluation of Student Learning</u>. ED 049 304 (New York: McGraw-Hill, 1971).

105. Blumberg, P. and others. "Should Taxonomic Levels be Considered in Developing Examinations?" <u>Educational and Psychological Measurement</u> 42: 1-7 (1982).

106. Blumberg, Phyllis. "A Practical Methodology for Developing Content Parallel Multiple Choice Tests." <u>Journal of Experimental Education</u> 50(2): 56-63 (1981-82).

107. Blumberg, Phyllis and Joel Felner. <u>A Practical Methodology for the Systematic Development of Multiple Choice Tests</u>. ED 189 198 (Arlington, VA: ERIC, 1980).

108. Blunt, A. "Subjective Estimation of Adult Learning: The Development of a Magnitude Estimation Scale." <u>Adult Education</u> 28: 38-52 (1977).

109. Board, Cynthia and Douglas R. Whitney. "The Effects of Selected Poor Item-writing Practices on Test Difficulty, Reliability and Validity." <u>Journal of Educational Measurement</u> 9(3): 225-33 (1972).

110. Bolden, Bernadine J. and Ann Stoddard. <u>The Effects of Language on Test Performance of Elementary School Children</u>. Paper presented at the annual meeting of the American Educational Research Association, 1980. ED 190 618 (Arlington, VA: ERIC, 1980).

111. Bollenbacher, Joan. "Standards for Educational & Psychological Tests." <u>Journal of Educational Measurement</u> 12(1): 55-6 (1975).

112. Bormuth, John. <u>Comments on Professor Alkin's paper entitled "Evaluating the Cost-effectiveness of Instructional Programs."</u> From the Proceedings of the Symposium on Problems in the Evaluation of Instruction, 1969. ED 031 777 (Arlington, VA: ERIC, 1969).

113. Bormuth, John R. <u>The Implications and Use of Cloze Procedure in the Evaluation of Instructional Programs</u>. ED 012 674 (Arlington, VA: ERIC, 1967).

114. Botterbusch, Karl F. <u>The Use of Psychological Tests With Individuals Who Are Severely Disabled</u>. ED 186 755 (Arlington, VA: ERIC, 1976).

115. Bowman, C. M. "Writing Thought-provoking Test Questions." <u>Social Studies</u> 67: 214-17 (1976).

116. Boyce, Max William. <u>Some Difficulties in Using Cloze Procedures to Assess Readability</u>. ED 110 921 (Arlington, VA: ERIC, 1974).

117. Boyd, Joseph L. Jr. <u>The Effect of Format Change on Test Item Difficulty</u>. ED 118 620 (Arlington, VA: ERIC, 1974).

118.   _____. *Word Processing for Item Banking and Test Production. Final Report*. ED 224 815 (Arlington, VA: ERIC, 1982).

119.   Boyd, Joseph L. Jr. and Benjamin Shimberg. *Developing Performance Tests for Classroom Evaluation*. ED 052 259 (Arlington, VA: ERIC, 1971).

120.   _____. *Handbook of Performance Testing: A Practical Guide for Test Makers*. ED 052 220 (Princeton, NJ: Educational Testing Service, 1971).

121.   Boyd, Rachel M. "Influence of Test Form on Assessment." *Australian Journal of Education* 15(2): 161-70 (1971).

122.   Boyd, Vivian S. "Neutralizing Sexist Titles in Holland's Self-directed Search: What Difference Does it Make." *Journal of Vocational Behavior* 9(2): 191-98 (1976).

123.   Boynton, Thomas J. *Construction of Survey Instruments*. ED 154 844 (Arlington, VA: ERIC, 1978).

124.   Bradley, Robert H. and Bettye M. Caldwell. "Home Observation for Measurement of the Environment: A Revision of the Preschool Scale." *American Journal of Mental Deficiency* 84(3): 235-44 (1979).

125.   Bramble, William J. and David E. Wiley. *Implications of a Class of Covariance Structure Models for the Development of Measuring Instruments*. ED 046 969 (Arlington, VA: ERIC, 1970).

126.   Braun, John R. "Forced-choice Self-report Devices: A Look at Some Unwarranted Claims." *Measurement Evaluation Guidance* 2(3): 153-55 (1969).

127.   Brennan, Robert L. *The Evaluation of Mastery Test Items. Final Report*. ED 092 593 (Arlington, VA: ERIC, 1974).

128.   _____. *Some Applications of Generalizability Theory to the Dependability of Domain-referenced Tests. ACT Technical Bulletin No. 32*. Paper presented at the annual meeting of the National Council on Measurement in Education, 1979. ED 167 577 (Arlington, VA: ERIC, 1979).

129.   Brickell, Henry M. "Needed: Instruments as Good as our Eyes." *Journal of Career Education* 2(3): 55-66. (1976).

130.   Bridgeford, Nancy J. *A Directory of Writing Assessment Consultants*. ED 209 325 (Arlington, VA: ERIC, 1981).

131.   Bridgeman, Brent. *A Duplicate Construction Experiment*. ED 091 400 (Arlington, VA: ERIC, 1974).

132.   Bridges, Claude F. *A New Approach to Developing Test Scales*. ED 223 689 (Arlington, VA: ERIC, 1981).

133.   Briggs, Leslie J. *Handbook of Procedures for the Design of Instruction*. ED 043 230 (Pittsburgh, PA: American Institute for Research, 1970).

134. Brown, Alan S. and Jerry M. Itzig. The Interaction of
      Humor and Anxiety in Academic Test Situations. ED 152 783
      (Arlington, VA: ERIC, 1976).

135. Brown, R. A. "Developing Classroom Tests." Agriculture
      Education 55: 16-17 (December 1982).

136. Brown, S. R. "Forced-free Distinction in Q Technique."
      Journal of Educational Management 8: 283-7 (1971).

137. Brown, Willard A. "A Computer Examination Compositor for
      the IBM 360/40." Educational Technology 13(3): 15-16
      (1973).

138. Broyles, David. Computer Techniques for Weekly Multiple-
      choice Testing. ED 014 288 (Arlington, VA: ERIC, 1966).

139. Bruell, Jan H. FIT: A New Computer-scorable Test. ED 116
      604 (Arlington, VA: ERIC, 1976).

140. Brzezinski, Evelyn and Randy Demaline. An Empirical
      Investigation of the Result of Two Different Test
      Development Strategies. Final Report for the Period March
      15, 1981-December 31, 1981. ED 217 079 (Arlington, VA:
      ERIC, 1982).

141. Buckley-Sharp, M.D. "A Multiple Choice Question Banking
      System." Educational Technology 13(3): 16-18 (1973).

142. Burdon, Barry E. and G. R. Teasdale. Construction of an
      Infant and Preschool Developmental Record. Final Report.
      ED 162 763 (Arlington, VA: ERIC, 1979).

143. Burry, James, ed. and Edys S. Quellmalz, ed. "Issues in
      Measurement and Methdology: CSE's 1978 Conference." ED
      179 585. Evaluation Comment 5(4) (1978).

144. Burtt, Harold E. and Harold V. Gaskill. "Suggestibility
      and the Form of the Question." Journal of Applied
      Psychology 16: 358-373 (1932).

145. Busch, W. M. "Look! Instructors. Let's Improve Our
      Standards to Meaningful Objective Measurement." Physical
      Education 31: 129-30 (1974).

146. Byars, Alvin Gregg. Practical Procedures for Constructing
      Mastery Tests to Minimize Errors of Classification and to
      Maximize or Optimize Decision Reliability. Paper
      presented at the annual meeting, National Council on
      Measurement in Education, 1980. ED 189 191 (Arlington,
      VA: ERIC, 1980).

147. Byrd, Manford Jr. Testing Under Fire: Chicago's Problem.
      Paper presented at the Conference of the Educational
      Records Bureau, 1970. ED 047 013 (Arlington, VA: ERIC,
      1970).

148. Byrne, Colin J. "Computerized Question Banking Systems:
      I--The State of the Art." British Journal of Educational
      Technology 7(2): 44-64 (1976).

149. Calder, J. R. "Programmed Learning--Inspires New Attitude to Testing Attainment." Visual Education 36-38 (1970).

150. Calhoun, W. Ford and Robert B. Frary. "Computer-supported Individualized Testing within Reach." Educational Technology 18(1): 45-8 (1978).

151. Calhoun, William Ford. Individualized Testing System. Report to Special Academic Programs. Improvement of Multiple Choice Testing. ED 131 100 (Arlington, VA: ERIC, 1976).

152. Callely, A. G. and D. E. Hughes. "Analytical Questions in Exams." Journal of Biological Education 6(5): 311-14 (1972).

153. Cameron, Bernard J. and others. Operational Evaluation from the Standpoint of the Program Manager. ED 069 747 (Arlington, VA: ERIC, 1971).

154. Campbell, Donald T. and Phillip J. Mohr. "The Effect of Ordinal Position Upon Responses to Items in a Checklist." Journal of Applied Psychology 34: 62-67 (1950).

155. Candor, Catherine. Writing Classroom Tests. ED 138 590 (Arlington, VA: ERIC, 1977).

156. Cappon, Daniel and Robin Banks. "The Birth of a Test: The Sensory Quotient." Perceptual and Motor Skills 31(2): 408-10 (1970).

157. Carter, Jamie E. "A Computerized Adaptive Version of the MMPI Based on the Rasch Model." Dissertation Abstracts International 43(4-B): 1248 (1982).

158. Carter, Robert C. and Harvey E. Sbisa. Human Performance Tests for Repeated Measurements: Alternate Forms of Eight Tests by Computer. Report NBDL-82R003 (New Orleans, LA: US Naval Biodynamics Laboratory, 1982).

159. Cason, Gerald J. Guidelines for Objective Testing of Students. ED 200 628 (Arlington, VA: ERIC, 1978).

160. Cassie, J. R. Bruce. "The Challenge to Testing." School Guidance Worker 32(4): 20-24 (1977).

161. Castleman, John Lavoid. "The Effect of an In-service Program Utilizing Bloom's 'Taxonomy' on Teachers' Self-concepts, Cognitive Level of Test Construction, and Attitudes of Students." Ed.D diss., North Texas State University, 1972. Dissertation Abstracts International 33(3-A): 1054 (1972).

162. Cattell, Raymond B. "How Good is the Modern Questionnaire? General Principles for Evaluation." Journal of Personality Assessment 38(2): 115-20 (1974).

163. Catts, Ralph. Q. How Many Options Should a Multiple-choice Question Have? (A) 2. (B) 3. (C) 4. At-a-glance Research Report. ED 173 354 (Arlington, VA: ERIC, 1978).

164.   Celce-Murcia, M. and others. "Goal: Good Multiple-choice Language-test Items." English Language Teaching Journal 28(3): 257-62 (1974).

165.   Cervantes, Robert. "Problems and Alternatives in Testing Mexican-American Students." Integrated Education 12(3): 33-37 (1974).

166.   Chen, Hui-chuan and others. "A Computer-based Examination System." Educational Research and Methods 9(2): 44-46 (1977).

167.   Christensen, P. R. "Computer-assisted Test-construction for Individualized-instruction." Educational Technology 19(3) 45-49 (1979).

168.   Church, Austin T. and David J. Weiss. Interactive Computer Administration of a Spatial Reasoning Test. Research Report 80-2. ED 191 892 (Arlington, VA: ERIC, 1980.)

169.   Cicciarella, Charles. "Test Writer." Classroom Computer News 2(4): 36-37 (1982).

170.   Clark, Cynthia L., ed. Proceedings of the First Conference on Computerized Adaptive Testing (Washington, D.C. June 12-13, 1975). ED 126 110 (Arlington, VA: ERIC, 1976).

171.   Cleary, T. A. and Robert L. Linn. Effect of Error of Measurement on the Power of Statistical Tests. Final Report. ED 017 006 (Arlington, VA: ERIC, 1967).

172.   Clopton, James R. and Charles Neuringer. "Fortran Computer Programs for the Development of New MMPI Scales." Educational and Psychological Measurement 37(3): 783-6 (1977).

173.   Cluff, Robert B. and Charles W. Smith. Humanizing the Testing Aspect of Evaluation. ED 076 498 (Arlington, VA: ERIC, 1973).

174.   Cohen, Eli. "Notes on the Reliability of Alternate Forms Constructed From a Table of Specifications." Journal of Experimental Education 46(1): 56-8 (1977).

175.   Cohen, Monroe D., ed. Testing and Evaluation: New Views. ED 109 143 (Arlington, VA: ERIC, 1975).

176.   Cohen, Perrin S. and Leila R. Cohen. "Computer Generated Tests for a Student Paced Course." Educational Technology 13(3): 18-19 (1973).

177.   Collins, Eugene A. and Dean C. Larsen. Computer Support for a Systems Approach to Instruction: Problem Statement and Data Entry Techniques. Paper presented at the annual conference of the Association for Educational Data Systems, 1976. ED 122 847 (Arlington, VA: ERIC, 1976).

178.   _____. "Computer Support for a Systems Approach to Instruction: Problem Statement, Data Entry, and Group

Formation." <u>Journal of Educational Technology Systems</u>
5(1): 3-14 (1977).

179. Collins, R. W. and S. J. Duff. "Automatic Program
Generation (APG) - Using Computer to Write Programs for
Computer-assisted Test-construction (CATC)." <u>Abstracts of
Papers of the American Chemical Society</u> 176: 23 (1978).

180. _____. "Computer-assisted Test-construction Via PROBGEN-
II--Using the Computer to Write Programs Automatically."
<u>Abstracts of Papers of the American Chemical Society</u> 177:
17 (1979).

181. <u>Computer Assisted Assembly of Tests at Educational
Testing Service</u>. Paper presented at the Computer Assisted
Test Construction Conference, 1974. ED 110 503
(Arlington, VA: ERIC, 1974).

182. "Computer Assisted Test Construction; Symposium."
<u>Educational Technology</u> 13: 9-44 (March 1973).

183. <u>Computer Program Pedage--SLEXTF-M2-F4</u>. ED 077 980
(Arlington, VA: ERIC, 1966).

184. Cone, Richard. <u>Educational Implications of Criterion-
referenced Tests</u>. Paper presented at the annual meeting
of the American Educational Research Association, 1976.
ED 121 852 (Arlington, VA: ERIC, 1976).

185. Connes, Bernard. "Course-component Evaluation II. A
Dynamic Computer System for Item Banking." <u>Journal of
Structural Learning</u> 4(1): 33-40 (1973).

186. Cook, Linda L. and Ronald K. Hambleton. <u>Application of
Latent Trait Models to the Development of Norm-referenced
and Criterion-referenced Tests</u>. Paper presented at the
annual meeting of the National Council on Measurement in
Education, 1978. ED 163 018 (Arlington, VA: ERIC, 1978).

187. Cooper, Mildred P., ed. <u>Special Report on Criterion-
referenced Test Development, Mid-Atlantic Region
Interstate Project 1972-73</u>. ED 078 046 (Arlington, VA:
ERIC, 1973).

188. Costin, Frank. "Difficulty and Homogeneity of Three-
choice Versus Four-choice Objective Test Items When
Matched for Content of Stem." <u>Teaching of Psychology</u>
3(3): 144-5 (1976).

189. Cowan, John and David Haldane. "Why Don't We Have More
Audio-visual Content in Examinations." <u>Programmed
Learning and Educational Technology</u> 13(2): 65-8 (1976).

190. Cox, Richard C. <u>Evaluative Aspects of Criterion-
referenced Measures</u>. Paper presented at the American
Educational Research Association Convention, 1970. ED 038
679 (Arlington, VA: ERIC, 1970).

191. _____. <u>Item Selection Techniques and Evaluation of
Instructional Objectives</u>. ED 014 805. Reprint from
Journal of Educational Measurement Vol. 2, 1965.

192.   Crambert, Albert C. Estimation of Validity for
       Criterion-referenced Tests. Paper presented at the annual
       meeting of the American Educational Research Association,
       1977. ED 151 418 (Arlington, VA: ERIC, 1977).

193.   Crehan, Kevin. Student Generated Items as an
       Instructional Tool. Paper presented at the annual meeting
       of the National Council on Measurement in Education,
       1979. ED 173 447 (Arlington, VA: ERIC, 1979).

194.   Cudeck, Robert A. and others. "Implied Orders Tailored
       Testing: Simulation with the Stanford-Binet." Applied
       Psychological Measurement 4(2): 157-63 (1980).

195.   _____. "TAILOR: A Fortran Procedure for Interactive
       Tailored Testing." Educational and Psychological
       Measurement 37(3): 767-9 (1977).

196.   Curlette, William L. and William M. Stallings. "Ten
       Issues in Criterion-referenced Testing: A Response to
       Commonly Heard Criticisms." Clearing House 53(3): 145-48
       (1979).

197.   Curtis, H. A., ed. The Development and Management of
       Banks of Performance Based Test Items. Symposium
       presented at the annual meeting of the National Council
       on Measurement in Education, 1972. ED 072 099 (Arlington,
       VA: ERIC, 1972).

198.   Dambrot, Faye. "Test Item Order and Academic Ability, or
       Should You Shuffle the Test Item Deck." Teaching of
       Psychology 7(2): 94-96 (1980).

199.   Darlington, Richard B. Evaluating the Use of Assessment
       Procedures Developed in One School in Other Schools. ED
       012 064 (Arlington, VA: ERIC, 1967).

200.   Davis, Frederick B. Item-analysis Data: Their
       Computation, Interpretation, and Use in Test
       Construction. (Cambridge: Harvard University, Harvard
       Education Papers Number 2, 1946).

201.   _____. 1971 AERA Conference Summaries: II. Criterion
       Referenced Measurement. ED 060 134 (Arlington, VA: ERIC,
       1972).

202.   Day, Gerald F. "Criterion-referenced Measurement."
       Man/Society/Technology 35(3): 84-6 (1975).

203.   Decotiis, Thomas A. "A Critique and Suggested Revision of
       Behaviorally Anchored Rating Scales: Developmental
       Procedures." Educational and Psychological Measurement
       38(3): 681-90 (1978).

204.   Delorenzo, Ronald A. "Computer Assisted Instruction and
       Computer Test Construction." Technological Horizons in
       Education 6(5): 50-51 (September 1979).

205.   Deni, R. "Basic Program for Objective Item Test-
       construction and Test Item Management." Teaching of
       Psychology 6(4): 241-42 (1979).

206.   Denova, Charles C. <u>Test Construction for Training</u>
       <u>Evaluation</u> (New York: Van Nostrand Reinhold/American
       Society for Training and Development, 1979).

207.   Denton, Jon J. "Pretests: How Do You Construct Them."
       <u>Science Teacher</u> 41(4): 42-43 (1974).

208.   Diamond, James J. and David V. Williams. <u>An</u>
       <u>Identification of the Process Response to Taxonomy-type</u>
       <u>Test Items</u>. Paper presented at the annual meeting of the
       American Educational Research Association, 1972. ED 111
       846 (Arlington, VA: ERIC, 1972).

209.   Diaz, A.P.D. "Construction Defect in Minnesota Clerical
       Test." <u>Professional Psychology</u> 9(1): 7-8 (1978).

210.   Dick, James and Joel Poetker. "Improving Essay Testing."
       <u>Social Science Record</u> 23(1): 32-3 (1975).

211.   Dimes, R. E. "Objective Tests and Their Construction."
       <u>Physics Education</u> 8(4): 251-54 (1973).

212.   Dinero, Thomas E. and Edward Haertel. <u>A Computer</u>
       <u>Simulation Investigating the Applicability of the Rasch</u>
       <u>Model With Varying Item Discriminations</u>. Paper presented
       at the annual meeting of the National Council on
       Measurement in Education, 1976. ED 120 240 (Arlington,
       VA: ERIC, 1976).

213.   Dizney, Henry. <u>Classroom Evaluation for Teachers</u>. ED 055
       113 (Dubuque: William C. Brown, 1971).

214.   Donlon, Thomas F. <u>Establishing Appropriate Time Limits</u>
       <u>for Tests</u>. Paper presented at the annual meeting of the
       Northeast Educational Research Association, 1973. ED 118
       590 (Arlington, VA: ERIC, 1973).

215.   _____ . <u>A Practical Assessment of Field</u>
       <u>Dependence/Independence</u>. Paper presented at the annual
       meeting of the New England Educational Research
       Organization, 1977. ED 139 827 (Arlington, VA: ERIC,
       1977).

216.   _____ . "The SAT in a Diverse Society: Fairness and
       Sensitivity." <u>College Board Review</u> 122: 16-21, 30-32
       (Winter 1981).

217.   Doran, Rodney L. and Milton O. Pella. <u>Development of Test</u>
       <u>Items Related to Selected Concepts Within the Scheme the</u>
       <u>Particle Nature of Matter</u>. Paper presented at the annual
       meeting of the National Association for Research in
       Science Teaching, 1970. ED 037 344 (Arlington, VA: ERIC,
       1970).

218.   Doran, Rodney L. and others. "Construction of Test Items
       to be Presented Via Motion Picture Film." <u>Audiovisual</u>
       <u>Instruction</u> 19(2): 52-56 (1974).

219.   Doyle, Kenneth O. Jr. and Scott Wattawa. "Programs for
       the Construction and Analysis of Custom Questionnaires
       and Rating Scales." Educational and Psychological

<u>Measurement</u> 37(1): 237-9 (1977).

220. Dragositz, Anna, ed. <u>Curriculum Innovations and
     Evaluation: Proceedings of the Association for
     Supervision and Curriculum Development Pre-conference
     Seminar (Princeton, March 8-9, 1968)</u>. ED 085 421
     (Arlington, VA: ERIC, 1969).

221. Drasgow, F. and H. E. Miller. "Psychometric and
     Substantive Issues in Scale Construction and Validation."
     <u>Journal of Applied Psychology</u> 67: 268-79 (June 1982).

222. Ducette, Joseph and Stephen Wolk. "Test Performance and
     the Use of Optional Questions." <u>Journal of Experimental
     Education</u> 40(3): 21-4 (1972).

223. Duckworth, Pauline A. <u>Construction of Questionnaires.
     Technical Study. TS-7-73-1</u>. ED 138 610 (Arlington, VA:
     ERIC, 1973).

224. Dudley, Thomas J. "How the Computer Assists in Pacing and
     Testing Students' Progress." <u>Educational Technology</u>
     13(3): 21-22 (1973).

225. Dudycha, Arthur L. and James B. Carpenter. "Effects of
     Item Format on Item Discrimination and Difficulty."
     <u>Journal of Applied Psychology</u> 58(1): 116 (1973).

226. Duncan, M. E. "Improving Instructor-made Tests."
     <u>Community College Frontiers</u> 9: 21-24 (Fall 1980).

227. Duncan, N. and C. Harris. "An Index of Effectiveness for
     Criterion Referenced Items Used in Pre-tests and Post-
     tests." <u>Programmed Learning and Educational Technology</u>
     11(3): 125-32 (1974).

228. Dunkleberger, Gary E. and Henry Heikkinen. "A Review of
     Computer-generated Repeatable Testing." <u>AEDS Journal</u>
     15(4): 218-25 (1982).

229. Dworkin, Nancy and Yehoash Dworkin. <u>Don't Say Anything,
     Just Hug Me</u>. Paper presented at the annual meeting of the
     College Reading Association, 1977. ED 170 690 (Arlington,
     VA: ERIC, 1977).

230. Dwyer, Carol Anne. <u>Test Content in Mathematics and
     Science: The Consideration of Sex</u>. Paper presented at the
     annual meeting of the American Educational Research
     Association, 1976. ED 129 886 (Arlington, VA: ERIC,
     1976).

231. Dyman, Daniel J. and Jerry J. Nisbet. "Test-assembly
     Method Saves Time and Money." <u>American Biology Teacher</u>
     36(2): 102-104 (1974).

232. Dziuban, Charles D. and Kenneth V. Vickery. "Criterion-
     referenced Measurement: Some Recent Developments."
     <u>Educational Leadership</u> 30(5): 483-6 (1973).

233. Ebel, Robert L. "Can Teachers Write Good True-false Test
     Items." Journal of Educational Measurement 12(1): 31-35

(1975).

234.   _____. The Comparative Effectiveness of True-false and
Multiple Choice Achievement Tests Items. Paper presented
at the annual meeting of the American Educational
Research Association, 1971. ED 050 148 (Arlington, VA:
ERIC, 1971).

235.   _____. Essentials of Educational Measurement. ED 073 168
(Englewood Cliffs: Prentice Hall, 1972).

236.   _____. "How to Write True-false Test Items." Educational
and Psychological Measurement 31(2): 417-26 (1971).

237.   _____. Ineffectiveness of Multiple True-false Test
Items." Educational and Psychological Measurement 38:
37-44 (Spring 1978).

238.   _____. 1971 AERA Conference Summaries: IV. Test
Development, Interpretation, and Use. ED 060 135
(Arlington, VA: ERIC, 1972).

239.   _____. "Proposed Solutions to Two Problems of Test
Construction." Journal of Educational Measurement 19(4):
267-78 (1982).

240.   _____. Test Development, Interpretation and Use. ED 073
141 (Arlington, VA: ERIC, 1973).

241.   Echternacht, Gary. "The Variances of Empirically Derived
Option Scoring Weights." Educational and Psychological
Measurement 35(2): 307-11 (1975).

242.   Educational Testing Service. Multiple-choice Questions: A
Close Look. (Princeton, N.J.: Test Development Division,
ETS, 1973).

243.   Edwards, J.S. "Computer-assisted Testing." Journal of
Research and Development in Education 14: 9-15 (Fall
1980).

244.   Eggleston, Jim F. "The Constructive Use of Examination
Results." Forum for the Discussion of New Trends in
Education 20(3): 81-3 (Summer 1978).

245.   _____. "Examinations -- An Alternative View." Forum for
the Discussion of New Trends in Education 18(3): 92-93
(1976).

246.   _____. "Prediction, Selection, Description and Choice."
Forum for the Discussion of New Trends in Education
16(2): 61-2 (1974).

247.   Eignor, Daniel R. and James B. Douglass. A Comparison of
the One-, the Modified Three-, and the Three-parameter
Item Response Theory Models in the Test Development Item
Selection Process. ED 214 994 (Arlington, VA: ERIC,
1982).

248.   Eignor, Daniel R. and Ronald K. Hambleton. Effects of
Test Length and Advancement Score on Several Criterion-

referenced Test Reliability and Validity Indices.
Laboratory of Psychometric and Evaluation Research Report
No. 86. Paper presented at the annual meeting of the
National Council on Measurement in Education, 1979. ED
206 723 (Arlington, VA: ERIC, 1979).

249. Eisenberg, Bernard. "Final Exams -- Let the Computer
      Write Them." Creative Computing 3(6): 103-6 (1977).

250. Ellis, J. A. and W. H. Wulfeck. Assuring Objective-test
      Consistency: A Systematic Procedure for Constructing
      Criterion-referenced Tests. (San Diego: NPRDC, Special
      Report 80-15, 1980).

251. Ellison, John W. "Visual Tests; An Alternative."
      Educational Technology 13(5): 50-52 (1973).

252. Embree, J.E. "Computer Assisted Test Construction." NASSP
      Bulletin 65: 116-18 (February 1981).

253. Enright, Brian E. Criterion-referenced Tests: A Guide to
      Separate Useful From Useless. Paper presented at the
      Annual International Convention of the Council for
      Exceptional Children, 1982. ED 218 816 (Arlington, VA:
      ERIC, 1982).

254. Epstein, Marion G. Classification Scheme for Items in
      CAAT. Paper presented at the Computer Assisted Test
      Construction Conference, 1974. ED 110 505 (Arlington, VA:
      ERIC 1974).

255. _____. "Computer Assisted Assembly of Tests at
      Educational Testing Service." Educational Technology
      13(3): 23-24 (1973).

256. Evers, Linda. "Computerizing the SATS." Popular Computing
      2(3): 58, 61-62, 64 (1983).

257. Feletti, Grahame I. "Reliability and Validity Studies on
      Modified Essay Questions." Journal of Medical Education
      55(11): 933-41 (1980).

258. Ferguson, R. L. "Model for Computer-assisted Criterion-
      referenced Measurement." Education 91: 25-31 (September
      1970).

259. Feuerman, Martin and Harvey Weiss. "A Mathematical
      Programming Model for Test Construction and Scoring."
      Management Science 19(8): 961-66 (1973).

260. Finn, Patrick J. "A Question Writing Algorithm." Journal
      of Reading Behavior 7(4): 341-67 (1975).

261. Fitzgibbon, Thomas J. Ethical Issues and Questions About
      Testing for Test Publishers. Paper presented at Session
      II of the Southeastern Invitational Conference on
      Measurement in Education, 1972. ED 075 465 (Arlington,
      VA: ERIC, 1972).

262. Foreman, Dale I. SCORE: A Flexible System for School
      Curriculum Objective-referenced Evaluation. Paper

presented at the annual meeting of the American
Educational Research Association, 1975. ED 117 168
(Arlington, VA: ERIC, 1975).

263.   Fox, Robert A. "Practical Multiple-choice Exams." Journal
of School Health 50(9): 514-16 (1980).

264.   Fremer, John and Ernest J. Anastasio. "Computer-assisted
Item Writing -- I (Spelling Items)." Journal of
Educational Measurement 6(2): 69-74 (1969).

265.   Fremer, John and others. Student Involvement in Test
Development. ED 069 699 (Arlington, VA: ERIC, 1972).

266.   Friel, S. and A. H. Johnstone. "Does the Position
Matter." Education in Chemistry 16(6): 175 (1979).

267.   Frigerio, Norman A. and Ralph S. Stowe. "Computer
Production of Randomized Examinations." Journal of
Medical Education 49(3): 286-88 (1974).

268.   Fuhs, F. Paul. RIBYT -- A Data Base System for Formal
Testing and Self-assessment. ED 193 324 (Arlington, VA:
ERIC, 1980).

269.   Gagne, Robert M. and David M. Merrill. "The Content
Analysis of Subject-matter: The Computer as an Aid in the
Design of Criterion-referenced Tests." Instructional
Science 5(1): 1-28 (1976).

270.   Geisinger, Kurt F. A Systems Approach to Item Production
and Review in a Computer Managed Instruction Project.
Paper presented at the annual meeting of the American
Educational Research Association, 1976. ED 121 280
(Arlington, VA: ERIC, 1976).

271.   Ghatala, Elizabeth S. and others. "Sources of
Interference When Testing for Students Learning from
Sentences." Contemporary Educational Psychology 6(1):
46-58 (1981).

272.   Gifford, Janice A. and Ronald K. Hambleton. Construction
and Use of Criterion-referenced Tests in Program
Evaluation Studies. Laboratory of Psychometric and
Evaluation Research Report No. 102. Paper presented at
the annual meeting of the American Educational Research
Association, 1980. ED 193 271 (Arlington, VA: ERIC,
1980).

273.   Gillmore, Gerald M. and William M. Stallings. "Problem
Solving: A Neglected Test Style." Improving College and
University Teaching 24(2): 122-3 (1976).

274.   Goheen, Howard W. and Samuel Kavruck. Selected References
on Test Construction, Mental Test Theory, and Statistics,
1929-1949. (Washington D.C.: U.S. Civil Service
Commission, 1950).

275.   Gorth, W. and A. Grayson. "A Program to Compose and Print
Tests for Instructional Testing Using Item Sampling."
Educational and Psychological Measurement 29(1): 173-74

(1969).

276.   Gorth, William P. "Computer Programs for Test Objective
        and Item Banking." Educational and Psychological
        Measurement 31(1): 245-50 (1971).

277.   Gould, R. Bruce and Raymond E. Christal. VARSEL: Variable
        Selection for Multiple-purpose Prediction Systems in the
        Absence of External Criteria. ED 126 112 (Arlington, VA:
        ERIC, 1976).

278.   Graham, Darol L. and Constance Bercquist. An Examination
        of Criterion-referenced Test Characteristics in Relation
        to Assumptions About the Nature of Achievement Variables.
        Paper presented at the annual meeting of the American
        Educational Research Association, 1975. ED 106 347
        (Arlington, VA: ERIC, 1975).

279.   Gray, William M. "A Comparison of Piagetian Theory and
        Criterion-referenced Measurement." Review of Educational
        Research 48(2): 223-49 (1978).

280.   _____. Development of a Piagetian-based Written Test: A
        Criterion-referenced Approach. Paper presented at the
        annual meeting of the American Educational Research
        Association, 1973. ED 079 325 (Arlington, VA: ERIC,
        1973).

281.   _____. Development of a Written Test Based Upon the Model
        of Piaget. Final Report. ED 109 196 (Arlington, VA: ERIC,
        1973).

282.   _____. Standardized Tests Based on Developmental Theory.
        Paper presented at the annual meeting of the American
        Educational Research Association, 1978. ED 163 028
        (Arlington, VA: ERIC, 1978).

283.   Green, Bert F. "A Primer of Testing." American
        Psychologist 36(10): 1001-11 (1981).

284.   Green, Donald Ross. Minimizing Bias in Educational
        Testing. Paper presented at the annual conference on
        Large Scale Assessment, 1979. ED 199 268 (Arlington, VA:
        ERIC, 1979).

285.   _____. Racial and Ethnic Bias in Test Construction. ED
        129 928 (Arlington, VA: ERIC, 1971).

286.   _____. Reducing Bias in Achievement Tests. Paper
        presented at the annual meeting of the American
        Educational Research Association, 1976. ED 126 126
        (Arlington, VA: ERIC, 1976).

287.   Green, Samuel B. and others. "Shortcut Methods for
        Deriving Behaviorally Anchored Rating Scales."
        Educational and Psychological Measurement 41(3): 761-75
        (1981).

288.   Griswold, George H. and George H. Kapp. Computer
        Processed Evaluation. Paper presented at the Conference
        on Computers in the Undergraduate Curricula, 1977. ED 156

215 (Arlington, VA: ERIC, 1977).

289.   Gronlund, Norman E. Measurement and Evaluation in
Teaching. 4th ed. (New York: Macmillan, 1981).

290.   _____. Preparing Criterion-referenced Tests for Classroom
Instruction (New York: Macmillan, 1973).

291.   Guggenheim, M. J. and P. Lazenby. "Micro-computer
Management of Learning for Tec Courses." Vocational
Aspect of Education 32(81): 13-17 (1980).

292.   Guttman, Louis and I. M. Schlesinger. Development of
Diagnostic Analytical and Mechanical Ability Tests
Through Facet Design and Analysis. ED 010 590 (Arlington,
VA: ERIC, 1966).

293.   Haak, Ruth Adlof and others. Student Evaluation of
Teacher Instrument, II. Manual. ED 080 574 (Arlington,
VA: ERIC, 1972).

294.   Haebara, Tomokazu. Least Squares Method for Equating
Logistic Ability Scales: A General Approach and
Evaluation. Iowa Testing Programs Occasional Papers,
Number 30. ED 211 609 (Arlington, VA: ERIC, 1981).

295.   Hahn, Christine T. Domain Referenced Testing. An
Annotated ERIC Bibliography. ED 152 803 (Arlington, VA:
ERIC, 1977).

296.   Haladyna, Thomas Michael. "Effects of Different Samples
on Item and Test Characteristics of Criterion-referenced
Tests." Journal of Educational Measurement 2(2): 93-100
(1974).

297.   _____. Measuring Performance: Teacher-made Tests. ED 143
688 (Arlington, VA: ERIC, 1977).

298.   Haladyna, Thomas Michael and Gale Roid. A Comparison of
Two Item Selection Procedures for Building Criterion-
referenced Tests. Paper presented at the annual meeting
of the American Educational Research Association, 1981.
ED 205 546 (Arlington, VA: ERIC, 1981).

299.   _____. "The Role of Instructional Sensitivity in the
Empirical Review of Criterion-referenced Test Items."
Journal of Educational Measurement 18(1): 39-53 (1981).

300.   _____. The Role of Instructional Sensitivity in the
Empirical Review of Criterion-referenced Test Items.
Paper presented at the annual meeting of the American
Educational Research Association, 1980. ED 185 100
(Arlington, VA: ERIC, 1980).

301.   Hales, Loyde W. "Method of Obtaining the Index of
Discrimination for Item Selection and Selected Test
Characteristics: A Comparative Study." Educational and
Psychological Measurement 32(4): 929-37 (1972).

302.   Hall, Eric. "Item Writing in Empirical Studies."
Educational Research 11(3): 223-25 (1969).

303.   Hambleton, Ronald K. The Effects of Item Order and
        Anxiety on Test Performance and Stress. ED 017 960
        (Arlington, VA: ERIC, 1968).

304.   _____. "Some Comments on Aikenhead's 'New Methodology for
        Test Construction.'" Journal of Research in Science
        Teaching 14(5): 473-75 (1977).

305.   Hambleton, Ronald K. and Daniel R. Eignor. Competency
        Test Development, Validation, and Standard-setting. Paper
        presented at the Minimum Competency Testing Conference of
        the American Educational Research Association, 1978. ED
        206 725 (Arlington, VA: ERIC, 1978).

306.   _____. Guidelines for Evaluating Criterion-referenced
        Tests and Test Manuals. Paper presented at the annual
        meeting of the National Council on Measurement in
        Education, 1975. ED 167 575 (Arlington, VA: ERIC, 1979).

307.   Hambleton, Ronald K. and Linda L. Cook. "Latent Trait
        Models and Their Use in the Analysis of Educational Test
        Data." Journal of Educational Measurement 14(2): 75-96
        (1977).

308.   Hambleton, Ronald K. and others. Criterion-referenced
        Testing and Measurement: A Review of Technical Issues and
        Developments. Paper presented at the annual meeting of
        the American Educational Research Association, 1975. ED
        107 722 (Arlington, VA: ERIC, 1975).

309.   _____. "Criterion-referenced Testing and Measurement: A
        Review of Technical Issues and Developments." Review of
        Educational Research 48(1): 1-47 (1978).

310.   _____. "Determining the Lengths for Criterion-referenced
        Tests." Journal of Educational Measurement 20(1): 27-38
        (1983).

311.   Hambleton, Ronald K. and Robert A. Simon. Steps for
        Constructing Criterion-referenced Tests. Laboratory of
        Psychometric and Evaluative Research Report No. 104.
        Paper presented at the annual meeting of the American
        Educational Research Association, 1980. ED 189 168
        (Arlington, VA: ERIC, 1980).

312.   Hambleton, Ronald K. and William P. Gorth. Criterion-
        referenced Testing: Issues and Applications. ED 060 025
        (Arlington, VA: ERIC, 1971).

313.   Hamer, Robert and Forrest W. Young. "TESTER: A Computer
        Program to Produce Individualized Multiple Choice Tests."
        Educational and Psychological Measurement 38(3): 819-21
        (1978).

314.   Hamersma, Richard J. Guttman Facet Design and Analysis: A
        Technique for Attitude Scale Construction. ED 058 286
        (Arlington, VA: ERIC, 1971).

315.   Haney, Walt. Standards for Tests and Test Use. National
        Consortium on Testing Staff Circular No. 3. ED 191 877
        (Arlington, VA: ERIC, 1978).

316. Hanna, Gerald S. Improving Reliability and Validity of
      Multiple-choice Tests with an Answer-until-correct
      Procedure. Paper presented at the joint session of the
      American Educational Research Association and the
      National Council on Measurement in Education, 1974. ED
      088 953 (Arlington, VA: ERIC, 1974).

317. _____. An Investigation of the "Don't Know" Option in
      Formative Evaluation. Paper presented at the annual
      meeting of the National Council of Measurement in
      Education, 1974. ED 087 822 (Arlington, VA: ERIC, 1974).

318. Hanna, Gerald S. and Fred R. Johnson. "Reliability and
      Validity of Multiple-choice Tests Developed by Four
      Distractor Selection Procedures." Journal of Educational
      Research 71(4): 203-6 (1978).

319. Hansen, Jo-Ida C. "Age Differences and Empirical Scale
      Construction." Measurement and Evaluation in Guidance
      11(2): 78-87 (1978).

320. _____. "Coding SCII Items According to Holland's
      Vocational Theory." Measurement and Evaluation in
      Guidance 10(2): 75-82 (1977).

321. Hanson, G. R. and others. Development and Validation of
      Sex-balanced Interest Inventory Scales. ED 141 392
      (Arlington, VA: ERIC, 1977).

322. Hardware Developments; Microcomputers and Processors;
      Grade School/High School Instructional; and Computer-
      aided Design. Papers presented at the Association for
      Educational Data Systems Annual Convention, 1976. ED 125
      662 (Arlington, VA: ERIC, 1976).

323. Harnisch, Delwyn L. and others. Development of a Shorter,
      More Reliable, and More Valid Measure of Test Motivation.
      Paper presented at the annual meeting of the National
      Council on Measurement in Education, 1980. ED 193 273
      (Arlington, VA: ERIC, 1980).

324. Harris, Chester W. and others. Problems in Criterion-
      referenced Measurement. CSE Monograph Series in
      Evaluation, 3. ED 171 732 (Arlington, VA: ERIC, 1974).

325. Harris, Margaret L. and Chester W. Harris. Item Analyses
      and Reliabilities for Reference Tests for Cognitive
      Abilities: Fifth Grade Boys and Girls. ED 070 020
      (Arlington, VA: ERIC, 1971).

326. _____. Newly Constructed Reference Tests for Cognitive
      Abilities. Report From the Project on a Structure of
      Concept Attainment Abilities. ED 072 114 (Arlington, VA:
      ERIC, 1971).

327. _____. Three Systems of Classifying Cognitive Abilities
      on Bases for Reference Tests. ED 070 021 (Arlington, VA:
      ERIC, 1971).

328. Hashway, Robert M. "New Software for Courses in Test
      Construction." Educational and Psychological Measurement

38(1): 159-66 (1978).

329. Hazlett, C. B. Medsirch: A Computerized System for the Retrieval of Multiple Choice Items. ED 049 633 (Arlington, VA: ERIC, 1970).

330. _____. "Medsirch: Multiple Choice Test Items." Educational Technology 13(3): 24-26 (1973).

331. Hedges, William D. and Derrick Mark Pauw. "Computer Generated Tests for Independent Study Programs." NASSP Bulletin 55(358): 91-8 (1971).

332. Heines, Jesse M. An Examination of the Literature on Criterion-referenced and Computer-assisted Testing. ED 116 633 (Arlington, VA: ERIC, 1975).

333. Helmstadter, G. C. Principles of Psychological Measurement. (New York: Appleton, 1964).

334. Henk, William A. "Selective Testing: A Viable Alternative for the Classroom." Teacher Educator 17(2): 11-15 (1981).

335. Henrysson, Sten and Ingemar Wedman. "Some Problems in Construction and Evaluation of Criterion-referenced Tests." Scandinavian Journal of Educational Research 18(1): 1-12 (1974).

336. Henson, Oleen M. "Current Trends in Evaluation of Students." Business Education Forum 33(7): 5-6 (1979).

337. Herbert, John and Carol Attridge. "A Guide for Developers and Users of Observation Systems and Manuals." American Educational Research Journal 12(1): 1-20 (1975).

338. Hermans, H. J. M. "Validity of Different Strategies of Scale Construction in Predicting Academic Achievement." Educational and Psychological Measurement 29: 877-83 (1983).

339. Hill, G. C. and G. T. Woods. "Multiple True-false Questions." Education In Chemistry 11(3): 86-87 (1974).

340. Hiscox, Michael D. and Evelyn J. Brzezinski. A Guide to Item Banking in Education. Prepared for the Annual Conference on Large-Scale Assessment, 1980. ED 196 945 (Arlington, VA: ERIC, 1980).

341. Hively, Wells. Domain-referenced Testing. ED 102 204 (Englewood Cliffs, NJ: Educational Technology Publications, 1974).

342. _____. "Introduction to Domain-referenced Testing." Educational Technology 14(6): 5-10 (1974).

343. Hoetker, James. On Writing Essay Topics for a Test of the Composition Skills of Prospective Teachers: With a Review of Literature on the Creation, Validation, and Effects of Topics on Essay Examination. Volume Four of Five. ED 194 615 (Arlington, VA: ERIC, 1979).

344.   Holdaway, Edward. "Different Response Categories and
        Questionnaire Response Patterns." Journal of Experimental
        Education 40: 57-60 (1971).

345.   Holliday, William G. and Louise A. Partridge.
        "Differential Sequencing Effects of Test Items on
        Children." Journal of Research in Science Teaching 16(5):
        407-11 (1979).

346.   Holloway, R. L. and J. S. Prestwood. "Domain-referenced
        Tests." Instructional Innovator 26: 39-40 (1981).

347.   Holtzman, Wayne H. Computer-assisted Instruction,
        Testing, and Guidance. ED 064 861 (New York: Harper and
        Row, 1970).

348.   Hopkins, P. G. E. "More Than One Choice in Objective
        Testing." English Language Teaching Journal 34(3): 221-23
        (1980).

349.   Howze, Glenn. "An Interactive Software System for
        Computer-assisted Testing." AEDS Journal 11(2): 31-7
        (1978).

350.   Hsu, Louis M. "Determination of the Number of Items and
        Passing Score in a Mastery Test." Educational and
        Psychological Measurement 40(3): 709-14 (1980).

351.   _____. "Ordering Power of Separate Versus Grouped True-
        false Tests: Interaction of Type of Test with Knowledge
        Levels of Examinees." Applied Psychological Measurement
        3(4): 529-36 (1979).

352.   Hsu, Tse-Chi. Empirical Data on Criterion-referenced
        Tests. Paper presented at the annual meeting of the
        American Educational Research Association, New York,
        1971. ED 050 139 (Arlington, VA: ERIC, 1971).

353.   Hsu, Tse-Chi and Marthena Carlson. "Test Construction
        Aspects of the Computer-assisted Testing Model."
        Educational Technology 13(3): 26-27 (1973).

354.   Hudson, H. T. and Carolyn K. Hudson. "Suggestions on the
        Construction of Multiple-choice Tests." American Journal
        of Physics 49(9): 838-41 (1981).

355.   Huntley, Renee M. and Barbara S. Plake. Effects of
        Selected Item-writing Practices on Test Performance: Can
        Relevant Grammatical Clues Result in Flawed Items. Paper
        presented at the annual meeting of the American
        Educational Research Association, 1980. ED 189 115
        (Arlington, VA: ERIC, 1980).

356.   Instructional (II); Computerized Testing; and CATC
        Discussion and Demonstration. Papers presented at the
        Association for Educational Data Systems, Annual
        Convention (Phoenix, Arizona, May 3-7 1976). ED 125 659
        (Arlington, VA: ERIC, 1976).

357.   Ivens, Stephen H. A Pragmatic Approach to Criterion-
        referenced Measures. Paper presented at a symposium at a

joint session of the annual meetings of the AERA and the National Council for Measurement in Education, 1972. ED 064 406 (Arlington, VA: ERIC, 1972).

358.   _____. The Promise of CRT: Panacea or Pandora. Paper presented at the annual meeting of the American Educational Research Association, 1979. ED 175 943 (Arlington, VA: ERIC, 1979).

359.   Izard, J. F. Construction and Analysis of Classroom Tests. ED 143 690 (Hawthorn, Victoria, Australia: Australian Council for Educational Research, 1977).

360.   Jacko, Edward J. and Schuyler W. Huck. The Effect of Varying the Response Format on the Statistical Characteristics of the Alpert-Haber Achievement Anxiety Test. Paper presented at the annual meeting of the American Educational Research Association, 1974. ED 093 992 (Arlington, VA: ERIC, 1974).

361.   Jackson, Rex. Developing Criterion-referenced Tests. ED 041 952 (Arlington, VA: ERIC, 1970).

362.   Jacobs, Paul I. Some Implications of Testing Procedures for Auto-instructional Programming. Final Report. ED 130 617 (Arlington, VA: ERIC, 1962).

363.   Jacobs, T. O. Developing Questionnaire Items: How To Do It Well. ED 103 454 (Arlington, VA: ERIC, 1974).

364.   Jenkins, Joseph R. and others. "Selection of Prose Material for Testing." Journal of Educational Measurement 9(2): 97-103 (1972).

365.   Jenkins, Joseph R. and Stanley L. Deno. "Assessing Knowledge of Concepts and Principles." Journal of Educational Measurement 8(2): 95-101 (1971).

366.   Jensen, Donald D. "Toward Efficient, Effective and Humane Instruction in Large Classes: Student Scheduled Involvement in Films, Discussions and Computer Generated Repeatable Tests." Educational Technology 13(3): 28-29 (1973).

367.   Jepsen, David A. and others. "Symposium: Testing for Career Counseling, Guidance, and Education. Trends and Applications." Measurement and Evaluation in Guidance 15(2): 141-68 (1982).

368.   Johnson, Stuart R. "When Should You Lie to Students?" Educational Technology 10(11): 51-53 (1970).

369.   Johnson, W. Russell, Nicholas A. Sieveking and Earl S. Clanton. "Effects of Alternative Positioning of Open-ended Questions in Multiple-choice Questionnaires." Journal of Applied Psychology 59: 776-78 (1974).

370.   Jones, Hazel C. "The Value of Self-test Items in Tape-slide Instruction." Medical Education 10(4): 729-83 (1976).

371.   Jones, John A. "How to Write Better Tests." Instructor
       89(3): 66-71 (1979).

372.   Kane, Robert B. Reducing Proximity Error in Administering
       the Semantic Differential. Final Report. ED 032 761
       (Arlington, VA: ERIC, 1968).

373.   Karras, Ray W. "Writing Multiple-choice Questions: The
       Problem and a Proposed Solution." History Teacher 11(2):
       211-8 (1978).

374.   Keller, Claudia Merkel. Criterion-referenced Measurement;
       a Bibliography. ED 060 014 (Arlington, VA: ERIC, 1972).

375.   Kibblewhite, D. "Test Reliability: A Practical Approach
       for the Teacher." Educational Studies 7(3): 205-13
       (1981).

376.   King, H. A. "QUIZ: An Interactive Program to Generate
       Content-referenced Objective Tests." Educational and
       Psychological Measurement 41: 185-7 (1981).

377.   Kishi, Akemi. Task Inventory Construction. Evaluation of
       the Marine Corps Task Analysis Program. Technical Report
       No. 14. ED 157 912 (Arlington, VA: ERIC, 1976).

378.   Klein, M. Frances. "Use of Taxomony of Educational
       Objectives (Cognitive Domain) in Constructing Tests for
       Primary School Pupils." Journal of Experimental Education
       40(3): 38-50 (1972).

379.   Klein, Stephen. Evaluating Tests in Terms of the
       Information They Provide. ED 045 699 (Arlington, VA:
       ERIC, 1970).

380.   Klein, Stephen P. Ongoing Evaluation of Educational
       Programs. Paper presented at the American Psychological
       Association Convention, 1972. ED 069 725 (Arlington, VA:
       ERIC, 1972).

381.   Klein, Stephen P. and Jacqueline Kosecoff. Issues and
       Procedures in the Development of Criterion Referenced
       Tests. ED 083 284 (Princeton, NJ: Educational Testing
       Service, ERIC TM Report 26, 1973).

382.   Kleinke, David J. Item Order, Response Format, and
       Examinee Sex and Handedness and Performance on a
       Multiple-choice Test. Paper presented at the annual
       meeting of the National Council on Measurement in
       Evaluation, 1979. ED 171 793 (Arlington, VA: ERIC, 1979).

383.   Koehler, Roger A. Coombs' Type Response Procedures. Paper
       presented at the annual meeting of the American
       Educational Research Association, 1972. ED 063 338
       (Arlington, VA: ERIC, 1972).

384.   Kolstad, Rosemarie K. and Robert A. Kolstad.
       "Applications of Conventional and Non-restrictive
       Multiple-choice Examination Items." Clearing House 56(4):
       153-55 (1982).

385.   Kosecoff, Jacqueline and Arlene Fink. The Appropriateness of Criterion-referenced Tests for Evaluation Studies. ED 135 841 (Arlington, VA: ERIC, 1976).

386.   _____. The Feasibility of Using Criterion-referenced Tests for Large-scale Evaluations. Paper presented at the annual meeting of the American Educational Research Association, 1976. ED 129 924 (Arlington, VA: ERIC, 1976).

387.   Kriewall, Thomas E. "Aspects and Applications of Criterion-referenced Tests." Illinois School Research 9(2): 5-18 (1972).

388.   Kriewall, Thomas E. and Edward Hirsch. The Development and Interpretation of Criterion-referenced Tests. Paper presented at the annual meeting of the American Educational Research Association, 1969. ED 042 815 (Arlington, VA: ERIC, 1969).

389.   Kruger, Irwin. "Computerized Test Generation According to Specified External Criteria." Journal of Educational and Psychological Measurement 34(1): 181-82 (1974).

390.   Landa, Suzanne. CAAPM: Computer-aided Admissible Probability Measurement on Plato IV. ED 129 850 (Arlington, VA: ERIC, 1976).

391.   Lange, Robert and others. Computer Based Test Development Center. Evaluation Report. ED 079 976 (Arlington, VA: ERIC, 1970).

392.   Larkin, Kevin C. and David J. Weiss. An Empirical Comparison of Two-stage and Pyramidal Adaptive Ability Testing. ED 106 317 (Arlington, VA: ERIC, 1975).

393.   _____. An Empirical Investigation of Computer-administered Pyramidal Ability Testing. Research Report No. 74-3. ED 096 343 (Arlington, VA: ERIC, 1974).

394.   Leclercq, Dieudonne. "Computerized Tailored Testing: Structured and Calibrated Item Banks for Summative and Formative Evaluation." European Journal of Education 15(3): 251-60 (1980).

395.   Lederhouse, Jonathan E. and James M. Lower. "Testing College Professors' Tests." College Student Journal 8(1): 68-70 (1974).

396.   Lennon, Roger T. "The Abiding Agenda of Measurement." Educational Measurement: Issues and Practice 1(1): 10-11 (1982).

397.   _____. "Standards for Educational & Psychological Tests." Journal of Educational Measurement 12(2): 135-7 (1975).

398.   LeSage, W. "Standardized Tests: What Are They? How Are They Made? How Are They Scored?" Instructor 82: 46-8 (1973).

399.   Lewy, Arieh and Rina Doron. Group Tailored Tests and Some

Problems of Their Utilization. Paper presented at the International Symposium on Educational Testing, 1977. ED 159 210 (Arlington, VA: ERIC, 1977).

400.   Linden, Kathryn W. and Wayne M. Garrison. "On Reporting Student Achievement: The Need for Meaningful Test Results." _NALLD Journal_ 11(2): 27-33 (1977).

401.   Linn, Robert. _Conceptualization of Issues in Construct and Content Validity. Studies in Measurement and Methodology, Work Unit No. 1: Conceptual and Design Problems in Competency-based Measurements_. ED 213 733 (Arlington, VA: ERIC, 1978).

402.   Linn Robert L. and others. "The Development and Evaluation of Several Programmed Testing Methods." _Educational and Psychological Measurement_ 29(1): 129-46 (1969).

403.   Lippey, Gerald. "Bibliography on Computer-assisted Test Construction." ED 095 909. _ACM Sigcue_ 7(4): 22-26 (1973).

404.   _____. A Comprehensive Question Retrieval Application to Serve Classroom Teachers_. ED 095 908 (Arlington, VA: ERIC, 1973).

405.   _____. "The Computer Can Support Test Construction in a Variety of Ways." _Educational Technology_ 13(3): 10-12 (1973).

406.   _____. "Computer-assisted Test Construction." _AEDS Monitor_ 12(10): 6 (1974).

407.   _____. Computer-assisted Test Construction_. ED 095 907 (Arlington, VA: ERIC, 1974).

408.   Lippey, Gerald and Nathan Partos. "Improvements to a Computer-assisted Test Construction System." _Educational Technology_ 16(12): 26-29 (1976).

409.   Lippey, Gerald, ed. _Computer-assisted Test Construction_. ED 096 948 (Englewood Cliffs, NJ: Educational Testing Publications, 1974).

410.   Livingston, Samuel A. "Criterion-referenced Applications of Classical Test Theory." _Journal of Educational Measurement_ 9(1): 13-26 (1972).

411.   Lockheed-Katz, Marlaine. _Sex Bias in Educational Testing: A Sociologist's Perspective. Research Memorandum No. 74-13_. ED 098 262 (Arlington, VA: ERIC, 1974).

412.   Logsdon, David M. _An Experimental Comparison of the Effectiveness of Two Domain Definition Strategies for Criterion-referenced Tests_. Paper presented at the annual meeting of the Eastern Educational Research Association, 1981. ED 206 714 (Arlington, VA: ERIC, 1981).

413.   Lord, Frederic M. _Individualized Testing and Item Characteristic Curve Theory_. ED 069 783 (Arlington, VA: ERIC, 1972).

414. _____. "Practical Applications of Item Characteristic Curve Theory." Journal of Educational Measurement 14(2): 117-38 (1977).

415. _____. "Robbins-Monro Procedures for Tailored Testing." Educational and Psychological Measurement 31(1): 3-31 (1971).

416. _____. "The Self-scoring Flexilevel Test." Journal of Educational Measurement 8(3): 147-51 (1971).

417. _____. Tailored Testing, An Application of Stochastic Approximation. ED 051 287 (Arlington, VA: ERIC, 1971).

418. _____. A Theoretical Study of the Measurement Effectiveness of Flexilevel Tests. ED 051 286 (Arlington, VA: ERIC, 1971).

419. Los Arcos, J. M. and E. Vano. "A New Computer-based Examination System." Educational Technology 18(11): 33-36 (1978).

420. Lucas, Peter A. and George W. McConkie. "The Definition of Test Items: A Descriptive Approach." American Educational Research Journal 17(2): 133-40 (1980).

421. MacAvoy, S. and L. B. Welch. "Tips on Test Construction." Journal of Nursing Education 20: 15-19 (1981).

422. McBride, James R. Adaptive Mental Testing: The State of the Art. ED 200 612 (Arlington, VA: ERIC, 1979).

423. McCauley, Donald E. Jr. and Magda Colberg. "Transportability of Deductive Measurement Across Cultures." Journal of Educational Measurement 20(1): 81-92 (1983).

424. McClain, Donald H. and Stephen W. Wessels. IPSIM: Additional System Enhancements Utilized in a Chemistry Application. Paper presented at the Conference on Computers in the Undergraduate Curricula, 1975. ED 111 356 (Arlington, VA: ERIC, 1975).

425. McClelland, G. "Ambiguity in Multiple-choice Items." Physics Education 13(2): 112-4 (1978).

426. McCormick, Douglas J. TAILOR-APL: An Interactive Computer Program for Individual Tailored Testing. Technical Report No. 5. ED 161 886 (Arlington, VA: ERIC, 1978).

427. McCormick, Douglas J. and Norman Cliff. "TAILOR-APL: An Interactive Computer Program for Individual Tailored Testing." Educational and Psychological Measurement 37(3): 771-4 (1977).

428. McGuire, Christine H. and others. Construction and Use of Written Simulations. ED 179 557 (New York: Psychological Corporation, 1976).

429. McKee, Barbara G. and Colleen Manning-Curtis. Teacher Constructed Classroom Tests: The Stepchild of Measurement

Research. Paper presented at the annual meeting of the National Council on Measurement in Education, 1980. ED 222 562 (Arlington, VA: ERIC, 1982).

430.   McKeegan, Hugh and Cathy C. Dennis. Applied Performance Tests: How to Judge Them; How to Develop Them. ED 187 752 (Arlington, VA: ERIC, 1975).

431.   McKenzie, Gary R. "Testing: Proceed with Caution." Elementary School Journal 76(5): 266-71 (1976).

432.   McKillip, William D. "Teacher-made Tests: Development and Use." Arithmetic Teacher 27(3): 38-43 (1979).

433.   McKinley, Mark B. A Comparison of an Audio-visual Test Mode with a Visual Test Mode as a Differential Variable in Test Performance. ED 120 247 (Arlington, VA: ERIC, 1975).

434.   McKinley, Robert L. and Mark D. Reckase. "Computer Applications to Ability Testing." AEDS Journal 13(3): 193-203 (1980).

435.   McMorris, Robert F. and others. "Effects of Violating Item Construction Principles." Journal of Educational Measurement 9(4): 287-94 (1972).

436.   McNamara, Walter J. and Ellis Weitzman. "The Effect of Choice Placement on the Difficulty of Multiple Choice Questions." Journal of Educational Psychology 36: 103-113 (1945).

437.   Madden, Theodore M. and Frederick J. Klopfer. "The 'Cannot Decide' Option in Thurstone-type Attitude Scales." Educational and Psychological Measurement 38(2): 259-64 (1978).

438.   Making the Classroom Test: A Guide for Teachers. ED 081 784 (Arlington, VA: ERIC, 1973).

439.   Mann, Irene T. and others. "An Examination of Methodological Issues Relevant to the Use and Interpretation of the Semantic Differential." Applied Psychological Measurement 3(2): 213-29 (1979).

440.   Manuel, Herschel T. Development of Inter-American Test Materials. ED 010 670 (Arlington, VA: ERIC, 1966).

441.   _____. The Preparation and Evaluation of Inter-language Testing Materials. ED 001 702 (Arlington, VA: ERIC, 1963).

442.   _____. Tests of General Ability and Reading, Inter-American Series. ED 003 857 (Arlington, VA: ERIC, 1963).

443.   Marco, Gary L. "Item Characteristic Curve Solutions to Three Intractable Testing Problems." Journal of Educational Measurement 14(2): 139-60 (1977).

444.   Marso, Ronald N. "Test Item Arrangement, Testing Time, and Performance." Journal of Educational Measurement

7(2): 113-8 (1970).

445.   Mason, Geoffrey P. "Test Purpose and Item Type." Canadian Journal of Education 4(4): 8-13 (1979).

446.   Masters, Geoff N. Looking Ahead in Educational Testing and Assessment. Paper presented at the Western Australian Institute for Educational Research, 1982. ED 221 599 (Arlington, VA: ERIC, 1982).

447.   Mathews, C. O. "The Effect of the Order of Printed Response Words on an Interest Questionnaire." Journal of Educational Psychology 20: 128-34 (1929).

448.   Mayo, Samuel T. Measurement in Education: Mastery Learning and Mastery Testing. ED 051 299 (Arlington, VA: ERIC, 1970).

449.   Mead, Ronald J. Basic Ideas in Item Banking. Paper presented at the annual meeting of the National Council on Measurement in Education, 1981. ED 208 029 (Arlington, VA: ERIC, 1981).

450.   Mehrens, W. A. and I. J. Lehmann. Measurement and Evaluation in Education and Psychology. 2nd ed. (New York: Holt, Rinehart & Winston, 1978).

451.   Mehrens, William A. "Scientific Test Construction -- Pure and Sterile." Contemporary Psychology 15(11): 666-7 (1970).

452.   Menne, John W. "Computer Assisted Test Assembly at Iowa State University." Educational Technology 13(3): 31-32 (1973).

453.   Mersand, Joseph. In Quest of the Perfect Test. ED 188 182 (Arlington, VA: ERIC, 1980).

454.   Mershon, Donald H. "An Inexpensive System for Producing Examinations with Minimal Typing and Proofreading." Teaching of Psychology 9(2): 108-9 (1982).

455.   Merz, William R. Methods of Assessing Bias and Fairness in Tests. ED 198 145 (Arlington, VA: ERIC, 1980.)

456.   Meskauskas, J. A. "Evaluation Models for Criterion-referenced Testing: Views Regarding Mastery and Standard-setting." Review of Educational Research 46: 133-58 (1976).

457.   Michener, R. Dean and others. Automating Exams for a Statistics Course: II. A Case Study. Paper presented at the annual convention of the Association for Educational Data Systems, 1978. ED 200 619 (Arlington, VA: ERIC, 1978).

458.   Miller, H. G., R. G. Williams and T. M. Haladyna. Beyond Facts: Objective Ways To Measure Thinking. (Englewood Cliffs, NJ: Educational Technology, 1978).

459.   Miller, Harry G. and Reed G. Williams. "Constructing

Higher Level Multiple Choice Questions Covering Factual Content." Educational Technology 13(5): 39-42 (1973).

460.   Miller, M. David. Test Construction Techniques for Building More Sensitive Indicators of Between-group Differences. ED 220 540 (Arlington, VA: ERIC, 1981).

461.   Miller, M. David and Leigh Burstein. Evaluation Design Project: Multilevel Interpretation of Evaluation Data Study. ED 212 649 (Arlington, VA: ERIC, 1981).

462.   Millman, Jason. Creating Domain-referenced Tests by Computer. Paper presented at the annual meeting of the American Educational Reseach Association, 1977. ED 135 852 (Arlington, VA: ERIC, 1977).

463.   _____. "Criterion-referenced Measurement." In Evaluation in Education: Current Applications edited by W. J. Popham. ED 123 236 (Berkeley, CA: McCutchan Publishing Corporation, 1974).

464.   _____. Determining Test Length. Passing Scores and Test Lengths for Objective-based Tests. ED 173 382 (Los Angeles: Instructional Objectives Exchange, 1972).

465.   _____. Passing Scores and Test Lengths for Domain-referenced Measures. Paper presented at the annual meeting of the American Educational Research Association, 1972. ED 065 555 (Arlington, VA: ERIC, 1972).

466.   _____. "Program Assessment, Criterion-referenced Tests, and Things Like That." Educational Horizons 52(4): 188-92 (1974).

467.   _____. "Sampling Plans for Domain-referenced Tests." Educational Technology 14(6): 17-21 (1974).

468.   Millman, Jason and Scott W. Outlaw. "Testing by Computer." AEDS Journal 11(3): 57-72 (1978).

469.   Mills, Craig N. and Robert Simon. A Method for Determining the Length of Criterion-referenced Tests Using Reliability and Validity Indices. Paper presented at the annual meeting of the American Educational Research Association, 1981. ED 205 594 (Arlington, VA: ERIC, 1981).

470.   Mione, Stephen A. Criterion-referenced Testing: A Critical Perspective. ED 147 757 (Arlington, VA: ERIC, 1977).

471.   Morgan, Penelope and others. It's the Metric That Counts; or, Criterion Referenced Schizophrenia. Paper presented at the annual meeting of the American Educational Research Association, 1976. ED 129 849 (Arlington, VA: ERIC, 1976).

472.   Morris, Lynn Lyons and Carol Taylor Fitz-Gibbon. How to Deal with Goals and Objectives. Program Evaluation Kit, 2. ED 175 887 (Beverly Hills, Ca: Sage Publications, 1978).

473. Morse, David T. "How to Write Good Test Items." Florida Vocational Journal 3(5): 11-5 (1978).

474. Muiznieks, Viktors and Richard J. Dennis. A Look at Computer-assisted Testing Operations. The Illinois Series on Educational Application of Computers, No. 12E. ED 183 191 (Arlington, VA: ERIC 1979).

475. Multiple Choice Questions: A Close Look. ED 081 783 (Arlington, VA: ERIC, 1973).

476. Murphy, Meg. "What's Your Classroom Testing Validity Quotient?" School Shop 40(5): 18-20,27 (1981).

477. Murphy, S. A. "Improving Teacher-made Tests in an Integrated Curriculum." Journal of Nursing Education 18: 41-45 (November 1979).

478. Murray, Norman B. Construction of a Thurstone Attitude Test. Paper presented at the annual convention of the California Educational Research Association, 1971. ED 058 306 (Arlington, VA: ERIC, 1971).

479. Nassif, Paula M. and others. Generating Parallel Test Forms for Minimum Competency Exams. Paper presented at the annual meeting of the National Council on Measurement in Education, 1979. ED 174 686 (Arlington, VA: ERIC, 1979).

480. Natarajan, V. "Question Banks: Their Use in Indian Examinations." New Frontiers in Education 5(8): 64-71 (1975).

481. Nelson, Jerald and Margaret Drennan. From Theory to Curriculum: Then (and Only Then) - Evaluation. Paper presented at the annual meeting of the California Educational Research Association, 1971. ED 054 227 (Arlington, VA: ERIC, 1971).

482. Nevo, Barukh. "Using Item Test-retest Stability (ITRS) as a Criterion for Item Selection: An Empirical Study." Educational and Psychological Measurement 37(4): 847-52 (1977).

483. Newbould, C. A. and A. J. Massey. "A Computerized Item Banking System (CIBS)." British Journal of Educational Technology 8(2): 114-23 (1977).

484. Newton, Nancy A. "Construction and Item Analysis of a Computerized Test for the Assessment of Memory for Verbal and Design Material." Dissertation Abstracts International 42(11-B): 4585-86 (1982).

485. Nimmer, Donald N. "Multiple True-false Classroom Tests." Clearing House 56(6): 257-58 (1983).

486. Nitko, Anthony J. A Model for Criterion-referenced Tests Based on Use. Paper presented at the annual meeting of the American Educational Research Association, 1971. ED 049 318 (Arlington, VA: ERIC, 1971).

487.   _____. Problems in the Development of Criterion-referenced Tests: The IPI Pittsburgh Experience. ED 120 250 (Arlington, VA: ERIC, 1974).

488.   Nixon, John E. "The Mechanics of Questionnaire Construction." Journal of Educational Research 47(7): 481-87 (1954).

489.   Noble, John W. "Computerized Testing: More Learning for Less Drudgery." Phi Delta Kappan 6(7): 485-86 (1980).

490.   Novick, Melvin R. and Charles Lewis. Prescribing Test Length for Criterion-referenced Measurement. I. Posttests. ACT Technical Bulletin No. 18. ED 152 830 (Arlington, VA: ERIC, 1974).

491.   Olander, C. P. and C. T. Merbitzer. "Using Technologies to Teach: An A/V, PSI Course with Computer-assisted Testing." Educational Technology 20: 50-2 (1980).

492.   Olsen, Henry D. and Robert S. Barcikowski. "Adopting to Multiple Choice Tests of Differing Item Arrangement." Child Study Journal 6(2): 91-98 (1976).

493.   _____. Test Item Arrangement and Adaptation Level. Paper presented at the American Educational Research Association annual meeting, 1974. ED 090 462 (Arlington, VA: ERIC, 1974).

494.   Olson, Leroy A. Writing Test Items. LES Papers on Learning and Teaching, Paper No. 50. ED 194 600 (Arlington, VA: ERIC, 1980).

495.   Oluikpe, G. C. "A Table of Upper-lower Number-right Difference (D) As An Index of Item Discriminatory Power." British Journal of Educational Psychology 52(1): 121-24 (1982).

496.   Olympia, P. L. Jr. "Computer Generation of Truly Repeatable Examinations." Educational Technology 14(6): 53-55 (1975).

497.   _____. Repetitive Domain-referenced Testing Using Computers: The TITA System. Paper presented at the Conference on Computers in Education in the Undergraduate Curricula, 1975. ED 111 358 (Arlington, VA: ERIC, 1975).

498.   Oosterhof, Albert C. and Douglas Glasnapp. Comparative Reliabilities of the Multiple Choice and True-false Formats. Paper presented at the annual meeting of the American Educational Research Association, 1972. ED 064 361 (Arlington, VA: ERIC, 1972).

499.   Oppenheim, A. N. Questionnaire Design and Attitude Measurement. (New York: Basic Books, 1966).

500.   O'Reilly, Robert P. and others. "Computer Assisted Test Construction: An Effort Based on an Evaluation Methodology." Educational Technology 13(3): 32-34 (1973).

501.   Osborne, R. J. and C. J. Potter. "Self-evaluation Tests

Using Interactive Computer Terminals." Assessment in Higher Education 4(3): 171-79 (1979).

502. Osburn, H. G. and David M. Shoemaker. Pilot Project on Computer Generated Test Items. ED 026 856 (Arlington, VA: ERIC, 1968).

503. Osgood, Charles, George J. Suci and Percy H. Tannenbaum. The Measurement of Meaning (Urbana, IL: University of Illinois Press, 1957).

504. Owens, Richard E. and William E. Cashin. Preparing Examinations: A Practical Guide for Idea Users. ED 171 217 (Arlington, VA: ERIC, 1977).

505. Ozenne, Dan Gilbert. Toward An Evaluative Methodology for Criterion-referenced Measures: Test Sensitivity. ED 061 263 (Arlington, VA: ERIC, 1971).

506. Parelius, Allen M. and others. Computerized Testing. Paper presented at the annual international convention of the Council for Exceptional Children, 1976. ED 122 496 (Arlington, VA: ERIC, 1976).

507. Pascale, Pietro J. Developing a Table of Specifications. ED 115 675 (Arlington, VA: ERIC, 1976).

508. Pask, Gordon. Strategic Disposition Tests and the Influence of Learning Strategy on the Performance and Breakdown of Skills. Interim Scientific Report. ED 073 374. (Springfield, VA: NTIS, 1972).

509. Pearlstein, R. B. and R. W. Swezey. Criterion-referenced Measurement in the Army: Development of a Research-based, Practical Test Construction Manual. (Alexandria, VA: U. S. Army Research Institute for the Behavioral and Social Sciences Technical Report TR-78-A31, 1978).

510. (The PEDAGE System.). ED 077 981 (Arlington, VA: ERIC, 1965).

511. Penfield, Douglas A. A Comparison of Some Nonparametric Tests for Scale. Paper presented at the annual meeting of the American Educational Research Association, 1972. ED 065 559 (Arlington, VA: ERIC, 1972).

512. Pickering, M. J. "Why Multiple Choice Language Tests are Sometimes Not." System 4(3): 164-173 (1976).

513. Pikulski, John J. Criterion Referenced Measures for Clinical Evaluations. Paper presented at the annual meeting of the College Reading Association, 1973. ED 085 660 (Arlington, VA: ERIC, 1973).

514. Planisek, S. L. and R. J. Planisek. A Description of Fifteen Test Statistics Based Upon Optically Scanned Instructor Made Multiple-choice Tests at Kent State University. ED 065 547 (Arlington, VA: ERIC, 1972).

515. Poetker, Joel S. "Practical Suggestions for Improving and

Using Essay Questions." High School Journal 61(1): 7-15 (1977).

516.   Poggio, John P. and Douglas R. Glassnapp. Item-sampling as a Classroom Evaluation Technique. Paper presented at annual meeting of the National Council on Measurement in Education, 1973. ED 076 692 (Arlington VA: ERIC, 1973).

517.   Polin, Linda and Eva L. Baker. Exploration of "Fuzzy Set" Procedures for Analysis of Item-specification Congruence. ED 212 657 (Arlington, VA: ERIC, 1978).

518.   _____. Qualitative Analysis of Test Item Attributes for Domain Referenced Content Validity Judgments. Studies in Measurement and Methodology, Work Unit 1: Design and Use of Tests. Paper presented a the annual meeting of the American Educational Research Assocation, 1979. ED 211 601 (Arlington, VA: ERIC, 1979).

519.   Poole, Richard L. Student Victimization and the Formulation of Test Construction Criteria. Paper presented at the annual meeting of the National Council on Measurement in Education, 1975. ED 111 871 (Arlington, VA: ERIC, 1975).

520.   _____. Writing and Improving Classroom Tests, A Teacher's Guide. Booklet 1. ED 091 230 (Arlington, VA: ERIC, 1973).

521.   Popham, W. James. Criterion-referenced Measurement (Englewood Cliffs, NJ: Prentice-Hall, 1978).

522.   _____. "Customized Criterion-referenced Tests." Educational Leadership 34(4): 258-59 (1977).

523.   _____. The Development of Criterion-referenced Tests: Technical Considerations. ED 173 383 (Los Angeles: Instructional Objectives Exchange, 1976).

524.   _____. Technical Travails of Developing Criterion-referenced Tests. Paper presented at the annual meeting of the National Council on Measurement in Education, 1974. ED 091 421 (Arlington, VA: ERIC, 1974).

525.   _____. "Well-crafted Criterion-referenced Tests." Educational Leadership 36(2): 91-95 (1978).

526.   Popham, W. James and Elaine Lindheim. "The Practical Side of Criterion-referenced Test Development." NCME Measurement in Education 10(4): 1-8 (1980).

527.   Popham, W. James, ed. Criterion-referenced Measurement: An Introduction. (Englewood Cliffs, NJ: Educational Technology·Publications, 1971).

528.   Pottinger, Paul S. and George O. Klemp. The Fund for the Improvement of Postsecondary Education. Final Report. ED 134 540 (Arlington, VA: ERIC, 1975).

529.   Poulter, Virgil L. "Computer-assisted Laboratory Testing." Modern Language Journal 53(8): 561-64 (1969).

530.   Poynor, Lee. General Assessment Techniques. ED 125 086
       (Austin, TX: Educational Systems Associates, 1974).

531.   Preece, P. F. W. "Test Item Analysis." School Science
       Review 55(192): 582-85 (1974).

532.   Preparation of a Filmstrip Unit on Basic Measurement
       Principles. Final Report. ED 091 444 (Arlington, VA:
       ERIC, 1973).

533.   Priestly, Michael and Paula M. Nassif. "From Here to
       Validity: Developing a Conceptual Framework for Test
       Item Generation in Criterion-referenced Measurement."
       Educational Technology 19(2): 27-32 (1979).

534.   Proceedings of the Annual Conference of the Military
       Testing Association (16th). Papers presented at the
       annual meeting of the Military Testing Association, 1974.
       ED 110 524 (Arlington, VA: ERIC, 1974).

535.   Prosser, Franklin. "Repeatable Tests." Educational
       Technology 13(3): 34-35 (1973).

536.   Pyrczak, Fred Jr. Objective Evaluation of the Quality of
       Multiple-choice Test Items. ED 069 703 (Arlington, VA:
       ERIC, 1972).

537.   Quellmalz, Edys and others. Studies in Test Design:
       Annual Report. ED 212 650 (Arlington, VA: ERIC, 1981).

538.   Quinto, Frances. "Teacher-made Tests -- An Alternative to
       Standardized Tests." Today's Education 66(2): 52-3
       (1977).

539.   Randall, Robert S. Contrasting Norm Referenced and
       Criterion Referenced Measures. ED 065 593 (Arlington, VA:
       ERIC, 1972).

540.   Reardon, Robert and William Kahnweiler. "Comparison of
       Pencil-and-paper and Tactile-board Forms of the Self-
       directed Search." Journal of Counseling Psychology 27(4):
       328-30 (1980).

541.   Reavis, William A. "About Tests." Mathematics Teacher
       70(2): 138-39 (1977).

542.   Reckase, Mark D. An Application of the Rasch Simple
       Logistic Model to Tailored Testing. Paper presented at
       the annual meeting of the American Educational Research
       Association, 1974. ED 092 585 (Arlington, VA: ERIC,
       1974).

543.   _____. The Effect of Item Choice on Ability Estimation
       When Using a Simple Logistic Tailored Testing Model.
       Paper presented at the annual meeting of the American
       Educational Research Association, 1975. ED 106 342
       (Arlington, VA: ERIC, 1975).

544.   _____. The Formation of Homogeneous Item Sets When
       Guessing is a Factor in Item Responses. ED 209 353
       (Arlington, VA: ERIC, 1981).

545.   . Item Pool Construction For Use With Latent Trait
    Models. Paper presented at the annual meeting of the
    American Educational Research Association, 1979. ED 173
    400 (Arlington, VA: ERIC, 1979).

546.   . Procedures for Criterion-referenced Tailored
    Testing. Final Report, 1977-1981. ED 209 354 (Arlington,
    VA: ERIC, 1981).

547.   . Tailored Testing, Measurement Problems and Latent
    Trait Theory. Paper presented at the annual meeting of
    the National Council on Measurement in Education, 1981.
    ED 207 987 (Arlington, VA: ERIC, 1981).

548.   . To Use or Not to Use -- (The One- or Three-
    parameter Logistic Model) That is the Question. Paper
    presented at the annual meeting of the American
    Educational Research Association, 1981. ED 206 642
    (Arlington, VA: ERIC, 1981).

549.   . "Unifactor Latent Trait Models Applied to
    Multifactor Tests: Results and Implications." Journal of
    Educational Statistics 4(3): 207-30 (1979).

550.   Ree, Malcolm James. Automated Test Item Banking. Final
    Report for Period January 1977-February 1978. ED 160 618
    (Arlington, VA: ERIC, 1978).

551.   . Development of Statistically Parallel Tests By
    Analysis of Unique Item Variance. ED 127 354 (Arlington,
    VA: ERIC, 1976).

552.   Reichman, Susan L. and Albert C. Oosterhof. Strategy
    Guidelines for the Construction of Mastery Tests. Paper
    presented at the annual meeting of the American
    Educational Research Association, 1976. ED 126 103
    (Arlington, VA: ERIC, 1976).

553.   Reilly, Richard R. Empirical Option Weighting with a
    Correction for Guessing. ED 073 132 (Arlington, VA: ERIC,
    1972).

554.   Remondini, David J. "Test Item System: A Method of
    Computer Assisted Test Assembly." Educational Technology
    13(3): 35-37 (1973).

555.   Rentz, R. Robert and Charlotte C. Rentz. Does the Rasch
    Model Really Work? A Discussion for Practitioners.
    ERIC/TM Report 67. ED 169 137 (Arlington, VA: ERIC,
    1978).

556.   Revelle, William. "Hierarchical Cluster Analysis and the
    Internal Structure of Tests." Multivariate Behavioral
    Research 14(1): 57-74 (1979).

557.   Rhoades, David J. "Student-made Tests." Journal of
    Counseling Services 2(2): 28-31 (1978).

558.   Riblet, Donald Campbell. "Environmental Knowledge and
    Opinion Scales -- Need, Design and Use: A Factor Analytic
    Study in Test Construction." Ed.D. diss., University of

Florida, 1971. *Dissertation Abstracts International* 32(12-A): 6747 (1971).

559.   Rindler, Susan Ellerin. "Pitfalls in Assessing Test Speededness." *Journal of Educational Measurement* 16(4): 261-70 (1979).

560.   Roberson, Don R. *Development and Use of Criterion-referenced Tests.* ED 125 097 (Austin, TX: Educational Systems Associates, 1975).

561.   Robertson, David W. and others. *Comparative Racial Analysis of Enlisted Advancement Exams: Item Differentiation. Final Report.* ED 166 246 (Arlington, VA: ERIC, 1977).

562.   Robinson, Michael E. and Peter Dicken. "Cloze Procedure and Cognitive Mapping." *Environment and Behavior* 11(3): 351-73 (1979).

563.   Rogers, Eric M. "Examinations: Powerful Agents for Good or Ill in Teaching." *American Journal of Physics* 37(10): 954-62 (1969).

564.   Roid, Gale H. and others. *Algorithms for Developing Test Questions From Sentences in Instructional Materials: An Extension of an Earlier Study.* ED 187 746 (Arlington, VA: ERIC, 1980).

565.   _____. *A Comparison of Item-writing Methods for Criterion-referenced Tests.* Paper presented at the Joint Annual Meetings of the American Educational Research Association and the National Council on Measurement in Education, 1980. ED 190 604 (Arlington, VA: ERIC, 1980).

566.   _____. *A Comparison of Methods for Transforming Sentences Into Test Questions for Instructional Materials. Technical Report #1.* ED 178 564 (Arlington, VA: ERIC, 1978).

567.   _____. *Item Writing for Domain-based Tests of Prose Learning.* Paper presented at the annual meeting of the American Educational Research Association, 1979. ED 170 365 (Arlington, VA: ERIC, 1979).

568.   Roid, Gale H. and Patrick J. Finn. *Algorithms for Developing Test Questions From Sentences in Instructional Materials. Interim Report. January-September 1977.* ED 163 024 (Arlington, VA: ERIC, 1978).

569.   _____. *Algorithms For Developing Test Questions From Sentences in Instructional Materials.* NPRDC Tech. Rep. 78-23 (San Diego: Navy Personnel Research and Development Center, 1978).

570.   Roid, Gale H. and T. M. Haladyna. "A Comparison of Objective-based and Modified-Bormuth Item Writing Techniques." *Educational and Psychological Measurement* 38(1): 19-28 (1978).

571.   _____. *A Comparison of Objective-based and Modified-*

Bormuth Item Writing Techniques. Paper presented at the annual meeting of the American Educational Research Association, 1976. ED 133 332 (Arlington, VA: ERIC, 1976).

572.   _____. A Comparison of Several Multiple-choice, Linguistic-based Item Writing Algorithms. Paper presented at the annual meeting of the American Educational Research Association, 1978. ED 159 183 (Arlington, VA: ERIC, 1978).

573.   _____. "The Emergence of an Item-writing Technology." Review of Educational Research 50(2): 293-314 (1980).

574.   _____. Handbook of Item Writing for Criterion-referenced Tests. (San Diego, California: NPRDC, Technical Note 80-8, 1980).

575.   _____. Handbook on Item Writing for Criterion-referenced Testing. (San Diego, California: Navy Personnel Research and Development Center, 1979).

576.   _____. A Review of Item Writing Methods for Criterion-referenced Tests in the Cognitive Domain. Paper presented at the annual meeting of the Military Testing Association, 1978. ED 178 562 (Arlington, VA: ERIC, 1976).

577.   _____. A Technology for Test-item Writing. (New York: Academic Press, 1982).

578.   Romoser, William V. "Teacher Utilization of Selected Principles of Test Construction." Ed.D. diss., University of Denver, 1963. Dissertation Abstracts International 24(12): 5253 (1963).

579.   Roth, Marjorie S. "Design Your Own Evaluation Tools." Audiovisual Instruction 23(8): 21-23 (1978).

580.   Roudabush, Glenn E. Item Selection for Criterion-referenced Tests. Paper presented at the annual meeting of the American Educational Research Association, 1973. ED 074 147 (Arlington, VA: ERIC, 1973).

581.   _____. Models for a Beginning Theory of Criterion-referenced Tests. Paper presented at the annual meeting of the National Council on Measurement in Education, 1974. ED 107 702 (Arlington, VA: ERIC, 1974).

582.   Roudabush, Glenn E. and Donald Ross Green. Aspects of a Methodology for Creating Criterion-referenced Tests. Paper presented at the annual meeting of the National Council for Measurement in Education, 1972. ED 099 411 (Arlington, VA: ERIC, 1972).

583.   _____. Some Reliability Problems in a Criterion-referenced Test. Paper presented at the annual meeting of the American Educational Research Association, 1971. ED 050 144 (Arlington, VA: ERIC, 1971).

584.   Rounds, James B. Jr. and others. "Comparability of

Multiple Rank Order and Paired Comparison Methods."
Applied Psychological Measurement 2(3): 415-22 (1978).

585.   Rovinelli, Richard J. and Ronald K. Hambleton. On the Use
       of Content Specialists in the Assessment of Criterion-
       referenced Test Item Validity. Paper presented at the
       annual meeting of the American Educational Research
       Association, 1976. ED 121 845 (Arlington, VA: ERIC,
       1976).

586.   Rubin, Donald L. Psychometric and Pedagogical Validity in
       Large Scale Assessments of Oral Communication Skills. ED
       206 666 (Arlington, VA: ERIC, 1979).

587.   Rudner, Lawrence M. Efforts Toward the Development of
       Unbiased Selection and Assessment Instruments. Paper
       presented at the International Symposium on Educational
       Testing, 1977. ED 148 899 (Arlington, VA: ERIC, 1977).

588.   _____. A Short and Simple Introduction to Tailored
       Testing. Paper presented at the annual meeting of the
       Eastern Educational Research Association, 1978. ED 166
       257 (Arlington, VA: ERIC, 1978).

589.   Ryan, Joseph P. and Debra W. Hamm. Practical Procedures
       for Increasing the Reliability of Classroom Tests by
       Using the Rasch Model. Paper presented at the annual
       meeting of the National Council on Measurement in
       Education, 1976. ED 129 901 (Arlington, VA: ERIC, 1976).

590.   Sacco, Steven J. The "Nuts and Bolts" of Test
       Construction. ED 216 541. Available as part of ED 216
       534, The OMLTA Yearbook: 1982. Ohio Modern Language
       Teachers Association, Columbus. (Arlington, VA: ERIC,
       1982).

591.   Saffir, M. A. "A Comparative Study of Scales Constructed
       by Three Psychophysical Methods." Psychometrika 2: 179-98
       (1937).

592.   Salisnjak, Julian. "Computer Aided Test Preparation: Six
       Years of Experience." Educational Technology 13(3): 37-38
       (1973).

593.   Sautter, Walter N. "A Time-saving Way to Effective Test
       Construction." Science Teacher 38(2): 50-51 (1971).

594.   Scheuneman, Janice. A New Method of Assessing Bias in
       Test Items. Paper presented at the annual meeting of the
       American Educational Research Association, 1975. ED 106
       359 (Arlington, VA: ERIC, 1975).

595.   Schmeiser, Cynthia Board and Douglas R. Whitney. The
       Effect of Selected Poor Item-writing Practices on Test
       Difficulty, Reliability and Validity: A Replication.
       Paper presented at the American Educational Research
       Association Meeting, 1973. ED 075 498 (Arlington, VA:
       ERIC, 1973).

596.   Schott, Robert W. "An Attempt at More Meaningful
       Examinations." Improving College and University Teaching

17(2): 112-14 (1969).

597. Schriber, Peter E. Cost Benefit Analysis of Comprehensive Achievement Monitoring for Classroom Evaluation. Paper presented at the annual meeting of the National Council of Measurement in Education, 1971. ED 053 181 (Arlington, VA: ERIC, 1971).

598. Schriber, Peter E. and William P. Gorth. Objective and Item Banking Computer Software and its Use in Comprehensive Achievement Monitoring. Paper presented at the annual meeting of the American Educational Research Association, 1971. ED 053 182 (Arlington, VA: ERIC, 1971).

599. Schrock, Timothy J. and Daniel J. Mueller. "Effects of Violating Three Multiple-Choice Item Construction Principles." Journal of Educational Research 75(5): 314-18 (1982).

600. Schulz, R. E. "Computer Aids for Developing Tests and Instruction." In H. F. O'Neil, Jr., Procedures for Instructional Systems Development (New York: Academic Press, 1979).

601. Schwartz, Steven A. "A Comprehensive System for Item Analysis in Psychological Scale Construction." Journal of Educational Measurement 15(2): 117-23 (1978).

602. Scott, C. Paul and James F. Watkins. "Criterion-referenced Testing." Journal of Studies in Technical Careers 4(4): 347-55 (1982).

603. Scott, Dennis L. and Leland F. Webb. "The Effects of Spacing and Handwritten or Typed Tests Upon Achievement of Students in Algebra and Geometry Classes." School Science and Mathematics 79(8): 663-69 (1979).

604. Seely, Oliver Jr. "Computer Assisted Test Construction - The View From California State University." Computers in Chemical Education Newsletter 5(4): 3-4 (1982).

605. Seely, Oliver Jr. and Van Willis. 'Socrates' Test Retrieval at the California State University and Colleges. Paper presented at the Conference on Computers in the Undergraduate Curricula, 1975. ED 112 828 (Arlington, VA: ERIC, 1975).

606. Selected References in Educational Measurement; Evaluation and Advisory Series. 3rd ed. ED 042 814 (Princeton, NJ: ETS, 1970).

607. Serlin, Ronald C. and Henry F. Kaiser. "A Computer Program for Item Selection Based on Maximum Internal Consistency." Educational and Psychological Measurement 36(3): 757-9 (1976).

608. Shann, Mary H. Measuring Problem Solving Skills and Processes in Elementary School Children. ED 135 807 (Arlington, VA: ERIC, 1976).

609. Shannon, Gregory A. The Construction of Matching Tests: An Empirical Statement. Paper presented at the National Council on Measurement in Education Meeting, 1975. ED 111 873 (Arlington, VA: ERIC, 1975).

610. Shaycoft, Marion F. Handbook of Criterion-referenced Testing: Development, Evaluation, and Use. ED 217 048 (Arlington, VA: ERIC, 1979).

611. Shayer, Michael. A New Approach to Data Analysis for the Construction of Piagetian Tests. ED 194 629 (Arlington, VA: ERIC, 1980).

612. Shepard, Lorrie. "Norm-referenced vs. Criterion-referenced Tests." Educational Horizons 58(1): 26-32 (1979).

613. Shively, Michael Jay. "Improving the Quality of Multiple Choice Examinations." Journal of Veterinary Medical Education 5(2): 71-6 (1978).

614. Shrigley, Robert L. "The Attitude of Preservice Science Teachers Toward a Low Anxiety Examination Model." School Science and Mathematics 76(1): 17-26 (1976).

615. Shrigley, Robert L. and C. R. Trueblood. "Designing a Likert-type Scale to Assess Attitude Toward Metrication." Journal of Research in Science Teaching 16: 73-8 (1979).

616. Shulman, Lee S. Test Design: A View From Practice. Paper presented at the Invitational Conference on Measurement and Methodology, 1978. ED 173 391 (Arlington, VA: ERIC, 1978).

617. Singh, Ishwar. "The Computer-assisted Test Construction and Marking System (CATCAMS)." Educational Technology 19(4): 46-48 (1979).

618. Sirotnik, Kenneth A. and others. "Some Methodological Issues in Developing Measures of Classroom Learning Environment: A Report of Work-in-Progress." Studies in Educational Evaluation 6(3): 279-89 (1980).

619. Sirotnik, Kenneth A. and Roger J. Wellington. "Scrambling Content in Achievement Testing: An Application of Multiple Matrix Sampling in Experimental Design." Journal of Educational Measurement 11(3): 179-88 (1974).

620. Sleeth, R. G. "Involving Students in Test-construction and Correction: Making Positive Use of True-False Ambiguity." Exchange Organizational Behavior Teaching Journal 4(3): 44-45 (1979).

621. Slem, Charles M. Modifying the Multiple Choice Test: A Short Answer Option. Paper presented at the annual convention of the American Psychological Association, 1981. ED 212 672 (Arlington, VA: ERIC, 1981).

622. Smith, A. G. "The Role of Question Banks in the Examining of Science." Australian Science Teachers Journal 18(3): 13-20 (1972).

623.   Smith, Charles W. "A Self-evaluation of Teacher-made
        Tests." College Student Journal 14 Monograph Supp: 1-11
        (Winter 1980).

624.   Smith, Douglas U. The Effects of Various Item Selection
        Methods on the Classification Accuracy and Classification
        Consistency of Criterion-referenced Instruments. Paper
        presented at the annual meeting of the American
        Educational Research Association, 1978. ED 159 222
        (Arlington, VA: ERIC, 1978).

625.   Smith, Jeffrey K. "Converging on Correct Answers: A
        Peculiarity of Multiple Choice Items." Journal of
        Educational Measurement 19(3): 211-20 (1982).

626.   _____. The Role of Measurement in the Process of
        Instruction. ED 189 164 (Arlington, VA: ERIC, 1979).

627.   Smith, Laura Spooner. Decisions and Dilemmas in
        Constructing Criterion-referenced Tests: Some Questions
        and Issues. CSE Report No. 110. ED 163 069 (Arlington,
        VA: ERIC, 1978).

628.   Smith, Paul. "The Tests and the Discipline." ADE Bulletin
        57: 26-9 (May 1978).

629.   Smith, R. "How Do Teachers' Tests Measure Up?" Momentum
        11: 19 (February 1980).

630.   Smith, Raymond G. and Harold J. Nichols. "Semantic
        Differential Stability as a Function of Meaning Domain."
        Journal of Communication 23(1): 64-73 (1973).

631.   Solomon, Warren and others. The Development, Use, and
        Importance of Instruments that Validly and Reliably
        Assess the Degrees to Which Experimental Programs are
        Implemented. ED 129 914 (Arlington, VA: ERIC, 1977).

632.   Spillman, B. M. "Development of an Instrument for the
        Dynamic Measurement of Consensus." Communication
        Monographs 46: 1-12 (March 1979).

633.   Spineti, John P. and Ronald K. Hambleton. "A Computer
        Simulation Study of Tailored Testing Strategies for
        Objective-based Instructional Programs." Educational and
        Psychological Measurement 37(1): 139-58 (1977).

634.   Spitze, Hazel Taylor and Mildred Barnes Griggs. Choosing
        Evaluation Techniques. ED 121 843 (Arlington, VA: ERIC,
        1976).

635.   Stallings, Jane A. The Development of the Contextual
        Observation System. Paper presented at the annual meeting
        of the American Educational Research Association, 1978).
        ED 166 211 (Arlington, VA: ERIC, 1978).

636.   "Standardized Tests: What Are They? How Are They Made?
        How Are They Scored." Instructor 82(7): 45-8 (1973).

637.   Stapleton, Peter T. "Make-it-yourself Exams for Do-it-
        yourself English: Self-directed Group Study." English

Journal 62(2): 275-77. (1973).

638.   Stephens, Will Beth and Surang Kowatrakul. Paper-and-
        pencil Versus Concrete Performance of Normals and
        Retardates on the ETS Written Exercises. Paper reprinted
        from the Proceedings, 77th Annual Convention, American
        Psychological Association, 1969). ED 035 442 (Washington,
        D.C.: APA, 1969).

639.   Stephenson, Robert W. and others. A Modular Approach to
        Proficiency Testing. Paper presented at the annual
        conference of the Military Testing Association, 1973. ED
        101 173 (Arlington, VA: ERIC, 1973).

640.   Stevens, J. M. and F. T. C. Harris. "The Display of
        Multiple Choice Question Bank on Microfilm." Medical
        Education 11(3): 190-1 (1977).

641.   Stewart, Roger G. "Some Effects of Reversing Certain
        Items in the Rokeach Dogmatism Scale." Educational and
        Psychological Measurement 30(2): 327-36 (1970).

642.   Stiggins, Richard J. "An Alternative to Blanket
        Standardized Testing." Today's Education 64(2): 38-40
        (1975).

643.   Stock, William and others. "A Conversational Random
        Access Computer-assisted Test Construction System." AEDS
        Monitor 15(7/8/9): 6-7,15 (1977).

644.   Strang, Harold R. "Effect of Technically Worded Options
        on Multiple-choice Test Performance." Journal of
        Educational Research 73(5): 262-65 (1980).

645.   Svinicki, Marilla D. "The Test: Uses, Construction and
        Evaluation." Engineering Education 66(5): 408-411 (1976).

646.   Swaminathan, H. and others. "A Bayesian Decision-
        theoretic Procedure for Use With Criterion-referenced
        Tests." Journal of Educational Measurement 12(2): 87-98
        (1975).

647.   Swezey, Robert W. "Toward the Development of Realistic
        Measures of Performance Effectiveness." Journal of
        Educational Technology Systems 5(4): 355-67 (1977). For
        related information see ED 125 577.

648.   Swezey, Robert W. and Richard B. Pearlstein. "Developing
        Criterion-referenced Tests." JSAS Catalog of Selected
        Documents in Psychology 5: 227 (1975).

649.   _____. Guidebook for Developing Criterion-referenced
        Tests. (Arlington, VA: U.S. Army Research Institute for
        the Behavioral and Social Sciences, 1975). For related
        information see ED 126 122.

650.   Swezey, Robert W., Richard B. Pearlstein and W. H. Ton.
        "Criterion-referenced Testing: A Discussion of Theory and
        Practice in the Army." (Arlington, VA: U.S. Army Research
        Institute Research Memorandum 75-11, December 1975). For
        related information see ED 178 548.

651.   Symposium: The Care and Feeding of Test Constructors.
       Symposium presented at the annual Military Testing
       Conference, 1974. ED 118 612 (Arlington, VA: ERIC, 1974).

652.   Talbott, Albert D. Q Technique and its Methodology: A
       Brief Introduction and Consideration. From the Symposium
       "The Use of Q Methodology for Research in Educational
       Administration" presented at the annual meeting of the
       American Educational Research Association, 1971. ED 060
       040 (Arlington, VA: ERIC, 1971).

653.   Taylor, Hugh. Construction, Administration and Analysis
       of a Classroom Test. Paper presented at the annual
       meeting of the National Council on Measurement in
       Education, 1979. ED 177 225 (Arlington, VA: ERIC, 1979).

654.   Taylor, Hugh and others. Construction and Use of
       Classroom Tests: A Resource Book for Teachers. ED 190 609
       (Arlington, VA: ERIC, 1979).

655.   Testing and the Public Interest. Proceedings of the ETS
       Invitational Conference, 1976. ED 150 191 (Arlington, VA:
       ERIC, 1977).

656.   Textbook Usage Inventories (4-12). ED 210 648 (Arlington,
       VA: ERIC, 1981).

657.   Thorndike, Robert L. "The Analysis and Selection of Test
       Items." In Problems in Human Assessment, edited by D. N.
       Jackson and S. Messick. (New York: McGraw-Hill, 1967).

658.   _____. Methodological Problems in Developing Instruments
       for Cross-national Studies. Paper presented at the annual
       meeting of the National Council on Measurement in
       Education, 1975. ED 111 881 (Arlington, VA: ERIC, 1974).

659.   Thurman, L. D. "Multiple Choice Testing Without
       Retyping." Journal of College Science Teaching 7: 42
       (1977).

660.   Tinkelman, Sherman N. Improving the Classroom Test: A
       Manual of Test Construction Procedures for the Classroom
       Teacher. ED 120 207 (Arlington, VA: ERIC, 1975).

661.   Tinsley, Howard E. A. and Rene V. Dawis. The Equivalence
       of Semantic and Figural Test Presentation of the Same
       Items. ED 068 515 (Arlington, VA: ERIC, 1972).

662.   Tisher, R. P. "A Piagetian Questionnaire Applied to
       Pupils in a Secondary School." Child Development 42(5):
       1633-6 (1971).

663.   Tittle, Carol Kehr. "Women and Educational Testing." Phi
       Delta Kappan 55(2): 118-19 (1973).

664.   Toben, Michael. "The Multiple Difficulties in the
       Construction of Multiple Choice Tests." English Teachers'
       Journal (Israel) 12: 40-42 (1974).

665.   Tokar, E. and D. Ruggles. "Using Pocket Calculators to
       Improve the Quality of Teacher-made Tests." Educational

Technology 21: 51-2 (1981).

666.   Tombari, Martin and Evangelina Mangino. How to Write
       Criterion-referenced Tests for Spanish-English Bilingual
       Programs. ED 161 281 (Austin, TX: Dissemination and
       Assessment Center for Bilingual Education, 1979).

667.   Torabi-Parizi, R. and N. J. Campbell. "Classroom Test-
       writing: Effects of Item Format on Test Quality."
       Elementary School Journal 83: 155-60 (1982).

668.   Towle, Nelson J. and others. A Case Study in the Use of
       Computers to Personalize Instruction. Paper presented at
       the Conference on Computers in the Undergraduate
       Curricula, 1973. ED 079 986 (Arlington, VA: ERIC, 1973).

669.   Towle, Nelson J. and Paul F. Merrill. "Effects of Anxiety
       Type and Item-difficulty Sequencing on Mathematics Test
       Performance." Journal of Educational Measurement 12(4):
       241-9 (1975).

670.   Trieber, J. Marshall. "The Use of Multiple-choice for
       Testing." Training and Development Journal 34(10): 24-28
       (1980).

671.   Tzeng, Oliver C. S. and Dan Landis. "Three-mode
       Multidimensional Scaling With Points of View Solutions."
       Multivariate Behavioral Research 13(2): 181-213 (1978).

672.   Urry, Vern W. "Tailored Testing: A Successful Application
       of Latent Trait Theory." Journal of Educational
       Measurement 14(2): 181-96 (1977).

673.   Valgeirsdottir, Sigridur Thora. "Adaptive Test
       Construction Using the Rasch Model of Measurement." Ph.D.
       diss., State University of New York at Buffalo, 1974.
       Dissertation Abstracts International 35(10-A): 6522
       (1974).

674.   Vanharskamp, F. and H. R. Vandongen. "Construction and
       Validation of Different Short Forms of Token Test."
       Neuropsychologia 15(3): 467-70 (1977).

675.   Vaughn, Joseph and Darrell Sabers. "Factors in Validating
       Affective Scales: An Applied Study." Journal of Reading
       Behavior 9(3): 253-8 (1977).

676.   Veal, L. Ramon and Edieann F. Biesbrock. "Primary Essay
       Tests." Journal of Educational Measurement 8(1): 45-6
       (1971).

677.   Vickers, F. D. "Creative Test Generators." Educational
       Technology 13(3): 43-44 (1973).

678.   Vierling, Anton F. "Computer-generated Drill and Test."
       American Journal of Physics 40(4): 631-32 (1972).

679.   Volans, Pamela J. "Pros and Cons of Tailored Testing: An
       Examination of Issues Highlighted by Experience with an
       Automated Testing System." International Journal of Man-
       machine Studies 17(3): 301-304 (1982).

680. Wahlstrom, M. W. and S. M. Hunka. "An Item Selection Algorithm." Journal of Experimental Education 41(2): 87-91 (1972).

681. Walker, R. A. and others. "Written Piagetian Task Instrument: Its Development and Use." Science Education 63: 211-20 (1979).

682. Walter, James and others. Computer-based Test Development Center Project. Final Report. ED 081 192 (Arlington, VA: ERIC, 1970).

683. Ward, Charles D. "Multiple-choice Question Writing: Research Participation and Exam Performance." Journal of College Science Teaching 3(1): 77-78 (1973).

684. Warren, Gordon. "Essay Versus Multiple Choice Tests." Journal of Research in Science Teaching 16(6): 563-67 (1979).

685. Warren, Richard D. and others. "Moderator Effects on Attitude Scale Construction." Home Economics Research Journal 1(4): 259-68 (1973).

686. Warthen, Frances Jean. "A Comparison of the Relative Effects of Various Methods of Test Construction Upon the Concurrent Validity of a Test." Ph.D. diss., Catholic University of America, 1964.

687. Washington, William N. and Richard R. Godfrey. "The Effectiveness of Illustrated Items." Journal of Educational Measurement 2(2): 121-24 (1974).

688. Wasik, J. L. "GENTEST: A Computer Program to Generate Individualized Objective Test Forms." Educational and Psychological Measurement 39: 653-6 (1979).

689. Waters, Carrie Wherry and A. G. Bayroff. "A Comparison of Computer-simulated Conventional and Branching Tests." Educational and Psychological Measurement 31(1): 125-36 (1971).

690. Weiss, David J. "Improving Measurement Quality and Efficiency with Adaptive Theory." Applied Psychological Measurement 6(4): 473-92 (1982).

691. Wesman, A. G. "Writing the Test Item." Chapter 4 in Educational Measurement, 2nd ed., ed. by R. L. Thorndike. (Washington, D.C.: American Council on Education, 1971).

692. Whaley, Donald L. Psychological Testing and the Philosophy of Measurement. ED 080 538 (Arlington, VA: ERIC, 1973).

693. Whitley, Theodore W. "Some Common Flaws in Multiple Choice Exam Questions." Nursing Outlook 27(7): 466-69 (1979).

694. Whitlock, Lawrence Robert. "Interactive Test Construction and Administration in the Generative Exam System." Ph.D. diss., University of Illinois at Urbana-Champaign, 1976.

Dissertation Abstracts International 37(10-B): 5215 (1976).

695.   Wiggers, Thomas B. "A Computerized Test Question Storage and Examination Preparation System." Educational Computer Magazine 2(2): 30-31 (1982).

696.   _____. "Utilization of the Apple Microcomputer for the Generation of Matching-type Examination Questions." Educational Computer 2(4): 32-33 (1982).

697.   Wilcox, Rand R. "Applying Ranking and Selection Techniques to Determine the Length of a Mastery Test." Educational and Psychological Measurement 39(1): 13-22 (1979).

698.   Wilkins, W. and G. Sisler. "Individualized Testing by Computer." Journal of Home Economics 63: 677-8 (1971).

699.   Williams, Robert L. and others. "Test Format as a Form of Bias for Black Students." Journal of Non-white Concerns in Personnel and Guidance 6(3): 141-7 (1978).

700.   Williams, Robert L., ed. "Culture-specific Testing: Part 1." Journal of Non-white Concerns in Personnel and Guidance 10(1): 3-48 (1981).

701.   Williams, Sheri S. "Criterion-referenced Tests." Improving College and University Teaching 27(1): 27-29 (1979).

702.   Wilson, H. A. A Humanistic Approach to Criterion Referenced Testing. ED 081 842 (Arlington, VA: ERIC, 1972).

703.   Wilson, Robert J. "Minimizing the Teaching-testing Conflict: Extended Multiple-choice." English Quarterly 7(2): 147-50 (1974).

704.   Wittmann, W. W. and R. Hampel. "Factor-analysis, Problems of Rotation and Implications for Test-construction -- Some Remarks to an Optimal Rotational Procedure With Empirical Data (FPI)." Archiv Fur Psychologie 128 (3-4): 219-39 (1976).

705.   Wofford, J. C. and T. L. Willoughby. "The Effects of Test Construction Variables Upon Test Reliability and Validity." California Journal of Educational Research 20(3): 96-106 (1969).

706.   Womer, F. B. "Reexamination of Multiple-choice Testing." Education 90: 285-9 (1970).

707.   Wood, Lewis Jay. Computer Assisted Test Construction in the BYU Library School. ED 144 602 (Arlington, VA: ERIC, 1976).

708.   Wood, Robert. "The Efficacy of Tailored Testing." Educational Research 11(3): 219-22 (1969).

709.   Woodson, M. I. Charles E. "The Issue of Item and Test

Variance for Criterion-referenced Tests." Journal of Educational Measurement 11(1): 63-4 (1974).

710. _____. "The Issue of Item and Test Variance for Criterion-referenced Tests: A Reply." Journal of Educational Measurement 11(2): 139-40 (1974).

711. Wright, B. D. and M. H. Stone. Best Test Design. (Chicago: Mesa Press, 1979).

712. Wright, Patricia. "Presenting People With Choices: The Effect of Format on the Comprehension of Examination Rubrics." Programmed Learning and Educational Technology 12(2): 109-14 (1975).

713. Yelland, Robert C. "Better Tests." Training and Development Journal 30(5): 42-4 (1976).

714. Zacharias, Jerrold R. "The People Should Get What They Need: An Optimistic View of What Tests Can Be." National Elementary Principal 58(2): 48-51 (1979).

715. Zwarts, Michel A. "On the Construction and Validation of Domain-referenced Measurements." Evaluation in Education: International Progress 5(2): 119-39 (1982).

Achievement Batteries

716. Adkins, Dorothy C. and others. Construction and Analysis of Achievement Tests. (Washington, D.C.: U.S. Civil Service Commission, 1947).

717. Aiken, Lewis R. The Case for Oral Achievement Testing. ED 222 578 (Arlington, VA: ERIC, 1979).

718. Alvidres, Maria D. and Randolph H. Whitworth. "The Development and Validation of an Entrance Examination in a Mexican University." Educational and Psychological Measurement 41(2): 503-9 (1981).

719. Anderson, Richard C. "How to Construct Achievement Tests to Assess Comprehension." Review of Educational Research 42(2): 145-70 (1972).

720. Asher, J. William and others. The Development of New Measures of Cognitive Variables in Elementary School Children (Phase II). Final Report. ED 078 888 (Arlington, VA: ERIC, 1970).

721. Bender, Timothy A. Processing Multiple Choice and Recall Test Questions. Paper presented at the annual meeting of the American Educational Research Association, 1980. ED 189 160 (Arlington, VA: ERIC, 1980).

722. Berk, Ronald A. "Application of Structural Facet Theory to Achievement Test Construction." Educational Research Quarterly 3(3): 62-72 (1978).

723. Bligh, Harold F. and others. Issues in the Development of an Individually-administered Achievement Test. Paper presented at the joint annual meetings of the American Educational Research Association and the National Educational Research Council on Measurement in Education, 1982. ED 219 397 (Arlington, VA: ERIC, 1982).

724. Boehm, Ann E. Assessing for Teaching with Young Children. ED 072 084 (Arlington, VA: ERIC, 1972).

725. Bormuth, J. R. On the Theory of Achievement Test Items.

(Chicago: University of Chicago Press, 1970).

726.   Boyle, T. A. and others. "Computer Mediated Testing: A Branched Program Achievement Test." _Modern Languages Journal_ 60: 428-40 (1976).

727.   Brickell, H. M. "Seven Key Notes on Minimal Competency Testing." _Educational Leadership_ 35: 551-2 (1978) and _Phi Delta Kappan_ 59: 589-92 (1978).

728.   Brooks, I. R. "Achievement Test for Indian Children (ATIC): Progress Report." _Northian_ 13(1): 20-7 (1978).

729.   Browning, Robert and others. "Technical Characteristics of the Peabody Individual Achievement Test as a Function of Item Arrangement and Basal and Ceiling Rules." _Psychology in the Schools_ 16(1): 4-7 (1979).

730.   Bull, Kay Sather and Jeffrey P. Feuquay. _Causal Attribution: A New Scale Developed to Minimize Existing Methodological Problems_. ED 199 258 (Arlington, VA: ERIC, 1980).

731.   Burrill, Lois E. _How A Standardized Achievement Test is Built. Test Service Notebook 125_. ED 178 588 (Arlington, VA: ERIC, 1970).

732.   Cahen, Leonard S. _The Development of a Selection Battery For Phase III-B. Beginning Teacher Evaluation Study. Technical Note Series. Technical Note III-1_. ED 151 380 (Arlington, VA: ERIC, 1976).

733.   Christie, Samuel G. and William A. Conniff. _A Case in Support of Using Locally Developed Non-normed Tests for Title I Program Evaluation_. Paper presented at the annual meeting of the American Educational Research Association, 1981. ED 206 658 (Arlington, VA: ERIC, 1981).

734.   Coffman, William E. _Classical Test Development Solutions. Number 23. Iowa Testing Programs Occasional Papers_. ED 175 913 (Arlington, VA: ERIC, 1979).

735.   _Constructing and Using Achievement Tests: A Guide For Navy Instructors_. ED 069 711 (Arlington, VA: ERIC, 1971).

736.   Costin, Frank. "The Optimal Number of Alternatives in Multiple-choice Achievement Tests: Some Empirical Evidence for a Mathematical Proof." _Educational and Psychological Measurement_ 30(2): 353-8 (1970).

737.   _____. "Three-choice Versus Four-choice Items: Implications for Reliability and Validity of Objective Achievement Tests." _Educational and Psychological Measurements_ 32(4): 1035-8 (1972).

738.   Coulson, Ronald R. and George K. Wood. "Using the High-speed Computer for Knowledge Test Construction." _Journal of Physical Education and Recreation_ 46(6): 28-9 (1975).

739.   Cox, Richard C. "An Empirical Investigation of the Effect of Item Selection Techniques on Achievement Test

Construction." Ph.D. diss., Michigan State University, 1964. Dissertation Abstracts International 25(11): 6386 (1964).

740.   Cox, Richard C. and Glenn T. Graham. The Development of a Sequentially Scaled Achievement Test. ED 010 206 (Arlington, VA: ERIC, 1966).

741.   Diamond, Esther E. "The AMEG Commission Report on Sex Bias in Achievement Testing." Measurement and Evaluation in Guidance 13(3): 135-47 (1980).

742.   Ebel, Robert L. Constructing Unbiased Achievement Tests. Paper presented at the National Institute of Education Test Bias Conference, 1975. ED 120 290 (Arlington, VA: ERIC, 1975).

743.   _____. "The Use of Item Response Times in Achievement Test Construction." Ph.D. diss., University of Iowa, 1947.

744.   Eggert, John. Developing Student Achievement Measures. Working Paper No. 3. ED 159 962 (Arlington, VA: ERIC, 1974).

745.   Eisenberg, Eric M. and Cassandra L. Book. Applying Latent Trait Theory to a Course Examination System: Administration, Maintenance, and Training. ED 193 266 (Arlington, VA: ERIC, 1980).

746.   Estes, Gary D. and others. A Criterion-referenced Basic Skills Assessment Program in a Large City School System. Paper presented at the annual meeting of the American Educational Research Association, 1976. ED 124 587 (Arlington, VA: ERIC, 1976).

747.   Filby, Nikola N. Progress Report on Reactivity Analyses (October-December Test Data). Beginning Teacher Evaluation Study. Technical Note Series. Technical Note III-5. ED 151 377 (Arlington, VA: ERIC, 1976).

748.   Filby, Nikola N. and Marilyn M. Dishaw. Construct Validation of Group-administered Achievement Tests Through Individual Testing. BTES. Beginning Teacher Evaluation Study. Technical Note Series. Technical Note III-4. Phase III-A. ED 160 637 (Arlington, VA: ERIC, 1977).

749.   _____. Development and Refinement of Reading and Mathematics Tests for Grades 2 and 5. Beginning Teacher Evaluation Study. Technical Report Series. Technical Report III-1. Continuation of Phase III A. ED 151 375 (Arlington, VA: ERIC, 1975).

750.   _____. Refinement of Reading and Mathematics Test Through an Analysis of Reactivity. Beginning Teacher Evaluation Study. Technical Report Series. Technical Report III-6. ED 151 376 (Arlington, VA: ERIC, 1976).

751.   Forbes, Dean W. The Use of Rasch Logistic Scaling Procedures in the Development of Short Multi-level

Arithmetic Achievement Tests for Public School
Measurement. Paper presented at the annual meeting of the
American Educational Research Association, 1976. ED 128
400 (Arlington, VA: ERIC, 1976).

752.   Gerberich, J. Raymond. Specimen Objective Test Items: A
Guide to Achievement Test Construction. (New York:
Longmans, Green & Co., 1956).

753.   Glaser, Robert and Richard C. Cox. Criterion-referenced
Testing for the Measurement of Educational Outcomes. ED
038 832 (Pittsburgh, PA: University of Pittsburgh,
Learning Research and Development Center, 1968).

754.   Gronlund, Norman E. Constructing Achievement Tests.
(Englewood Cliffs, N.J.: Prentice-Hall, 1968).

755.   _____. Constructing Achievement Tests, 3rd edition.
(Englewood Cliffs, N.J.: Prentice-Hall, 1982).

756.   Guttman, Louis and I. M. Schlesinger. The Analysis of
Diagnostic Effectiveness of a Facet Design Battery of
Achievement and Analytical Ability Test. ED 014 773
(Arlington, VA: ERIC, 1967).

757.   Haladyna, Thomas Michael and Gale Roid. A Theoretical and
Empirical Comparison of Three Approaches to Achievement
Testing. ED 148 903 (Arlington, VA: ERIC, 1976).

758.   Kennedy, E. G. and others. Position Paper on Standardized
Testing. ED 066 445 (Arlington, VA: ERIC, 1972).

759.   Klausmeier, Herbert J. and others. Development of
Conceptual Learning and Development Assessment Series I:
Equilateral Triangle. Technical Report No. 430. Reprinted
December 1977. ED 154 008 (Arlington, VA: ERIC, 1973).

760.   _____. Development of Conceptual Learning and Development
Assessment Series I: Equilateral Triangle. Working Paper
No. 119. ED 103 482 (Arlington, VA: ERIC, 1973).

761.   _____. Development of Conceptual Learning and Development
Assessment Series II: Cutting Tool. Technical Report No.
431. Reprinted December 1977. ED 154 010 (Arlington, VA:
ERIC, 1973).

762.   _____. Development of Conceptual Learning and Development
Assessment Series II: Cutting Tool. Working Paper No.
120. ED 103 483 (Arlington, VA: ERIC, 1973).

763.   _____. Development of Conceptual Learning and Development
Assessment Series III: Noun. Working Paper No. 121. ED
103 484 (Arlington, VA: ERIC, 1973).

764.   _____. Development of Conceptual Learning and Development
Assessment Series IV: Tree. Working Paper No. 126. ED 103
485 (Arlington, VA: ERIC, 1974).

765.   _____. An Individually Administered Test to Assess Level
of Attainment and Use of the Concept Equilateral
Triangle. ED 088 931 (Arlington, VA: ERIC, 1973).

766.   . Second Cross-sectional Study of Attainment of the Concepts "Equilateral Triangle," "Cutting Tool," "Noun," and "Tree" by Children Age 6 to 16 of City A. Technical Report No. 367. ED 128 395 (Arlington, VA: ERIC, 1976).

767.   . Second Cross-sectional Study of Attainment of the Concepts "Equilateral Triangle," "Cutting Tool," "Noun," and "Tree" by Children Age 6 to 16 of City B. Technical Report No. 347. ED 128 394 (Arlington, VA: ERIC, 1976).

768. McLean, Leslie D. and Ronald G. Ragsdale. "The Rasch Model for Achievement Tests -- Inappropriate in the Past, Inappropriate Today, Inappropriate Tomorrow." Canadian Journal of Education 8(1): 71-6 (1983).

769. Manzo, Anthony V. and Ula Price Casale. Description and Factor Analysis of a Broad Spectrum Battery for Assessing "Progress Toward Reading Maturity." ED 223 972 (Arlington, VA: ERIC, 1982).

770. Merwin, Jack C. An Author's Perspective of Standardized Achievement Tests. Paper presented at the annual meeting of the National Council on Measurement in Education, 1979. ED 177 195 (Arlington, VA: ERIC, 1979).

771. Morris, Lynn Lyons and Carol Taylor Fitz-Gibbon. How to Measure Achievement. Program Evaluation Kit, 6. ED 175 892. (Beverly Hills, CA: Sage Publications, 1978).

772. Mosher, Frederic A. Final Report on the Instrumentation Study. ED 166 195 (Arlington, VA: ERIC, 1976).

773. Mueller, Daniel J. "An Assessment of the Effectiveness of Complex Alternatives in Multiple Choice Achievement Test Items." Educational and Psychological Measurement 35(1): 135-41 (1975).

774. The National Item Analysis Program. Metropolitan Achievement Tests, 1978 Edition. Special Report Number 7. ED 194 560 (Arlington, VA: ERIC, 1978).

775. Patalino, Marianne. Rationale and Use of Content-relevant Achievement Tests for the Evaluation of Instructional Programs. ED 041 044 (Arlington, VA: ERIC, 1970).

776. Popham, W. James. Development of Readability Controlled Basic Skills Tests. Paper presented at the annual meeting of the American Educational Research Association, 1981. ED 205 542 (Arlington, VA: ERIC, 1981).

777. Sako, Sydney. "Writing Proficiency and Achievement Tests." TESOL Quarterly 3(3): 237-49 (1969).

778. Sanders, James R. and Stephen L. Murray. "Alternatives for Achievement Testing." Educational Technology 16(3): 17-23 (1976).

779. Schratz, Mary K. and Barrie Wellens. Minority Panel Review in the Development of an Achievement Test. Paper presented at the annual meeting of the American Psychological Association, 1981. ED 209 350 (Arlington,

VA: ERIC, 1981).

780.   Shoemaker, David M. "Toward a Framework for Achievement
        Testing." Review of Educational Research 45(1): 127-47
        (1975).

781.   Shoemaker, David M. and H. G. Osburn. "Computer-aided
        Item Sampling for Achievement Testing: A Description of a
        Computer Program Implementing the Universe Defined Test
        Concept." Educational and Psychological Measurement
        29(1): 165-72 (1969).

782.   _____. "A Simulation Model for Achievement Testing."
        Educational and Psychological Measurement 30(2): 267-72
        (1970).

783.   Smith, Donald M. Determining Learning Sequences from a
        Difficulty-scaling of Test Items. Paper presented at the
        annual meeting of the American Educational Research
        Association, 1974. ED 093 900 (Arlington, VA: ERIC,
        1974).

784.   Technical Recommendations for Achievement Tests. Prepared
        by the Committees on Test Standards of the American
        Educational Research Association and the National Council
        on Measurements Used in Education. (Washington, D.C.:
        American Educational Research Association, National
        Education Association, 1955).

785.   Travers, R.M.W. How to Make Achievement Tests. (New York:
        The Odyssey Press, 1950).

786.   Yen, Wendy M. Use of Three-parameter Item Response Theory
        in the Development of CTBS, Form U, and TCS. Paper
        presented at the annual meeting of the National Council
        on Measurement in Education, 1982. ED 220 514 (Arlington,
        VA: ERIC, 1982).

English

787. Berry, Sharon R. "A Criterion Referenced Test of Written Language Syntax of Hearing Impaired Students." Dissertation Abstracts International 43(3-A): 753-4 (1982).

788. Bond, James T. The High/scope Productive Language Assessment Tasks: Effects of the Cognitively Oriented Curriculum on Follow Through Children's Written Language Production. ED 142 560 (Arlington, VA: ERIC, 1975). Appendices available from High/scope Educational Research Foundation, Ypsilanti, MI.

789. Breneman, Beth. Reaction: The Cloze and the Composition Process. Paper presented at the annual meeting of the National Council of Teachers of English, 1975. ED 117 699 (Arlington, VA: ERIC, 1975).

790. Britt, Morris F. An Exploratory Study of a Color Association Exercise for the Assessment of Verbal Creative Ability. ED 021 267 (Arlington, VA: ERIC, 1967).

791. Byrd, Marquita L. and Hampton S. Williams. Language Attitudes and Black Dialect: An Assessment. (1) Language Attitudes in the Classroom. (2) A Reliable Measure of Language Attitudes. Paper presented at the annual meeting of the Speech Communication Association, 1981. ED 213 062 (Arlington, VA: ERIC, 1981).

792. Carruthers, Robert B. Building Better English Tests: A Guide for Teachers of English in the Secondary School. ED 038 385 (Champaign, IL: National Council of Teachers of English, 1963).

793. Celce-Murcia, M. and others. "Goal: Good Multiple-choice Language-test Items." English Language Teaching Journal 28: 257-62 (1974).

794. Chew, Charles R. The Writing Test for New York State Elementary Schools: Development, Form, Implications. ED 224 046 (Arlington, VA: ERIC, 1982).

795.   Cronnell, Bruce. Language Competency Testing in the Elementary School. Paper presented at the Southwest Regional NCTE Conference, 1980. ED 199 278 (Arlington, VA: ERIC, 1980).

796.   Curry, Robert L. and Lynna Geis. Development and Standardization of Parallel Forms of the Curry-Geis Syllabication Skills Test (including Curry-Geis Syllabication Skills Test Form A and Form B). ED 129 922 (Arlington, VA: ERIC, 1977).

797.   _____. Syllabication Skills of College Students. Paper presented at the National Reading Conference, 1974. ED 124 871 (Arlington, VA: ERIC, 1974).

798.   Day, Richard R. and others. The Standard English Repetition Test (SERT); A Measure of Standard English Performance for Hawaii Creole English-speaking Children. Technical Report #15. ED 160 607 (Arlington, VA: ERIC, 1975).

799.   Dew, Donald and Paul J. Jensen. "The Phonetic Transcription Proficiency Test: Description and Preliminary Evaluation." Speech Monographs 40(1): 38-48 (1973).

800.   Di Giulio, Robert C. "Measuring Teacher Attitudes Toward Black English: A Pilot Project." Florida FL Reporter 2(1 & 2): 25-6, 49 (1973).

801.   Evans, William H., comp. "Testing in English." Illinois English Bulletin 52(5): 1-35 (1965).

802.   Finnegan, Denis Edward. "Receptive Phoneme Sequencing Knowledge of Kindergarten and Elementary School Age Children." Ph.D. diss., University of Wisconsin, Madison, 1976. ED 141 809. Available from University Microfilms, Ann Arbor, MI.

803.   Floriani, Bernard P. and John T. Wolinski. "Divide and Conquer: Syllabication Assessment and Older Students." Reading Horizons 22(1): 49-53 (1981).

804.   Ford, James and others. Report on the Working Conference on the SCRDT (Stanford Center for Research and Development in Teaching) Black English Tests for Teachers (February 19-20, 1976). Occasional Paper No. 15. ED 128 804 (Arlington, VA: ERIC, 1976).

805.   Gallimore, Ronald and Roland G. Tharp. Studies of Standard English and Hawaiian Islands Creole English: KEEP Linguistic Research, 1971-1976. Technical Report No. 59. ED 153 447 (Arlington, VA: ERIC, 1976).

806.   Geis, Lynna. Development and Standardization of Parallel Forms of a Syllabication Skills Test. Paper presented at the annual meeting of the International Reading Association Southwestern Regional Conference, 1976. ED 132 508 (Arlington, VA: ERIC, 1976).

807.   Golub, Lester S. and others. Measuring Language Arts

Concept Attainment: Boys and Girls. Technical Report No. 199. ED 065 894 (Arlington, VA: ERIC, 1971).

808.   Goodwin, Coleen Rawson. "The Development of a Diagnostic Test for Determining Secondary Students' Knowledge and Understanding of Certain Basic Language Concepts." Ed.D. diss., Arizona State University, 1974. ED 097 686. Available from University Microfilms, Ann Arbor, MI.

809.   Graham, Norman. "Towards a Test of Language Production." Educational Review 24(1): 34-46 (1971).

810.   Herrington, Anne J. Judgment: Designing a Proficiency Exam. Paper presented at the annual meeting of the Conference on College Composition and Communication, 1979. ED 176 259 (Arlington, VA: ERIC, 1979).

811.   Hisel, Wanda Coffield. "The Informal Language Inventory: Practical Language Assessment Form for Elementary Classroom Usage." Ph.D. diss., Kansas State University, 1974. ED 112 396. Available from University Microfilms, Ann Arbor, MI.

812.   Hollomon, John W. and others. Eliciting Covert Mental Operations, Concepts and Oral Language Skills in Young Bilingual Children. ED 138 123 (Arlington, VA: ERIC, 1975).

813.   Hoover, Mary R. and others. CERAS Test Battery: Tests of Black English for Teachers of Bidialectal Students (TBETB). Test I. History and Structure--Forms A and B; Test II. Language Arts Pedagogy--Forms A and B. ED 173 827 (Arlington, VA: ERIC, 1979).

814.   Horner, Judith. "How Do We Know How Well Kids Write? A Program for Testing Writing: Close-up: Evaluating and Revising Composition." English Journal 67(7): 60-61 (1978).

815.   Humes, Ann. Constructing Items for Assessing English Writing Skills. Technical Note. ED 192 337 (Arlington, VA: ERIC, 1980).

816.   Humes, Ann and others. Specifications for 1-6 Writing Skills Assessment Part I: Mechanics. Technical Note. ED 192 371 (Arlington, VA: ERIC, 1980).

817.   _____. Specifications For 1-6 Writing Skills Assessment Part II: Spelling. Technical Note. ED 192 372 (Arlington, VA: ERIC, 1980).

818.   _____. Specifications For 1-6 Writing Skills Assessment Part III: Language. Technical Note. ED 192 373 (Arlington, VA: ERIC, 1980).

819.   _____. Specifications For 1-6 Writing Skills Assessment Part IV: General Discourse. Technical Note. ED 192 374 (Arlington, VA: ERIC, 1980.).

820.   _____. Specifications For 1-6 Writing Skills Assessment Part V: Discourse Products. Technical Note. ED 192 375

(Arlington, VA: ERIC, 1980).

821.   Jacobs, Paul H. and William H. Evans. Illinois Tests in
       the Teaching of High School English. Interim Report. ED
       031 497 (Arlington, VA: ERIC, 1969).

822.   Johnson, Dale D. and others. The Assessment of Structural
       Analysis Skills. ED 185 539 (Arlington, VA: ERIC, 1979).

823.   _____. Interim Report: The Refinement of the Test Battery
       to Assess Word Identification Skills. Report From the
       Project on Studies in Language: Reading and
       Communication. ED 194 575 (Arlington, VA: ERIC, 1980).

824.   _____. The Word Identification Test Battery: A New
       Approach to Mastery and the Assessment of Word
       Identification Skills. Report From the Project on Studies
       in Language: Reading and Communication. ED 194
       590 (Arlington, VA: ERIC, 1980).

825.   Johnson, Dale D. and Richard Venezky. An Instrument for
       Testing Pronunciations of Vowel Clusters. Part I:
       Linguistic Background. ED 046 626 (Arlington, VA: ERIC,
       1970).

826.   Lawson, James Herbert. "The Development of a Poetry Test
       for Grades Eleven and Twelve." Ph.D. diss., University of
       Kansas, 1968. ED 041 012. Available from University
       Microforms, Ann Arbor, MI.

827.   Lederman, Marie Jean. The CUNY Writing Assessment Test:
       1976-1980. Paper presented at the annual meeting of the
       New York State English Council, 1980. ED 194 893
       (Arlington, VA: ERIC, 1980).

828.   Lindamood, Charles, H. and Patricia C. Lindamood.
       Conceptualization of Auditory Patterns. Paper presented
       at the International Reading Association Conference,
       1970. ED 044 253 (Arlington, VA: ERIC, 1970).

829.   Lutz, William D. How to Read 55,000 Essays a Year, and
       Love It. Paper presented at the annual meeting of the
       Conference on College Composition and Communication,
       1980. ED 185 563 (Arlington, VA: ERIC, 1980).

830.   Matalene, Carolyn B. "Objective Testing: Politics,
       Problems, Possibilities." College English 44(4): 368-81
       (1982).

831.   Maxwell, Marilyn Griffith. "The Development and
       Evaluation of a Test of Certain Expository Abilities."
       Ed.D. diss., Boston University, 1969. ED 048 260.
       Available from University Microfilms, Ann Arbor, MI.

832.   O'Donnell, Roy C. A Test of Perception of Syntactic
       Alternatives. Studies in Language Education, Report No.
       2. ED 077 025 (Arlington, VA: ERIC, 1973).

833.   Politzer, Robert L. and Dwight Brown. "A Production Test
       in Black Standard and Nonstandard Speech." Florida FL
       Reporter 2(1 & 2): 21 (1973).

834. Politzer, Robert L. and others. A Test of Proficiency in
      Black Standard and Nonstandard Speech. Research and
      Development Memorandum #101. Paper presented at the
      Doctoral Seminar, University of Georgia, 1971. ED 075
      479. Contained in ED 075 470. (Arlington, VA: ERIC,
      1973).

835. Prather, Elizabeth M. and others. "A Mini-screening
      Language Test for Adolescents." Language, Speech, and
      Hearing Services in the Schools 12(2): 67-73 (1981).

836. Purves, Alan C. "Competence in English: Can We Test It."
      Curriculum Review 17(1): 29-31 (1978).

837. Ralph, Ruth S. "Measuring Effects of General Semantic
      Personality Adjustment." ETC: A Review of General
      Semantics 29(1): 13-19 (1972).

838. Reynell, Joan and R.M.C. Huntley. "New Scales for the
      Assessment of Language Development in Young Children."
      Journal of Learning Disabilities 4(10): 549-57 (1971).

839. Robertson, William J. and Jerry F. Garner. The
      Development of a Diagnostic Instrument to be Used for
      Identifying Nonstandard Dialect Patterns of Disadvantaged
      Negro Students. Final Report. ED 040 261 (Arlington, VA:
      ERIC, 1970).

840. Rose, Suzanna and others. The Development of a Measure to
      Evaluate Language Communication Skills of Young Children.
      Paper presented at the American Educational Research
      Association Meeting, 1973. ED 076 665 (Arlington, VA:
      ERIC, 1973).

841. Ross, Raymond S. and others. Speech Fright Problems of
      Grade School Students. ED 015 198 (Arlington, VA: ERIC,
      1966).

842. Rudegeair, Robert E. Assessment of Early Childhood
      Language Proficiency. ED 111 004 (Arlington, VA: ERIC,
      1972).

843. Schuessler, B. F. and others. "Development of Scales
      Measuring Teacher Attitudes Toward Instruction in Written
      Composition: A Preliminary Investigation." Research in
      Teaching English 15: 55-63 (1981).

844. Shackford, Helen Greene. "Junior High School Students'
      Knowledge of Grammatical Structure and its Relation to
      Reading Comprehension." Ed.D. diss., Boston University,
      1976. ED 125 592. Available from University Microfilms,
      Ann Arbor, MI.

845. Sherman, M. and M. Zieky, eds. Handbook for Conducting
      Task Analyses and Developing Criterion-referenced Tests
      of Language Skills. (Princeton, N.J.: Educational Testing
      Service, 1974).

846. Snider, Sarah J. "Developing Non-essay Tests to Measure
      Affective Response to Poetry." English Journal 67(7):
      38-40 (1978).

847.   Yoder, A. C. "Testing Speeches; Student Prepared Tests."
        Communication Education 26: 76-7 (1977).

LITERATURE

848.   McAleer, Nancy Marie. "The Development and Validation of
        a Scale to Measure the Attitudes of Fifth Grade Children
        Toward Literature." Ed.D. diss., University of Florida,
        1974. ED 114 832. Available from University Microfilms,
        Ann Arbor, MI.

849.   Purves, Alan C. "Designing the Board's New Literature
        Achievement Test." College Board Review 67: 16-20 (1968).

SPELLING

850.   Bowers, Thomas A. and Richard R. Cole. How to Construct
        Your Own Exam on Spelling, Grammar and Punctuation. Paper
        presented at the annual meeting of the Association for
        Education in Journalism, 1974. ED 097 706 (Arlington VA:
        ERIC, 1974).

851.   Gentry, Larry A. An Analysis of the Content of Seven
        Spelling Series. Technical Note. Paper presented at the
        annual meeting of the Association for Education in
        Journalism, 1980. (Arlington, VA: ERIC, 1979).

852.   Gibson, Susanne K. Computer-aided Construction of
        Categorized Spelling Tests. ED 039 226 (Arlington, VA:
        ERIC, 1969).

853.   Johnson, Dale D. and others. A New Approach to the
        Assessment of Phonics Skills. ED 186 846 (Arlington, VA:
        ERIC, 1979).

854.   Shores, Jay H. and Albert H. Yee. "Spelling Achievement
        Tests: What is Available and Needed." Journal of Special
        Education 7(3): 301-9 (1973).

VOCABULARY

855.   Bayer, Maria L. Primary Grade Understanding Vocabulary as
        Measured by Orally Administered Basic Word Vocabulary
        Test. M. Ed. thesis, Rutgers University, 1976. ED 131 417
        (Arlington, VA: ERIC, 1976).

856.   Bellugi-Klima, Ursula. Some Language Comprehension Tests.
        ED 040 765 (Arlington, VA: ERIC, 1970).

857.   Duffelmeyer, Frederick A. "A Non-traditional Technique
        for Testing Vocabulary." Reading Horizons 21(3): 179-82
        (1981).

858.   Faizunisa, Ali and Joan Costello. Modification of the
        Peabody Picture Vocabulary Test. ED 033 752 (Arlington,
        VA: ERIC, 1969).

859.   Haroian, Rose D. "Haroian Early Language Picture Test: A
        Picture Test of Early Language Development." Dissertation
        Abstracts International 43(2): 426 (1982).

860.   Hutchings, Geoffrey. "Colourless Green Ideas: Multiple-
        choice Vocabulary Tests." English Language Teaching
        25(1): 68-71 (1970).

861.   Johnson, Dale D. and others. Format Effects on Vocabulary
        Assessment. ED 173 355 (Arlington, VA: ERIC, 1978).

862.   Levy, Stine. "Use of the Peabody Picture Vocabulary Test
        with Low-functioning Autistic Children." Psychology in
        the Schools 19(1): 24-7 (1982).

863.   McBride, James R. and David J. Weiss. A Word Knowledge
        Item Pool for Adaptive Ability Measurement. Research
        Report No. 74-2. ED 096 339 (Arlington, VA: ERIC, 1974).

864.   O'Donnell, Roy C. An Instrument to Explore Category
        Features as Determinants of Choice in Pairing Words.
        Studies in Language Education. Report No. 13. ED 099 856
        (Arlington, VA: ERIC, 1975).

865.   The Rationale, Development, and Standardization of a
        Basic Word Vocabulary Test: A Methodological Report on
        the Conceptual Representation and Measurement of
        American-English Basic Word Vocabulary Acquisition. Data
        Evaluation and Methods Research, Series 2, No. 60. ED 094
        373 (Arlington, VA: ERIC, 1974).

866.   Taft, Jerome and Melvin Tennis. The Development of a Test
        to Assess the Occurrence of Selected Features of Non-
        standard English in the Speech of Disadvantaged Primary
        Children. ED 015 790 (Arlington, VA: ERIC, 1968).

867.   Wiener, Florence D. and others. Spanish Picture
        Vocabulary Test. Prueba Ilustrada de Vocabulario Espanol.
        An Adaptation of the Peabody Picture Vocabulary Test.
        Manual (and) Plates. Research Project 1978. ED 181 056
        (Arlington, VA: ERIC, 1978).

Fine Arts

ART

868. Force, Lorraine S. An Experimental Study to Examine the
      Responses of Sixth Grade Students to Programmed Art
      Instruction and Evaluative Instruments Designed to
      Correspond to Selected Ability Trait Variables. ED 051
      638 (Arlington, VA: ERIC, 1970).

869. Henton, Richard Wayne. "FAFT: An Evaluation Technique in
      Furniture Arrangement." Studies in Art Education 13(2):
      44-50 (1972).

870. Stuckhardt, Michael H. and Jerry W. Morris. "The
      Development of a Scale to Measure Attitudes Held Towards
      Arts Education." Studies in Art Education 21(2): 50-56
      (1980).

871. Taylor, Anne P. and G. C. Helmstadter. A Preliminary Pair
      Comparison Test for Measuring Aesthetic Judgment in Young
      Children. Paper presented at the annual meeting of the
      American Educational Research Association, 1971. ED 048
      351 (Arlington, VA: ERIC, 1971).

MUSIC

872. Abeles, Harold F. "Development and Validation of a
      Clarinet Performance Adjudication Scale." Journal of
      Research in Music Education 21: 246-55 (Fall 1973).

873. Beazley, Herschel V. "Development and Validation of a
      Music Education Competency Test." Journal of Research in
      Music Education 29(1): 5-10 (1981).

874. Brown, Merrill. "The Optimum Length of the Musical
      Aptitude Profile Subtests." Journal of Research in Music
      Education 17(2): 240-47 (1969).

875. Bryce, Jennifer. ACER and University of Melbourne Music
      Evaluation Kit. Handbook and Report. ED 183 585

(Arlington, VA: ERIC, 1979).

876.   Chalmers, B. A. "Development of a Measure of Attitude Toward Instrumental Music Style." Journal of Research in Music Education 26: 90-6 (Summer 1978).

877.   Davies, J. B. "New Tests of Musical Aptitude." British Journal of Psychology 62(4): 557-65 (1971).

878.   Gorder, Wayne Douglas. "Divergent Production Abilities as Constructs of Musical Creativity." Journal of Research in Music Education 28(1): 34-42 (1980).

879.   Herrold, Rebecca. The Development and Trial of a Computer Managed Test of Music Fundamentals. Paper presented at the Oregon Council for Research in Teacher Education, 1977. ED 171 312 (Arlington, VA: ERIC, 1977).

880.   Kaminska, B. "Designing and Preliminary Verification of the Knowledge of Music Test." Bulletin of the Council for Research in Music Education 59: 48-9 (Summer 1979).

881.   Karma, Kai. The Ability to Structure Acoustic Material as a Measure of Musical Aptitude. 4. Experiences with Modifications of the Acoustic Structuring Test. Research Bulletin No. 51. ED 177 172 (Arlington, VA: ERIC, 1978).

882.   _____. The Ability to Structure Acoustic Material as a Measure of Musical Aptitude: I. Background Theory and Pilot Studies. Research Bulletin 38. ED 092 440 (Arlington, VA: ERIC, 1973).

883.   _____. The Ability to Structure Acoustic Material as a Measure of Musical Aptitude: Part 2. Test Construction and Results. Research Bulletin 43. ED 110 402 (Arlington, VA: ERIC, 1975).

884.   Kidd, Robert Lee. "Construction and Validation of a Scale of Trombone Performance Skills." Ed.D. diss., University of Illinois, 1975. Critique by H. Abeles in Bulletin of the Council for Research in Music Education 65: 80-83 (Winter 1981).

885.   Legore, Sharon H. "Development and Validation of a Test to Measure Music Reading Readiness." D.M.A. thesis, Catholic University of America, 1981. Critique by D. W. Roach in Bulletin of the Council for Research in Music Education 72: 87-91 (Fall 1982).

886.   Long, Newell H. Pilot Study for the Development of Music Discrimination Tests for Elementary School Children. Final Report. ED 048 318 (Arlington, VA: ERIC, 1970).

887.   Oldefendt, Susan J. Scoring Instrumental and Vocal Musical Performances. Paper presented at the annual convention of the National Council on Measurement in Education, 1976. ED 129 839 (Arlington, VA: ERIC, 1976).

888.   Rider, M. S. "Assessment of Cognitive Functioning Level Through Musical Perception." Journal of Music Therapy 18:

110-19 (1981).

889.   Schmalstieg, Emily. "The Construction of a Reliable Test
       for Assessing Musical Performance." Journal of Research
       in Music Education 20(2): 280-2 (1972).

890.   Shaw, C. N. and M. Tomcala. "Music Attitude Scale for Use
       with Upper Elementary School Children." Journal of
       Research in Music Education 24: 73-80 (1976).

891.   Simons, Gene M. "A Criterion-referenced Test of
       Fundamental Music Listening Skills." Child Study Journal
       6(4): 223-34 (1976).

892.   Tomcala, Maryjane Pickles. "Construction and Comparison
       of a Verbal and Nonverbal Measure of Attitudes Toward
       Musical Activities in Grades Three, Four, and Five."
       Ed.D. diss., University of Georgia, 1977. Critique by D.
       W. Roach in Bulletin of the Council for Research in Music
       Education 63: 39-42 (Summer 1980).

893.   Wifler, Raymond Charles. "Development and Application of
       an Instrument to Identify Music-affect Shift Resulting
       from a College Music Appreciation Course." Ph.D. diss.,
       Michigan State University, 1978. Critique by H.
       Froehlich in Bulletin of the Council for Research
       in Music Education 64: 48-54 (Fall 1980).

894.   Wood, Stanley Dean. "Development and Evaluation of a
       Teaching Performance Test for Elementary Classroom
       Music." Ph.D. diss., Ohio State University, 1978.
       Critique by R. J. Tuley in Bulletin of the Council
       for Research in Music Education 72: 63-6 (Fall 1982).

895.   Zander, Alex Joseph. "Development and Validation of the
       Vernon-Zander Harmonic Discrimination Test." Ph.D. diss.,
       Northwestern University, 1975. Critique by R. H. Edwards
       in Bulletin of the Council for Research in Music
       Education 61: 1-5 (Winter 1980).

Foreign Languages

896. Agrawal, K. C. "Short Tests of Linguistic Skills and their Calibration." TESOL Quarterly 13: 185-208 (June 1979).

897. Aitken, Kenneth G. "Discrete Structure-point Testing: Problems and Alternatives." ED 142 034 TESL Reporter 9(4): 7-9, 18-20 (1976).

898. _____. TESL Applications of the Cloze Procedure: An Annotated Bibliography. ED 109 922 (Arlington, VA: ERIC, 1975).

899. _____. "Using Cloze Procedure as an Overall Language Proficiency Test." TESOL Quarterly 11(1): 59-67 (1977).

900. Bartz, Walter H. Testing Oral Communication in the Foreign Language Classroom. Language in Education: Theory and Practice, No. 17. ED 176 590 (Arlington, VA: ERIC, 1979).

901. Boynton, Damon. A Study-conference to Determine Acceptable Specifications for Standardized Foreign Language Reading Proficiency Tests for Graduate Students. Final Report. ED 010 476 (Arlington, VA: ERIC, 1961).

902. Brooks, Nelson. Language and Language Learning, Theory and Practice. Second Edition. ED 020 698 (New York: Harcourt, Brace and World, 1964).

903. Bryan, Miriam M. "The MLA Cooperative Foreign Language Tests." Revue de Louisiane/Louisiana Review 1(2): 143-8 (1972).

904. _____. Tests With a New Look and a New Purpose--The MLA Cooperative Foreign Language Tests. ED 012 154 (Arlington, VA: ERIC, 1966).

905. Carroll, John B. Foreign Language Testing: Will the Persistent Problems Persist. Paper presented at the ATESOL Conference, 1973. ED 079 432 (Arlington, VA: ERIC, 1973).

906.   Carroll, John B. and others. An Investigation of "Cloze" Items in the Measurement of Achievement in Foreign Languages. ED 021 513 (Arlington, VA: ERIC, 1959).

907.   Clark, John L. D., ed. Direct Testing of Speaking Proficiency: Theory and Application. ED 172 523 (Arlington VA: ERIC, 1978).

908.   Cohen, Andrew D. Testing Language Ability in the Classroom. ED 198 720 (Rowley, MA: Newbury House, 1980).

909.   Del Olmo, Guillermo. "The MLA Foreign Language Proficiency Tests for Teachers and Advanced Students." Contact 10: 18-22 (December 1967).

910.   Evans, Joyce S. Spanish/English Language Performance Screening: Technical Report. Final Report. ED 142 040 (Arlington, VA: ERIC, 1976).

911.   Evans, Joyce S. and others. The Spanish/English Language Performance Screening (S/ELPS): Extension of Reliability and Validity Studies with Cuban, Puerto Rican, and Mexican American Children, Preschool Through Third Grade. ED 142 041 (Arlington, VA: ERIC, 1977).

912.   Faulkner, James C. Objective Testing and Standardized Tests in Modern Foreign Languages. ED 011 169 (Arlington, VA: ERIC, 1968).

913.   Gardner, Robert C. and Padric C. Smythe. Second Language Acquisition: A Social Psychological Approach. Research Bulletin No. 332. ED 163 754 (Arlington, Va: ERIC, 1975).

914.   Irving, Evelyn Uhrhan. Testing in the Language Laboratory. Paper presented at the Mountain Interstate Foreign Language Conference, 1970. ED 069 170 (Arlington, VA: ERIC, 1970).

915.   Jakobovits, Leon A. "A Functional Approach to the Assessment of Language Skills." Journal of English as a Second Language 4(2): 63-76 (1969).

916.   Jorstad, Helen L. New Approaches to Assessment of Language Learning. Paper presented at the Northeast Conference on the Teaching of Foreign Languages, 1980. ED 191 308 (Middlebury, VT: Northeast Conference, 1980).

917.   King, Gail and Diane Nadeau. "An Evaluation of Oral/Aural Testing in Modern Foreign Languages at Boston University." NALID Journal 16(1): 5-15 (1981).

918.   Lado, Robert. Language Testing: The Construction and Use of Foreign Language Tests. A Teacher's Book. ED 032 799 (New York: McGraw-Hill, 1961).

919.   Ladu, Tora and others. Modern Foreign Languages: A Four-year Program (and) a Six-year Program. ED 046 307 (Arlington, VA: ERIC, 1971).

920.   Low, Graham D. "The Direct Testing of Academic Writing in a Second Language." System 10(3): 247-57 (1982).

921.   Luft, Max and others. Development of a Test Instrument to
        Determine Language Dominance of Primary Students: Test of
        Language Dominance (TOLD). Paper presented at the annual
        meeting of the American Educational Research Association,
        1977. ED 141 393 (Arlington, VA: ERIC, 1977).

922.   Matluck, Joseph H. and Betty J. Mace-Matluck. "Language
        and Culture in the Multi-ethnic Community: Spoken-
        language Assessment." Modern Language Journal 59(5-6):
        250-55 (1975).

923.   _____. Language and Culture in the Multi-ethnic
        Community: Spoken Language Assessment. Paper presented at
        the annual meeting of the Pacific Northwest Council on
        Foreign Languages, 1975. ED 138 053 (Arlington, VA: ERIC,
        1975).

924.   _____. The MAT-SEA-CAL Instruments for Assessing Language
        Proficiency. Paper presented at the annual meeting of the
        American Educational Research Association, 1976). ED 129
        877 (Arlington, VA: ERIC, 1976).

925.   _____. The Multilingual Test Development Project: Oral
        Language Assessment in a Multicultural Community. Paper
        presented at the National Conference of the Teachers of
        English to Speakers of Other Languages, 1975. ED 119 498
        (Arlington, VA: ERIC, 1975).

926.   Mazeika, Edward J. The Description of an Instrument to
        Assess the Receptive Language of Monolingual or Bilingual
        (Spanish/English) Children 12 to 36 Months of Age.
        Occasional Papers on Linguistics, No. 1. Proceedings of
        the International Conference on Frontiers in Language
        Proficiency and Dominance Testing, 1977. ED 144 411
        (Arlington, VA: ERIC, 1977).

927.   Meara, Paul. "Two Tests of Overall Ability in a Foreign
        Language." Audio-visual Language Journal 12(3): 233-6
        (1974-75).

928.   Petersen, Calvin R. and Antoine R. Ali-Haik. "The
        Development of the Defense Language Aptitude Battery
        (DLAB)." Educational and Psychological Measurement 36(2):
        369-80 (1976).

929.   Politzer, Robert L. and Maryann McKay. "A Pilot Study
        Concerning the Development of a Spanish/English Oral
        Proficiency Test." Bilingual Review 2(1/2): 112-37
        (1975).

930.   _____. A Pilot Study Concerning the Development of a
        Spanish/English Oral Proficiency Test. Research and
        Development Memorandum No. 120. ED 108 400 (Arlington,
        VA: ERIC, 1974).

931.   Proposal for the Development of a Language Testing
        Program for the Peace Corps. From the "Final Report on
        Peace Corps Language Coordinators Workshop," 1970. ED 043
        024 (Arlington, VA: ERIC, 1970).

932.   Robinson, Peter. <u>Basic Factors in the Choice, Composition and Adaption of Second Language Tests</u>. Paper presented at the third annual TESOL Convention, 1969. ED 027 540 (Arlington, VA: ERIC, 1969).

933.   _____. "The Composition, Adaptation, and Choice of Second-language Tests." <u>English Language Teaching</u> 25(1): 60-68 (1970).

934.   _____. "Towards a Basic Procedure in the Composition of Second Language Tests." <u>IRAL</u> 8(1): 49-58 (1970).

935.   Rosenbluth, Annabelle R. "The Feasibility of Test Translation Between Unrelated Languages: English to Navajo." <u>TESOL Quarterly</u> 19(1): 33-44 (1976).

936.   Schevill, Karl E. and James C. Stone. <u>PEEL Evaluation Report</u>. ED 190 644 (Arlington, VA: ERIC, 1980).

937.   Seaton, Ian. <u>A Review of Issues Raised in the Production of the English Language Testing Service</u>. Proceedings of the International Language Testing Symposium of the Interuniversitare Sprachtesgruppe, 1981. ED 217 736. Contained in ED 217 724. (Arlington, VA: ERIC, 1981).

938.   <u>Specialised Bibliography 1. Foreign Language Testing</u>. ED 083 881 (Arlington, VA: ERIC, 1971).

939.   Spolsky, Bernard. "Language Testing--The Problem of Validation." <u>Florida FL Reporter</u> 7(1): 100-102, 163-4 (1969).

940.   Stansfield, Charles. <u>The Assessment of Language Proficiency in Bilingual Children: An Analysis of Theories and Instrumentation</u>. ED 212 149 (Ypsilanti, MI: Eastern Michigan University, Bilingual Program, 1981).

941.   <u>Testing and Evaluation. Foreign Languages in Virginia Schools, No. 3.</u> ED 153 453 (Arlington, VA: ERIC, 1977).

942.   Valette, Rebecca M. <u>Modern Language Testing. Second Edition</u>. ED 153 489 (New York: Harcourt, Brace, Jovanovich, 1977).

943.   Wesche, Marjorie Bingham. "Communicative Testing in a Second Language." <u>Modern Language Journal</u> 67(1): 41-55 (1983).

944.   William, U. "The Construction of Standardized Tests for Welsh-speaking Children." <u>Educational Research</u> 14(1): 29-34 (1971).

945.   Wipf, Joseph A. "Measuring and Evaluating Progress in Reading." <u>Foreign Language Annals</u> 9(6): 569-76 (1976).

946.   Zdenek, Joseph W. "Twenty-five Pointers on Foreign Language Testing." <u>Foreign Language Annals</u> 13(5): 419-21 (1980).

ENGLISH

947.   Angelis, Paul J. Student Evaluation. ED 043 033
        (Arlington, VA: ERIC, 1970).

948.   Baldauf, Richard B. Jr. and Ivan K. Propst Jr. Measuring
        ESL Reading Achievement With Matching Cloze. Paper
        presented at the Micronesian Educators Conference, 1979.
        ED 186 468 (Arlington, VA: ERIC, 1979).

949.   Berger, Louis S. and others. A Methodology to Achieve
        Secure Administration of English Comprehension Level
        Tests--Phase 1. Final Report. ED 054 659 (Arlington, VA:
        ERIC, 1971).

950.   Blatchford, Charles H. "A Theoretical Contribution to ESL
        Diagnostic Test Construction." TESOL Quarterly 5(3):
        209-15 (1971). For related information see ED 055 484.

951.   Cahill, William and others. "Assessing Student
        Achievement." TESL Talk 6(1): 29-44 (1975).

952.   Culhane, P. T., ed. and J. White, ed. Testing. Occasional
        Papers 21. eD 191 324 (Arlington, VA: ERIC, 1979).

953.   Cziko, Gary A. "Improving the Psychometric, Criterion-
        referenced, and Practical Qualities of Integrative
        Language Tests." TESOL Quarterly 16(3): 367-79 (1982).

954.   Darnell, Donald K. "Clozentropy: A Procedure for Testing
        English Language Proficiency of Foreign Students." Speech
        Monographs 37(1): 36-46 (1970).

955.   Davidson, David M. Assessing Writing Ability of ESL
        College Freshman. Paper presented at the meeting of the
        New York State Teachers of English to Speakers of Other
        Languages, 1977. ED 135 247 (Arlington, VA: ERIC, 1976).

956.   English as a Second Language in Kindergarten--Testing
        Young Children. Preschool Education Series, No. 3.
        Indochinese Refugee Education Guides. ED 116 478
        (Arlington, VA: ERIC, 1975).

957.   English Placement Test (EPT) Project Technical Report for
        May Test 1977. ED 152 817 (Arlington, VA: ERIC, 1977).

958.   Estes, Gary D. and Carole Estes. What is the Criterion of
        Interest in Identifying Limited-English Speaking
        Students: Language Dominance or Proficiency. Paper
        presented at the annual meeting of the American
        Educational Research Association, 1979. ED 178 613
        (Arlington, VA: ERIC, 1979).

959.   Gaies, Stephen J. "Toward the Measurement of Functional
        Proficiency: Contextualization of the Noise Test." TESOL
        Quarterly 11(1): 51-7 (1977).

960.   Garcia-Zamor, Marie and David Birdsong. Testing in
English as a Second Language: A Selected, Annotated
Bibliography. CAL-ERIC/CLL Series on Languages and
Linguistics, No. 40. ED 135 206 (Arlington, VA: ERIC,
1977).

961.   Gewirtz, Agatha. "Some Observations on Testing and
Motivation." English Language Teaching Journal 31(3):
240-44 (1977).

962.   Gipps, Caroline and Elizabeth Ewen. "Tests of English for
Immigrant Children." Trends in Education 33: 31-5 (1974).

963.   Harris, David P. Testing English as a Second Language. ED
027 533 (New York: McGraw-Hill, 1969).

964.   Hernandez, Alberto and Susan L. Melnick. Modular
Sequence: English as a Second Language, Methods and
Techniques. TTP 001.15 Testing. Teacher Corps Bilingual
Project. ED 095 143 (Arlington, VA: ERIC, 1974).

965.   Hisama, Kay K. and others. A New Direction in Measuring
Proficiency in English as a Second Language. Paper
presented at the annual meeting of the American
Educational Research Association, 1977. ED 150 198
(Arlington, VA: ERIC, 1977).

966.   Hisama, Kay Keiko Washiya. Design and Empirical
Validation of the Cloze Procedure for Measuring Language
Proficiency of Non-native Speakers. ED 147 800 (Ann
Arbor, Michigan: University Microfilms, 1976).

967.   Ilyin, Donna. Assessing Oral Communication in Adult
Program English Second Language Classes. Revised edition
of paper presented at the annual meeting of the Teachers
of English to Speakers of Other Languages (TESOL), 1971.
ED 119 463 (Arlington, VA: ERIC, 1976).

968.   _____. Developing a Placement Test for Adults in
English-second-language Programs in California. Paper
presented at the Adult Education Research Conference,
1970. ED 036 766 (Arlington, VA: ERIC, 1970).

969.   _____. "Structure Placement Tests for Adults in English-
second-language Programs in California." TESOL Quarterly
4(4): 323-30 (1970).

970.   Jonz, Jon. "Improving on the Basic Egg: The M-C Cloze."
Language Learning 26(2): 255-65 (1976).

971.   Kjellmer, Goran. "On Active Versus Passive Proficiency in
Pronunciation, Universitetspedagogiska Utredningen
Projekt MUP (Mal, Undervisning Prov) (University
Pedagogical Investigation Project (Speech, Instruction
Test)." ED 027 801 Moderna Sprak 62(3): 1-8 (1968).

972.   Levine, Josie. "An Outline Proposal for Testing
Communicative Competence." English Language Teaching
Journal 30(2): 128-34 (1976).

973.   Madsen, Harold S. "New Alternatives in EFL Exams or, 'How
        to Avoid Selling English Short.'" English Language
        Teaching Journal 30(2): 135-43 (1976).

974.   Mares, Sharon. Non-discriminatory Assessment: Formal and
        Informal Assessment of Limited English Proficient
        Children. Paper presented at the Council for Exceptional
        Children Conference on the Exceptional Bilingual Child,
        1981. ED 209 834 (Arlington, VA: ERIC, 1981).

975.   Mendelsohn, David. Problems in Testing the Intonation of
        Advanced Foreign Learners. ED 158 602 (Arlington, VA:
        ERIC, 1978).

976.   Olguin, Leonard and William B. Michael. "The Development
        and Preliminary Validation of the Olguin Diagnostic Test
        of Auditory Perception for Spanish Language-oriented
        Children." Educational and Psychological Measurement
        39(4): 985-97 (1979).

977.   Porter, D. "Modified Cloze Procedure: A More Valid
        Reading Comprehension Test." English Language Teaching
        Journal 39(2): 151-55 (1976).

978.   Rivera, Charlene and Maria Lombardo. The Validaton of the
        English as a Second Language Assessment Battery (ESLAB).
        ED 185 073 (Arlington, VA: ERIC, 1979).

979.   Rivers, Wilga M. Testing and Student Learning. Paper
        presented at the First International Conference of the
        Association of Teachers of English to Speakers of Other
        Languages, 1973. ED 086 003 (Arlington, VA: ERIC, 1973).

980.   Teaching English as a Second Language: Perspectives and
        Practices. A Series of Six Texts. Testing: Fourth of a
        Series. ED 162 528 (Arlington, VA: ERIC, 1978).

981.   Testing English Language Proficiency. General Information
        Series, No. 2. Indochinese Refugee Education Guides. ED
        116 487 (Arlington, VA: ERIC, 1975).

FRENCH

982.   Bourque, Lorraine Y. and Marvin Boss. Development of the
        Perceived Instrumentality of French as a Second Language
        Scale. Paper presented at the annual meeting of the
        American Educational Research Association, 1979. ED 177
        214 (Arlington, VA: ERIC, 1979).

983.   Howard, Francoise. "Testing Communicative Proficiency in
        French as a Second Language: A Search for Procedures."
        Canadian Modern Language Review 36(2): 272-89 (1980).

984.   McLean, L. D. Separating the Effect of More Hours of
        Instruction From General Language Development on
        Achievement in French as a Second Language. ED 212 128
        (Arlington, VA: ERIC, 1980).

985.   O'Callaghan, Delma. I.T.E. Experimental Test in Spoken
        French: Report on Work Carried Out on the Development of
        an Aural-oral Language Test in French at Leaving
        Certificate Level. Publication No. 9 (B). ED 179 112
        (Arlington, VA: ERIC, 1978).

986.   Osman, Neile. The Design of Objective Diagnostic and
        Attainment Tests of a Reading-writing Command of French.
        ED 010 936 (Arlington, VA: ERIC, 1965). Available also in
        Babel 1(3) October 1965.

987.   _____. The Design of Objective Diagnostic and Attainment
        Tests of an Aural-oral Command of French. ED 011 170
        (Arlington, VA: ERIC, 1965). Available also in Babel 1(2)
        July 1965.

988.   Roger, Derek and others. "The Construction and Validation
        of a Questionnaire for Measuring Attitudes Towards
        Learning Foreign Languages." Educational Review 33(3):
        223-30 (1981).

GERMAN

989.   Lange, Dale L. and Gerhard Clausing. "An Examination of
        Two Methods of Generating and Scoring Cloze Tests With
        Students of German on Three Levels." Modern Language
        Journal 65(3): 254-61 (1981).

990.   Lofgren, H. Measuring Proficiency in the German Language:
        A Study of Pupils in Grade 7. ED 044 426 (Arlington, VA:
        ERIC, 1969).

991.   Matthews, Susan and David Matthews. "Multiple-choice
        Tests for A-level German." Audio-visual Language Journal
        15(1): 107-8 (1977).

992.   Miller, Ann and David Phillips. "Towards a New Language
        Aptitude Test." British Journal of Language Teaching
        20(2): 97-100 (1982).

993.   Steinke, Elisabeth. Computer Aided Tests. ED 072 076
        (Arlington, VA: ERIC, 1974).

RUSSIAN

994.   Bennett, Pearl S. Examinations--Their Use and Abuse. ED
        013 019 (Arlington, VA: ERIC, 1966).

SPANISH

995.   Andrade, Manuel and others. Measurement of Speaking
        Skills in Elementary Level Spanish Instruction. Denver-
        Stanford Project on the Context of Instructional
        Television, Report No. 9. ED 018 153 (Arlington, VA:
        ERIC, 1968).

996.   Blanco, George M. Spanish-language Assessment in a
        Bilingual Teacher Education Program. Paper presented at
        the annual meeting of the American Educational Research
        Association, 1976. ED 161 878 (Arlington, VA: ERIC,
        1976).

997.   Ife, Anne E. and Peter Standish. Advanced-level Testing
        of Foreign Language Proficiency: An Interim Report of the
        Post A-level Spanish Project. ED 053 582 (Arlington, VA:
        ERIC, 1971).

998.   Obrecht, Dean H. A Proposal to Plan and Develop a Sample
        Set of Drill and Testing Materials, Based on Audio and
        Visual Environmental and Situational Stimuli, Aimed at
        Training and Testing in the Creation of Original
        Utterances by Foreign Language Students at the Secondary
        and College Levels. ED 055 534 (Arlington, VA: ERIC,
        1971).

999.   Stansfield, Charles W. Testing Standard Spanish as a
        Second Dialect. ED 117 980 (Arlington, VA: ERIC, 1975).

1000.   Turner, D. "Confessions of a Test Development Chairman:
        Fifteen Years With the AATSP National Spanish
        Examinations. Hispania 57: 948-51 (1974).

Intelligence

1001. Allen, R. R. and others. The Development of the Wisconsin Tests of Testimony and Reasoning Assessment (WISTTRA). Report From the Concepts in Verbal Argument Project. ED 036 521 (Arlington, VA: ERIC, 1969).

1002. Blank, Marion. The Analysis of Cognitive Abilities in the Preschool Age. Paper presented at the annual meeting of the American Psychological Association, 1972. ED 078 922 (Arlington, VA: ERIC, 1972).

1003. Boone, James A. "Racial Differences in Standard I.Q. = Cultural Bias." Negro Educational Review 28(3,4): 183-8 (1977).

1004. Burgart, Herbert J. The Development of a Visual-verbal Measure of General Creativity-The Symbol Test of Originality. Final Report. ED 019 801 (Arlington, VA: ERIC, 1968).

1005. Burney, Gilbert McCollum. The Construction and Validation of an Objective Formal Reasoning Instrument. Ed.D. diss., University of Northern Colorado, 1974. ED 110 335 (Ann Arbor, MI: University Microfilms, 1974).

1006. Cattell, Raymond B. "Are Culture Fair Intelligence Tests Possible and Necessary." Journal of Research and Development in Education 12(2): 3-13 (1979).

1007. Cattell, Raymond B. and John L. Horn. "Check on the Theory of Fluid and Crystallized Intelligence with Description of New Subtest Designs." Journal of Educational Measurement 15(3): 139-64 (1978).

1008. Cillizza, Joseph Edward. The Construction and Evaluation of a Test of Critical Thinking Ability, Grades 7-8. Ed.D. diss., Boston University, 1970. ED 075 181 (Ann Arbor, MI: University Microfilms, 1970).

1009. Cocking, Rodney R. and others. Reconstructive Memory: A
       Non-traditional Approach to Assessing Young Children's
       Intelligence. Paper presented at the American Educational
       Research Association, 1980. ED 193 327 (Arlington, VA:
       ERIC, 1980).

1010. Conoley, Colleen W. and Jill L. Conoley. "Blow the
       Teacher's Mind With an Ethnic Test in Kind." Integrated
       Education 15(4): 8-9 (1977).

1011. Curtis, W. Scott. Development and Application of
       Intelligence Tests for the Blind: A Research Utilization
       Conference. Final Report. ED 080 595 (Arlington, VA:
       ERIC, 1972).

1012. Dupuy, Harold J. and Gunnar Gruvaeus. The Construction
       and Utility of Three Indexes of Intellectual Achievement:
       An Intellectual-development (ID) Index; A Socio-
       intellectual-status (SIS) Index; A Differential-
       intellectual-development (DID) Index. U.S. Children and
       Youths, 6-17 Years. Vital and Health Statistics. Data
       Evaluation and Methods Research. Series 2-Number 74. ED
       160 630 (Arlington, VA: ERIC, 1977).

1013. Gaudia, Gil. "Piaget's Theory and Psychometric
       Intelligence." Elementary School Journal 73(1): 37-43
       (1972).

1014. Goh, David S. "Empirical Versus Random Item Selection in
       the Design of Intelligence Test Short Forms--The WISC-R
       Example." Applied Psychological Measurement 3(1): 75-82
       (1979).

1015. Gonda, Judith and K. Warner Schaie. Age-appropriate
       Measures and Intellectual Competence in Three Age
       Groups. Paper presented at the annual convention of the
       American Psychological Association, 1978. ED 203 223
       (Arlington, VA: ERIC, 1978).

1016. Green, Russel F. and Juan N. Martinez. Standardization of
       a Spanish Language Adult Intelligence Scale. Final
       Report. ED 013 045 (Arlington, VA: ERIC, 1967).

1017. Guthrie, George M. and others. A Culture-fair Information
       Test of Intelligence. ED 054 212 (Arlington, VA: ERIC,
       1970).

1018. Hooper, Frank H. and others. A Representative Series of
       Piagetian Concrete Operations Tasks. Theoretical Paper
       No. 57. ED 124 416 (Arlington, VA: ERIC, 1975).

1019. Jacobson, L. I., M. A. Prio, M.A. Ramirez, A. I.
       Fernandez, and M. L. Hevia. "Construction and Validation
       of an Intelligence-test for Cubans." Revista
       Interamericana de Psicologia 12(1): 39-45 (1978).

1020. Kaufman, Alan S. "A Short Form of the Wechsler Preschool
       and Primary Scale of Intelligence." Journal of Consulting
       and Clinical Psychology 39(3): 361-9 (1972).

1021. Kelly, Edward M. "The Myth of Intellectual Testing."
       Clearing House 51(6): 271-3 (1978).

1022. King, Lynda A. and Daniel W. King. "Wechsler Short Forms:
       A Brief Status Report." Psychology in the Schools 19(4):
       433-8 (1982).

1023. Lusk, Donald V. "The Lusk Gifted and Talented Program
       Screening Test." Dissertation Abstracts International
       43(3-B): 854 (1982).

1024. Pandey, Tej N. and Anne T. Cleary. The Wisconsin Test of
       Adult Basic Education (WITABE). Paper presented at the
       annual meeting of the American Educational Research
       Association, 1972. ED 064 352 (Arlington, VA: ERIC,
       1972).

1025. Pinsent, A. The Construction and Use of Standardised
       Tests of Intelligence and Attainment. Pamphlet No. 3. ED
       117 958 (Arlington, VA: ERIC, 1960).

1026. "Psychological Testing." Exceptional Parent 1(6): 24-8
       (1972).

1027. Ray, Steven. "Adapting the WISC-R for Deaf Children."
       Diagnostique 7(3): 147-57 (1982).

1028. Rosenberg, Leon A. The Johns Hopkins Perceptual Test--Its
       Development and Current Status as a Measure of
       Intellectual Functioning. ED 014 754 (Arlington, VA:
       ERIC, 1966).

1029. Rosenberg, Leon A. and others. The Johns Hopkins
       Perceptual Test, the Development of a Rapid Intelligence
       Test for the Pre-school Child. ED 020 787 (Arlington, VA:
       ERIC, 1966).

1030. Schaie, K. Warner and Kathy Gribbin. The Impact of
       Environmental Complexity Upon Adult Cognitive
       Development. Paper presented at the Biennial Conference
       of the International Society for the Study of Behavioral
       Development, 1975. ED 148 895 (Arlington, VA: ERIC,
       1975).

1031. Staver, J. R. "Piagetian Logical Operations Test: A
       Group-assessment Method of Measuring Formal Reasoning
       Patterns." School Science and Mathematics 82: 169-73
       (February 1982).

1032. Staver, J. R. and D. L. Gabel. "Development and Construct
       Validation of a Group-administered Test of Formal
       Thought." Journal of Research in Science Teaching 16:
       535-44 (November 1979).

1033. _____. "Development and Construct Validation of a Group-
       administered Test of Formal Thought. Discussion." Journal
       of Research in Science Teaching 19: 91-2 (January 1982).

1034. Sympson, James B. The Assessment of Basic Competencies: A New Test Battery. Paper presented at the American Psychological Association Annual Meeting, 1979. ED 181 061 (Arlington, VA: ERIC, 1979).

1035. Veroff, Joseph and others. Measuring Intelligence and Achievement Motivation in Surveys. Final Report to U.S. Department of Health, Education and Welfare. Office of Economic Opportunity. ED 146 177 (Arlington, VA: ERIC, 1971).

1036. Ward, J. "New British Intelligence Scale: A Brief Progress Report." Journal of School Psychology 10: 307-13 (1972).

1037. Wechsler, David. "Historical Review: The Psychometric Tradition. Developing the Wechsler Adult Intelligence Scale." Contemporary Educational Psychology 6(2): 82-5 (1981).

SPECIFIC

1038. Alpern, Gerald D. and Carolyn C. Kimberlin. "Short Intelligence Test Ranging From Infancy Levels Through Childhood Levels for Use With the Retarded; Cattell-Binet Short Form." American Journal of Mental Deficiency 75(1): 65-71 (1970).

1039. Bart, William M. A Construction and Validation of Formal Operational Reasoning Instruments. Paper presented at the annual meeting of the American Educational Research Association, 1970. ED 042 806 (Arlington, VA: ERIC, 1970).

1040. Begle, E. G. Inductive Reasoning Test for Grade Five. SMESG Working Paper No. 3. ED 142 416 (Arlington, VA: ERIC, 1973).

1041. Hadar, N. and L. Henkin. "Children's Conditional Reasoning Part II: Towards a Reliable Test of Conditional Reasoning Ability." Educational Studies in Mathematics 9(1): 97-114 (1978).

Mathematics

1042. Anderson, Lorin W. and Jo Craig Anderson. "Functional Literacy Tests: A Case of Anticipatory Validity." Educational Evaluation and Policy Analysis 3(2): 51-5 (1981).

1043. Bernstein, Margery R. Evaluation of Elementary Math Program. ED 108 971 (Arlington, VA: ERIC, 1973).

1044. Brown, P. G. "Tests of Development in Children's Understanding of the Laws of Natural Numbers." British Journal of Educational Psychology 40: 354 (1970).

1045. Burton, C. R. and W. A. Marosz. "Construction and Uses of CATIA, a Computerized Mathematics Testbank." Two Year College Mathematics Journal 8: 212-16 (1977).

1046. Canadore Comprehensive Achievement Monitoring (CAM) Mathematics: An Introduction and Overview. ED 129 837 (Arlington, VA: ERIC, 1977).

1047. The Certificate of Secondary Education: Experimental Examinations--Mathematics. Examinations Bulletin No. 2. ED 068 474 (London: Her Majesty's Stationery Office, S.O. Code No. 27-364-2, 1964).

1048. The Certificate of Secondary Education: Experimental Examinations--Mathematics 2. Examinations Bulletin No. 7. ED 068 479 (London: Her Majesty's Stationery Office, S.O. Code No. 27-364-7, 1965).

1049. Chase, Clinton I. and Judith J. Johnson. Q-Analogies: A Test of Quantitative Reasoning. ED 191 921 (Arlington, VA: ERIC, 1980).

1050. Ebeling, David George. The Ability of Sixth Grade Students to Associate Mathematical Terms With Related Algorithms. Ed.D. diss., Indiana University, 1973. ED 107 500 (Ann Arbor: University Microfilms, 1973).

1051. Ferguson, Richard L. and Tse-Chi Hsu. The Application of Item Generators for Individualizing Mathematics Testing and Instruction. ED 053 935 (Arlington, VA: ERIC, 1971).

1052. Gourgey, Annette F. Development of a Scale for the Measurement of Self-concept in Mathematics. ED 223 702 (Arlington, VA: ERIC, 1982).

1053. Harris, Margaret L. and Thomas A. Romberg. Measuring Mathematics Concept Attainment: Boys and Girls. ED 070 659 (Arlington, VA: ERIC, 1971).

1054. Horn, Dorothy M. "Development of a Pool of Mathematics Test Items for Grades 7 and 8." Arithmetic Teacher 16(7): 543-5 (1969).

1055. _____. The Writing of Multiple-choice Mathematics Test Items. ED 044 313 (West Toronto, Ontario: Ontario Institute for Studies in Education, 1970).

1056. Jeffery, Jay M. "Psychological Set in Relation to the Construction of Mathematics Tests." Math Teacher 62(8): 636-8 (1969).

1057. Jones, Chancey O. and others. "An Overview of the Mathematics Achievement Tests Offered in the Admissions Testing Program of the College Entrance Examination Board." Mathematics Teacher 70(3): 197-208 (1977).

1058. Klein, Mary F. and others. Logical Error Analysis and Construction of Tests to Diagnose Student "Bugs" In Addition and Subtraction of Fractions. ED 212 496 (Arlington, VA: ERIC, 1981).

1059. Knights, George and Phil Waite. "Assessing the Mathematical Abilities of Children." Mathematics Teaching 68: 16-18 (1974).

1060. McNaughton, A. E. Evaluation in Secondary School Mathematics. ED 065 275 (Arlington, VA: ERIC, 1970).

1061. Math Resource Items for Minimal Competency Testing. A Collection of Math Items for State and Local Education Agencies to Draw Upon in Custom-building Their Own Minimal Competency Instruments. ED 173 395 (Arlington, VA: ERIC, 1977).

1062. Mathematics Objectives: Second Assessment. ED 156 439 (Arlington, VA: ERIC, 1978).

1063. Michaels, Linda A. and Robert A. Forsyth. "Construction and Validation of an Instrument Measuring Certain Attitudes Toward Mathematics." Educational and Psychological Measurement 37(4): 1043-9 (1977).

1064. Palmer, Chester. "Using an Item Bank to Construct a Local College Mathematics Placement Test." Measurement and Evaluation in Guidance 15(4): 259-66 (1983).

1065. Plake, Barbara S. and Claire S. Parker. "The Development and Validation of a Revised Version of the Mathematics Anxiety Rating Scale." Educational and Psychological Measurement 42(2): 551-7 (1982).

1066. Purakam, Orasri. "Some Issues in Mathematics Evaluation." Journal of Science and Mathematics Education in Southeast Asia 11(1): 7-16 (1979).

1067. Reys, Robert E. and Robert E. Rea. The Comprehensive Mathematics Inventory: A Research Instrument For Assessing Mathematics Achievement in Early Years. ED 065 549 (Arlington, VA: ERIC, 1972).

1068. Richardson, F. C. and R. M. Suinn. "Mathematics Anxiety Rating Scale: Psychometric Data." Journal of Counseling Psychology 19: 551-4 (1972).

1069. Robitaille, David F. and others. Mathematics Achievement Test Project. Technical Manual. ED 187 531 (Arlington, VA: ERIC, 1980).

1070. Romberg, Thomas A. The Development and Validation of a Set of Mathematical Problem-solving Superitems. Executive Summary of the NIE/ECS Item Development Project. ED 219 246 (Arlington, VA: ERIC, 1982).

1071. Romberg, Thomas A. and James W. Wilson. NLSMA Reports, No. 7, The Development of Tests. ED 084 112 (Pasadena, CA: A. C. Vroman, 1969).

1072. Romberg, Thomas A. and others. The Development of Mathematical Problem-solving Superitems. A Report on the NIE/ECS Item Development Project. Paper presented at the Education Commission of the States Annual Conference on Large Scale Assessment, 1982. ED 222 559 (Arlington, VA: ERIC, 1982).

1073. Romberg, Thomas A., ed. Four Studies on Aspects of Assessing Computational Performance. Technical Report No. 297. ED 115 490 (Arlington, VA: ERIC, 1975).

1074. Sheehan, D. S. and R. G. Davis. "Development and Validation of a Criterion-referenced Mathematics Battery." School Science and Mathematics 79: 125-32 (1979).

1075. Sovchik, Robert J. "An Analysis of Cognitive Achievement in a Number Systems Course for Prospective Elementary School Teachers." School Science and Mathematics 77(1): 66-70 (1977).

1076. _____. "The Reliability of a Metric System Attitude Scale." School Science and Mathematics 80(4): 327-30 (1980).

1077. Suydam, Marilyn N. Evaluation in the Mathematics Classroom: From What and Why To How and Where. ED 086 517 (Arlington, VA: ERIC, 1974).

1078. Swadener, Marc and D. Franklin Wright. "Testing in the
       Mathematics Classroom." Mathematics Teacher 68(1): 11-17
       (1975).

1079. Van Houten, Carel A. Setting Standards of Performance:
       Towards a Teacher Referenced Test System. Paper presented
       at the fourth International Symposium on Educational
       Testing, 1980. ED 193 288 (Arlington, VA: ERIC, 1980).

1080. Wadkins, J. R. Jefferson. "The GRE Advanced Mathematics
       Test." American Mathematical Monthly 85(9): 703-19
       (1978).

1081. Wall, Janet and William J. Geppert. "Initiating School
       Change Through a Statewide Testing Program in
       Mathematics." School Science and Mathematics 81(1): 51-4
       (1981).

ALGEBRA

1082. Caldwell, James R. and others. "Comparative Validities
       and Working Times for Composites of Structure-of-
       intellect Tests and Algebra Grades and Composites of
       Traditional Test Measures and Algebra Grades in the
       Prediction of Success in Tenth-grade Geometry."
       Educational and Psychological Measurement 30(4): 955-9
       (1970).

1083. Forester, D. L. and W. B. Michael. "Comparison of the
       Validities of a Traditional Item-allocation Method and of
       an Item-sampling Procedure in the Construction of In-
       class Examinations in Intermediate Algebra." Educational
       and Psychological Measurement 36: 933-8 (Winter 1976).

1084. Ray, Kenneth Larry. "The Effects of Computer-assisted
       Test Construction on Achievement in First-year Algebra."
       Ph.D. diss., University of Southern California, 1977.
       Dissertation Abstracts International 38(8-A): 4758
       (1977).

ARITHMETIC

1085. Burns, Edward. A Computer Program for Generating
       Sequences of Primary Arithmetic Facts in Random Order. ED
       108 973 (Arlington, VA: ERIC, 1975).

1086. Connolly, Austin Jay. "An Instrument of Measurement to
       Appraise the Arithmetic Abilities of Educable Mentally
       Retarded Children Ages Thirteen Through Sixteen." ED 025
       434 (Ann Arbor, MI: University Microfilms, 1968).

1087. Hively, W. W., H. C. Patterson and S. Page. "A Universe-
       defined System of Arithmetic Achievement Tests." Journal
       of Educational Measurement 5: 225-90 (1968).

1088. Kwansa, Kofi Bassa. Investigation of the Relative Content
       Validity of Norm-referenced and Domain-referenced
       Arithmetic Tests. Ph.D. diss, University of Pittsburgh,
       1972. ED 077 742 (Ann Arbor, MI: University Microfilms,
       1972).

1089. Long, L. "Writing an Effective Arithmetic Test."
       Arithmetic Teacher 29: 16-18 (1982).

1090. Meeker, M. "Relevance of Arithmetic Testing to Teaching
       Arithmetic Skills: SOI Learning Abilities Test." Gifted
       Child Quarterly 23: 297-303 (Summer 1979).

1091. Sachar, Jane. Use of Performance Models in Developing
       Standardized Tests. Paper presented at the annual meeting
       of the American Psychological Association, 1976. ED 135
       836 (Arlington, VA: ERIC, 1976).

1092. Smith, Robert Francis. A Diagnostic Study of Pupil
       Performance on a Test of Skills Relevant to the Mastery
       of Place-value Tasks. Ph.D. diss., Fordham University,
       1972. ED 077 665 (Ann Arbor, MI: University Microfilms,
       1972).

1093. Trocchi, Robert F. "Computer-based Arithmetic Test
       Generation." Journal of Educational Data Processing
       10(3): 10-18 (1973).

GEOMETRY

1094. Hanna, Gerald S. "Testing Students' Ability to do
       Geometric Proofs: A Comparison of Three Objective Item
       Types." Journal For Research in Mathematics Education
       2(3): 213-17 (1971).

1095. Wallrabenstein, Hartmut. "Development and Signification
       of a Geometry Test." Educational Studies in Mathematics
       5(1): 81-9 (1973).

Miscellaneous

1096. Canale, Michael. "The Method Effect in Communicative Testing." _Medium_ 6(4): 43-55 (1981).

1097. Cory, Charles H. and others. _The Development and Statistical Evaluation of a Recruit Training Performance Test_. ED 081 852 (Arlington, VA: ERIC, 1973).

1098. Cunningham, Clarence J. _Measures of Leader Behavior and Their Relation to Performance Levels of County Extension Agents_. Ph.D. diss., Ohio State University, 1964. ED 020 333. Available from University Microfilms, Ann Arbor, MI.

1099. Deschin, Celia S. _Families in Trouble: A Comprehensive Family Rating Technique_. ED 050 515 (Arlington, VA: ERIC, 1970).

1100. _Development of the Brief Test of Literacy. National Center for Health Statistics. Series 2, No. 27_. ED 113 693 (Arlington, VA: ERIC, 1968).

1101. "Development of the DDI: A Seriousness Scale for Delinquency." _Evaluation Review_ 5(6): 788-809 (1981).

1102. Ferrell, George. _Development and Use of a Test of Test-wiseness_. Paper presented at the annual meeting of the Western College Reading Association, 1977. ED 154 374 (Arlington, VA: ERIC, 1977).

1103. Fillenbaum, Gerda G. and Michael A. Smyer. "The Development, Validity, and Reliability of the OARS Multidimensional Functional Assessment Questionnaire." _Journal of Gerontology_ 36(4): 428-34 (1981).

1104. _Final Report on the Development of Essential Competencies and Matching Evaluation Instruments for Evaluating the Performance of First-year Typewriting Students in the High Schools of Pennsylvania_. ED 164 566 (Arlington, VA: ERIC, 1978).

1105. Finn, Jerry and Rose Sheldon. "Development and Validation of the Interview Skills Role-play Test." Social Work Research & Abstracts 18(2): 21-7 (1982).

1106. Franklin, Margery and Judith Cobb. Head Start Evaluation and Research Center. Progress Report of Research Studies 1966 to 1967. Document 3, An Experimental Approach to Studying Non-verbal Representation in Young Children. ED 021 625 (Arlington, VA: ERIC, 1967).

1107. Fraser, Barry J. "Development and Validation of a Test of Enquiry Skills." Journal of Research in Science Teaching 17(1): 7-16 (1980).

1108. _____. Test of Enquiry Skills (and) Handbook. ED 181 082 (Arlington, VA: ERIC, 1979).

1109. Fredrick, Wayne C. and others. Analysis of the Linguistic Ability Test, Grades 4 & 6. ED 040 401 (Arlington, VA: ERIC, 1970).

1110. Gerst, Marvin S. and Rudolf H. Moos. "Social Ecology of University Student Residences." Journal of Educational Psychology 63(6): 513-25 (1972).

1111. Grohsmeyer, Frederick and Richard R. Johnson. A Comparison of Two Techniques of Teaching Scientific Method in Introductory Psychology Laboratories: Stage 1, The Development of an Evaluative Instrument. Final Report. ED 035 941 (Arlington, VA: ERIC, 1968).

1112. Gulley, S. Beverly and others. The Development of a Reliable Instrument for Observing the Behaviors of Infant Caregivers - BOSIC. Final Report. ED 197 840 (Arlington, VA: ERIC, 1980).

1113. Horner, Walter R. and others. The Development, Test, and Evaluation of Three Pilot Performance Reference Scales. ED 058 320 (Arlington, VA: ERIC, 1970).

1114. Hughes, Charles P. and others. "A New Clinical Scale for the Staging of Dementia." British Journal of Psychiatry 140: 566-72 (1982).

1115. Isaacs, Patricia A. Preparation and Validation of a Videotaped Test of Conservation Suitable for Grade 6 Students in Jamaica. ED 205 384 (Arlington, VA: ERIC, 1981).

1116. Johnson, Deborah. In-law Relations: A Research Note. Paper presented at the annual conference of the National Council on Family Relations, 1977. ED 165 035 (Arlington, VA: ERIC, 1977).

1117. Kralj, M. M. and others. The Measurement of Parenting Locus of Control. ED 219 138 (Arlington, VA: ERIC, 1981).

1118. Leathers, Dale G. and Ted H. Emigh. "Decoding Facial Expressions: A New Test With Decoding Norms." Quarterly Journal of Speech 66(4): 418-36. (1980).

1119. Liu, I. M., B. H. Chang and Y. T. Yang. "Constructing a Word-construction Test." Acta Psychologica Taiwanica 21(2): 85-90 (1979).

1120. Loesch, Larry C. and Roderick J. McDavis. "A Scale for Assessing Counseling-orientation Preferences." Counselor Education and Supervision 17(4): 262-71 (1978).

1121. Marko, George Franklin. "Civil Defense: An Analysis of Attitudes and Knowledge." M.S. thesis, Indiana University, 1968. ED 036 741 (Arlington, VA: ERIC, 1968).

1122. Matthews, Doris B. and Jimmy L. Quinn. The Development of the Checklist for Parents of Preadolescent Children. Paper presented at the annual convention of the American Personnel and Guidance Association, 1981. ED 208 285 (Arlington, VA: ERIC, 1981).

1123. Meyer, Mortimer M. "Family Relations Test." Journal of Projective Techniques 27: 309-14 (1963).

1124. Norbeck, Jane S., Ada M. Lindsey and Virginia L. Carrier. "The Development of an Instrument to Measure Social Support." Nursing Research 30(5): 264-69 (1981).

1125. Olson, Norma Jean. "Design and Validation of a Straight-copy Typewriting Prognostic Test Using Kinesthetic Sensitivity." Business Education Forum 33(5): 33-6 (1979).

1126. _____. "Design and Validation of a Straight-copy Typewriting Prognostic Test Using Kinesthetic Sensitivity." Delta Pi Epsilon Journal 22(3): 13-27 (1980).

1127. Palmore, Erdman and others. "The Facts on Aging Quiz: A Review of Findings and a Revision of Palmore's Facts on Aging Quiz." Gerontologist 20(6): 669-79 (1980).

1128. Parrish, Berta W. "A Test to Test Test-wiseness." Journal of Reading 25(7): 672-75 (1982).

1129. Ringenbach, Susan and others. Development of a Problem Solving Inventory Involving Three-dimensional Models of Problem Situations. Paper presented at the joint session of NCME-AREA, 1973. ED 074 078 (Arlington, VA: ERIC, 1973).

1130. Ritzler, Barry A. and others. A Comprehensive Projective Alternative to the TAT. ED 179 567 (Arlington, VA: ERIC, 1979).

1131. Rocha Bastos, Lilia Da and others. "Empirical Test of the Validity of a Unitary Construct Underlying a Modified Form of the Barrett-Lennard Relationship Inventory." Educational and Psychological Measurement 39(2): 499-504 (1979).

1132.   Rubin, Rebecca B. <u>Assessment of College-level Speaking and Listening Skills</u>. Paper presented at the annual meeting of the American Educational Research Association, 1981. ED 208 032 (Arlington, VA: ERIC, 1981).

1133.   _____. <u>The Development and Refinement of a Communication Competency Assessment Instrument</u>. Paper presented at the annual meeting of the Speech Communication Association, 1981. ED 210 732 (Arlington, VA: ERIC, 1981).

1134.   Schaefer, Charles E. "The Cottage Life Questionnaire: A New Measure of Social Climate in Children's Residential Centers." <u>Child Care Quarterly</u> 3(4): 255-8 (1974).

1135.   Skull, J. and A. Wilkinson. "Construction of an Oral Composition Quality Scale." <u>British Journal of Educational Psychology</u> 39: 272-7 (November 1969).

1136.   Smith, Gerald R. and others. <u>The SAS Inventory: A Measure of the Extent to Which Alternative and Conventional High Schools Meet Student Needs</u>. Paper presented at the annual meeting of the American Educational Research Association, 1981. ED 204 397 (Arlington, VA: ERIC, 1981).

1137.   Whiteman, V. L. "Development and Validation of the Macropractice Social Work Knowledge Test." <u>Educational and Psychological Measurement</u> 42: 311-16 (1982).

1138.   Zalar, Marianne K. "Development and Initial Validation of the Human Sexuality Clinical Situation Test." <u>Dissertation Abstracts International</u> 42(11-A): 4801 (1982).

AGRICULTURE

1139.   McCormick, Floyd G. <u>The Development of an Instrument for Measuring the Understanding of Profit-maximizing Principles</u>. Ph.D. diss., Ohio State University, 1964. ED 020 339. Available from University Microfilms, Ann Arbor, MI.

1140.   Mityga, Henry G. and others. "A Standardized Achievement Test for High School Horticulture Students." <u>Journal of the American Association of Teacher Educators in Agriculture</u> 19(2): 11-16,30 (1978).

BLIND

1141.   Bauman, M. K. "Interest Inventory for the Visually Handicapped." <u>Education of the Visually Handicapped</u> 5: 78-83 (October 1973).

1142.   Bourgeault, Stanley E. and Richard W. Woodcock. <u>Construction and Standardization of a Battery of Braille Skill Tests</u>. ED 003 298 (Arlington, VA: ERIC, 1964).

1143. Dauterman, William L. and Richard M. Suinn. Stanford-Ohwaki-Kohs Tactile Block Design Intelligence Test for the Blind. Part One-Final Report. ED 012 119 (Arlington, VA: ERIC, 1966).

1144. Davidson, Terry. "Braille Tests With Tactual Response Buttons Allow for Unaided Test-taking." New Outlook for the Blind 67(4): 158-60 (1973).

1145. The Development and Application of Intelligence Tests for the Blind: A Research Utilization Conference. Final Report. ED 074 655 (Arlington, VA: ERIC, 1972).

1146. Harley, Randall K. and others. "The Development of a Scale in Orientation and Mobility for Multiply Impaired Blind Children." Education of the Visually Handicapped 7(1): 1-5 (1975).

1147. Lord, F. E. "Development of Scales for the Measurement of Orientation and Mobility of Young Blind Children." Exceptional Children 36(2): 77-81 (1969). For related information see ED 024 198.

1148. Ludlow, Larry H. A Residual is More Than a Chi-square: Patterns in Attitudes Toward Blindness. Paper presented at the annual meeting of the National Council on Measurement in Education, 1982. ED 222 523 (Arlington, VA: ERIC, 1982).

1149. Newland, T. Ernest. The Blind Learning Aptitude Test. ED 031 867 (Arlington, VA: ERIC, 1969).

1150. Tobin, M. J. and S. O. Myers. Memory Span Tests for the Deaf-blind. ED 175 206 (Arlington, VA: ERIC, 1978).

BUSINESS EDUCATION

1151. Davis, R. E. "Construction of Evaluation Devices and Interpreting Results: Subject Matter Areas." National Business Education Yearbook 16: 152-69 (1978).

1152. Hilton, Thomas L. and others. Performance Criteria in Graduate Business Study: Parts I and II--Development of Rating Scales, Background Data Form and the Pilot Study. ED 164 549 (Arlington, VA: ERIC, 1970).

1153. Reitzel, David. "Business Law--Construction Guides for the Essay Test." Journal of Business Education 46(4): 157-58 (1971).

1154. _____ . "Business Law--Construction Guides for the Essay Test, Part II." Journal of Business Education 46(5): 206-8 (1971).

1155. Vincent, W. S. "Construction of Evaluation Devices and Interpreting Results: Skill Subjects." National Business Education Yearbook 16: 141-51 (1978).

COURTSHIP AND MARRIAGE

1156.   Davidson, J. Kenneth Sr. and Gerald R. Leslie.
        "Premarital Sexual Intercourse: An Application of
        Axiomatic Theory Construction." Journal of Marriage and
        the Family 39(1): 15-25 (1976).

1157.   Foster, Arthur Lee. "The Sexual Compatibility Test."
        Journal of Consulting and Clinical Psychology 45(2):
        332-3 (1977).

1158.   Herold, Edward S. "A Dating Adjustment Scale for College
        Students." Adolescence 8(29): 51-9 (1973).

1159.   Mathes, Eugene W. and Nancy Severa. Jealousy, Romantic
        Love, and Liking. ED 147 671 (Arlington, VA: ERIC, 1974).

1160.   Miller, William R. and Harold I. Lief. "The Sex Knowledge
        and Attitude Test (SKAT)." Journal of Sex and Marital
        Therapy 5(3): 282-87 (1979).

1161.   Raschke, Helen J. The Development of a Post
        Separation/Post Divorce Problems and Stress Scale. Paper
        presented at the annual meeting of the National Council
        on Family Relations, 1978. ED 170 619 (Arlington, VA:
        ERIC, 1978).

1162.   Rayman, J. R. "Sex and the Single Interest Inventory: The
        Empirical Validation of Sex-balanced Interest Inventory
        Items." Journal of Counseling Psychology 23: 239-46
        (1976).

1163.   Roach, Arthur J. and others. "The Marital Satisfaction
        Scale: Development of a Measure for Intervention
        Research." Journal of Marriage and the Family 43(3):
        537-46 (1981).

1164.   Schaefer, Mark T. and David H. Olson. "Assessing
        Intimacy: The Pair Inventory." Journal of Marital and
        Family Therapy 7(1): 47-60 (1981).

1165.   Tamashiro, Roy T. "Adolescents' Concepts of Marriage: A
        Structural-Developmental Analysis." Journal of Youth and
        Adolescence 8(4): 443-52 (1979).

1166.   Waring, E. M. and John R. Reddon. "The Measurement of
        Intimacy in Marriage: The Waring Intimacy Questionnaire."
        Journal of Clinical Psychology 39(1): 53-7 (1983).

1167.   Weiss, Robert L. and Mary C. Cerreto. "The Marital Status
        Inventory: Development of a Measure of Dissolution
        Potential." American Journal of Family Therapy 8(2): 80-
        85 (1980).

DRIVING AND SAFETY EDUCATION

1168.   Keenan, Donna and others. "Oral Drivers' Test: Solution
        to a Lifelong Learning Problem." Lifelong Learning: The
        Adult Years 5(7): 6-8 (1982).

1169. McKnight, James and Molly A. Green. Safe Driving
       Knowledge Dissemination and Testing Techniques. Volume I:
       General Findings. ED 152 972 (Arlington, VA: ERIC, 1977).

1170. _____. Safe Driving Knowledge Dissemination and Testing
       Techniques. Volume II: Final Report. ED 153 074
       (Arlington, VA: ERIC, 1977).

1171. _____. Safe Driving Knowledge Dissemination and Testing
       Techniques. Volume III: Handbook. Final Report. ED 152
       957 (Arlington, VA: ERIC, 1977).

1172. Pollock, William T. and Thomas L. McDole. Development of
       a National Item Bank for Tests of Driving Knowledge. ED
       128 403 (Springfield, VA: NTIS, PB 234-226, 1976).

1173. _____. Handbook for Driving Knowledge Testing. ED 105 149
       (Springfield, VA: NTIS, PB 235-916, 1974).

EDUCATION

1174. Abbott, Robert D. and David Perkins. "Development and
       Construct Validation of a Set of Student Rating-of-
       instruction Items." Educational and Psychological
       Measurement 38(4): 1069-75 (1978).

1175. Bailey, John E. III and David B. Ellis. Development of an
       Instrument to Measure Educational Situational Variables
       and Preschool Competencies Desired by Parents. ED 109 219
       (Arlington, VA: ERIC, 1974).

1176. Balderson, James H. The Bureaucratization of Teacher
       Behavior Scale and the Measurement of School
       Organizational Structure. Paper presented at the annual
       meeting of the American Educational Research Association,
       1977. ED 139 841 (Arlington VA: ERIC, 1977).

1177. Bemis, Katherine A. and Max Luft. Relationships Between
       Teacher Behavior, Pupil Behavior, and Pupil Achievement.
       Paper presented at the annual meeting of the American
       Educational Research Association, 1970. ED 038 189
       (Arlington, VA: ERIC, 1970).

1178. Blair, Mark W. and Keith M. Kershner. Assessment of
       Student Attitudes Toward Learning Environments. Paper
       presented at the annual meeting of the American
       Educational Research Association, 1975. ED 110 500
       (Arlington, VA: ERIC, 1975).

1179. Boersma, Frederic J. and others. Technical Data on the
       Student's Perception of Ability Scale: An Instrument for
       Measuring Academic Self-concept in Elementary School
       Children. Research and Information Report. ED 166 233
       (Arlington, VA: ERIC, 1978).

1180. Bolton, Charles D. and others. Patterns and Determinants
       of Student Affiliation at a Public Urban Commuter
       College. Final Report. ED 024 088 (Arlington, VA: ERIC,
       1968).

1181. Boshier, R. "Development and Use of a Dropout Prediction
       Scale: Personality and Educational Environment Scales and
       Dropout Prediction Scale." Adult Education 22: 87-99
       (Winter 1972).

1182. Bourke, S. F. and others. Performance in Literacy and
       Numeracy: 1980. ED 208 056 (Arlington, VA: ERIC, 1981).

1183. Bowers, John J. Developing an Instrument to Assess Non-
       technical Outcomes of Occupational Education. ED 223 693
       (Arlington, VA: ERIC, 1982).

1184. Brehman, George E. Jr. Attitude Toward School Learning:
       The Development of a Seventh Grade Level Instrument for
       Measurement of Goal IV of the Pennsylvania Educational
       Quality Assessment Program. Paper presented at the annual
       meeting of the American Educational Research Association,
       1972. ED 062 391 (Arlington, VA: ERIC, 1972).

1185. Brenner, L. P. "On-line Item Banking in Health Sciences
       Education." Journal of Educational Technology Systems
       9(3): 213-27 (1980-81).

1186. Briers, Gary E. and David L. Williams. "Research
       Procedures For Assessing the Effectiveness of
       Instructional Materials For Vocational Education."
       Journal of Vocational Education Research 4(3): 41-55
       (1979).

1187. Browne, John Robert. Multicultural Press in Elementary
       School Classrooms: A Function of Selected Learning
       Conditions. ED 124 628 (Ann Arbor, MI: Xerox University
       Microfilms, 76-5317, 1975).

1188. Bunting, C. E. "Development and Validation of the
       Educational Attitudes Inventory." Educational and
       Psychological Measurement 41: 559-65 (Summer 1981).

1189. Carden, Thomas E. The Development of a Student
       Satisfaction Questionnaire for Adult Learners at Piedmont
       Technical Institute. ED 153 686 (Arlington, VA: ERIC,
       1978).

1190. Carter, H. D. "Measurement of Attitudes Toward School."
       California Journal of Educational Research 20: 186-92
       (September 1969).

1191. Cartwright, Glenn F. and Jeffrey L. Derevensky. "The
       Development of Computer-assisted Testing as an Adjunct to
       Traditional Instructional Processes in Educational
       Psychology." British Journal of Educational Technology
       9(3): 166-69 (1978).

1192. Carver, Leslee R. and Kathleen J. Lewis. "A Nutrition
       Knowledge Test for Elementary School Teachers." Journal
       of Nutrition Education 11(2): 68-71 (1979).

1193. Casey, Jean Marie. A Pre-kindergarten Screening. ED 145
       966 (Arlington, VA: ERIC, 1976).

1194. Cataldo, Michael F. and Todd R. Risley. Development of a Standardized Measure of Classroom Participation. Paper presented at the American Psychological Association Convention, 1973. ED 087 792 (Arlington, VA: ERIC, 1973).

1195. Cervero, Ronald. Development of an Instrument for Grouping Students Who Are Preparing for the General Educational Development (GED) Test. Paper presented at the Adult Education Research Conference, 1977. ED 141 515 (Arlington, VA: ERIC, 1977).

1196. Chase, Craig. Development and Use of the Chase Outdoor Education Inventory. ED 038 231 (Arlington, VA: ERIC, 1968).

1197. Chiarelott, Leigh and others. "Evaluating Pre-service Teacher Candidates." Clearing House 53(6): 295-99 (1980).

1198. Christner, C. A. and others. Competency-based Teacher Evaluation in a School District: Validation of the Competencies' Importance by District Administrators, Professionals, Students and Parents. Publication Number 78.69. Paper presented at the annual meeting of the American Educational Research Association, 1979. ED 177 213 (Arlington, VA: ERIC, 1979).

1199. Claus, Richard N. "The Development and Evaluation of the Prekindergarten Readiness Screening Device." Dissertation Abstracts International 42(12-A): 5094 (1982).

1200. Coe, Richard M. The Politics of Testing. Paper presented at the annual meeting of the Conference on College Composition and Communication, 1980. ED 188 236 (Arlington, VA: ERIC, 1980).

1201. Coffman, William E., ed. Frontiers of Educational Measurement and Information Systems-1973. Proceedings of an invitational conference on the occasion of the dedication of the Lindquist Center for Measurement, University of Iowa, 1973. ED 091 442 (Boston: Houghton Mifflin, 1973).

1202. Colwell, David and others. Development and Validation of an Instrument for Measuring Attitudes of Primary Students in a Large Urban School System. ED 110 475 (Arlington, VA: ERIC, 1975).

1203. Competency Based Education Inservice for Part Time Community College Occupational Education Teachers. Objective Referenced Tests: Module #3. ED 189 411 (Arlington, VA: ERIC, 1980).

1204. Comprehensive Evaluation Project. Final Report. ED 037 571 (Arlington, VA: ERIC, 1969).

1205. Conlin, Bernard J. and others. The Comparison of Telelecture and Regular Lecture in the Transfer of Knowledge to Adults. ED 070 946 (Arlington, VA: ERIC, 1973).

1206. Connecticut Ninth-grade Proficiency Test 1980-81 Summary
       Report: Mathematics, Basic Writing Skills in the Language
       Arts, Reading. ED 206 724 (Arlington, VA: ERIC, 1981).

1207. Conti, Gary J. Principles of Adult Learning Scale. Paper
       presented at the annual Adult Education Research
       Conference, 1979. ED 179 713 (Arlington, VA: ERIC, 1979).

1208. Cooke, Madeline A. "A Pair of Instruments for Measuring
       Student Attitudes Toward Bearers of the Target Culture."
       Foreign Language Annals 11(2): 149-63 (1978).

1209. Cortes, Juan B. and others. Relationship Between Measures
       of Academic Motivation and Achievement in College. Final
       Technical Report. ED 014 764 (Arlington, VA: ERIC, 1967).

1210. Corwin, Ronald G. The Development of an Instrument for
       Examining Staff Conflicts in the Public Schools. Final
       Report. ED 001 124 (Arlington, VA: ERIC, 1963).

1211. Cote, Marianne and Gregory F. Harper. A Systems Approach
       to Kindergarten Screening: Systems Intervention and Test
       Development. ED 119 049 (Arlington, VA: ERIC, 1976).

1212. Crowley, Robert J. The Institutional Renewal (IRS) Scale:
       An Instrument to Measure Attitudes Toward Educational
       Innovation. ED 156 678 (Arlington, VA: ERIC, 1976).

1213. Crowther, Henry I. G. and Peter F. W. Preece. "The
       Development and Validation of Several Measures of
       Confidence and Self-image in Relation to Science for Two
       Samples of Preservice Elementary School Teachers."
       Educational and Psychological Measurement 39(1): 169-74
       (1979).

1214. _____. "The Factorial Validity of a Measure of Students'
       Perceptions of the Learning Environment for Science in
       Preservice Elementary Teacher Education." Educational and
       Psychological Measurement 39(1): 175-80 (1979).

1215. Cruickshank, Donald and James Leonard. The Identification
       and Analysis of Perceived Problems of Teachers in Inner-
       city Schools. Occasional Paper One. NDEA National
       Institute for Advanced Study in Teaching Disadvantaged
       Youth. ED 026 335 (Arlington, VA: ERIC, 1967).

1216. Darom, Efraim and others. "The Development and Validation
       of a Multidimensional Scale for Assessment of Teachers'
       Attitudes Toward Small-group Teaching." Educational and
       Psychological Measurement 38(4): 1233-38 (1978).

1217. Davis, John N. and James Moriel Jr. Using the Rasch Model
       to Establish Equivalent Certification Tests. Paper
       presented at the annual meeting of the American
       Educational Research Association, 1980. ED 191 865
       (Arlington, VA: ERIC, 1980).

1218. Deaton, William L. and others. A Scale to Assess the
       Affective Entry Level of Students. Paper presented at the
       annual meeting of the National Council on Measurement in
       Education, 1977. ED 146 209 (Arlington, VA: ERIC, 1977).

1219. Development and Initial Testing of Instrumentation to Measure Five Functions of Schooling. Final Report. Volume I--Summary Report. ED 147 356 (Arlington, VA: ERIC, 1976).

1220. Development and Initial Testing of Instrumentation to Measure Five Functions of Schooling. Final Report. Volume II--Technical Reports. ED 147 357 (Arlington, VA: ERIC, 1976).

1221. Dickinson, Gary. Introduction to Teaching Adults. Module 4: Using Evaluation Instruments. ED 208 204 (Arlington VA: ERIC, 1981).

1222. Dickson, Gary L. and others. "The Resident Assistant Stress Inventory--A Focus on Individualized RA In-service Education." Journal of College and University Student Housing 7(1): 22-5 (1977).

1223. Dixon, Nancy Powell. The Development of a Test to Measure the Ability of Students in Teacher Education to Identify Comprehension Activities in Terms of Categories of Comprehension Skills. ED 122 254 (Ann Arbor, MI: University Microfilms, 1975).

1224. Docking, Russell A. PRISM--Profile of Real/Ideal Scholastic Motivation. User's Manual. ED 194 552 (Arlington, VA: ERIC, 1979).

1225. Doran, Rodney L. and others. "Assessing Students' Awareness of Environmental Problems." Journal of Environmental Education 5(4): 14-18 (1974).

1226. Doss, David A. and Glynn D. Ligon. The BRC: A Practical, Economical, Reliable, and Valid Measure of Student Classroom Behavior. Publication No. 78.78. Paper presented at the annual meeting of the American Educational Research Association, 1979. ED 177 212 (Arlington, VA: ERIC, 1979).

1227. Downey, Ronald G. and others. "Development and Validation of a Set of University Involvement Scales." Measurement and Evaluation in Guidance 13(3): 158-68 (1980).

1228. Downs, Gary E. "Development of an Affective Instrument For Measuring High School Science Students' Behaviors." School Science and Mathematics 79(3): 217-22 (1979).

1229. Doyle, Kenneth O. Jr. "Development of the Student Opinion Survey." Educational and Psychological Measurement 37(2): 439-43 (1977).

1230. Doyle, Kenneth O. Jr. and Ross E. Moen. "Toward the Definition of a Domain of Academic Motivation." Journal of Educational Psychology 70(2): 231-6 (1978).

1231. Dunn, James A. The Investigation of Children's School Anxiety: A Theory, Procedure, and Results. Paper presented in Symposium at Western Psychological Association meeting, 1969. ED 069 698 (Arlington, VA: ERIC, 1969).

1232.   Dusewicz, Russell A. The Pennsylvania Preschool
         Inventory. Testing Manual (and) Test Plates. ED 205 585
         (Arlington, VA: ERIC, 1976).

1233.   Eash, Maurice J. and others. "Evaluating Teacher Behavior
         from Student Perceptions." Studies in Educational
         Evaluation 6(3): 293-95 (1980).

1234.   Eckard, Pamela J. Design and Validation of an Observation
         Schedule and Self-report for the Measurement of Self-
         concept in an Educational Setting. Paper presented at the
         annual meeting of the American Educational Research
         Association, 1976. ED 164 569 (Arlington, VA: ERIC,
         1976).

1235.   Ellison, Robert L. and others. The Measurement of
         Academic Climate in Elementary Schools. Expanded version
         of a paper presented at the annual meeting of the
         American Psychological Association, 1973. ED 109 142
         (Arlington, VA: ERIC, 1973).

1236.   Elsworth, Gerald R. and Frank Coulter. Aspiration and
         Attainment: The Measurement of Professional Self
         Perception in Student Teachers. Occasional Paper No. 11.
         ED 198 169 (Arlington, VA: ERIC, 1977).

1237.   Farrar, Carroll D. Developing and Utilizing Undergraduate
         Program Objectives for Developing Evaluative Instruments.
         Paper presented at the annual meeting of the Mid-South
         Educational Research Association, 1980. ED 206 729
         (Arlington, VA: ERIC, 1980).

1238.   Feild, H.S. and L. F. Schoenfeldt. "Development and
         Application of a Measure of Students' College
         Experiences; College Experience Inventory." Journal of
         Applied Psychology 60: 491-97 (August 1975).

1239.   Feldhusen, John F. and Margaret Britton Kolloff. "ME: A
         Self-concept Scale for Gifted Students." Perceptual and
         Motor Skills 53(1): 319-23 (1981).

1240.   Ferguson, Richard L. "The Development, Implementation,
         and Evaluation of a Computer-assisted Branched Test for a
         Program of Individually Prescribed Instruction." Ph.D.
         diss., University of Pittsburgh, 1969. ED 034 406 (Ann
         Arbor, MI: University Microfilms, 1969).

1241.   Fillbrandt, James R. and William R. Merz. "Minimum
         Proficiencies and the Fine Art of Setting Standards."
         NASSP Bulletin 62(415): 70-80 (1978).

1242.   Finch, C. R. "Instrument to Assess Student Attitude
         Toward Instruction." Journal of Educational Measurement
         6: 257-8 (Winter 1969).

1243.   Finding Kids With Special Needs: The Background,
         Development, Field Test and Validation. ED 087 183
         (Arlington, VA: ERIC, 1974).

1244. Fletcher, Jerry L. and William G. Spady. The Development of Instrumentation to Measure the Alternative Operational Manifestations of Five Basic Functions of Schooling. Paper presented at the annual meeting of the American Educational Research Association, 1975. ED 109 181 (Arlington, VA: ERIC, 1975).

1245. Flora, Ben V. Jr. "Diagnosing Selected Behavior Characteristics of Teachers of Secondary School Mathematics." Journal for Research in Mathematics Education 3(1): 7-20 (1972).

1246. Flynn, T. M. "Quantifying Teachers' Recall of Student Behavior." Psychology in the Schools 11(4): 408-11 (1974).

1247. Foster, Dennis R. and others. Evidence for a Student-centered Course Evaluation Form. ED 109 241 (Arlington, VA: ERIC, 1975).

1248. Fraser, Barry J. "Development of Short Forms of Several Classroom Environment Scales." Journal of Educational Measurement 19(3): 221-27 (1982).

1249. _____. Validity and Use of Individualized Classroom Environment Questionnaire. Paper presented at the annual meeting of the American Educational Research Association, 1981. ED 204 351 (Arlington, VA: ERIC, 1981).

1250. Fraser, Barry J. and Darrell L. Fisher. "Development and Validation of Short Forms of Some Instruments Measuring Student Perceptions of Actual and Preferred Classroom Learning Environment." Science Education 67(1): 115-31 (1983).

1251. Frye, Helen B. Development and Initial Validation of the Teaching Situation Reaction Test (Elementary Form), A Measure of Teacher Effectiveness. ED 074 050 (Arlington, VA: ERIC, 1972).

1252. Gardner, P. L. and S. M. Taylor. "A Transmission-interpretation Scale." British Journal of Educational Psychology 50(2): 186-87 (1980).

1253. Garfunkel, Frank. Productivity of Young Children: The Development of the Classroom Behavior Scales (CRB). ED 052 227 (Arlington, VA: ERIC, 1970).

1254. Gillan, Robert E. The Middle School Questionnaire. ED 160 617 (Arlington, VA: ERIC, 1978).

1255. Goehring, Harvey J. Jr. Perceptions of Secondary School Professional Personnel in Relation to Teacher Training in Pupil Evaluation Procedures. ED 209 264 (Arlington, VA: ERIC, 1981).

1256. Golmon, Melton E. "Assessing Teaching Opinions of Pre-service Science Teachers." School Science and Mathematics 75(4): 338-42 (1975).

1257. Goolsby, Thomas M. Jr. and Grace A. Wray. Practice Test for Pre-primary and Beginning First Grade. ED 054 219 (Arlington, VA: ERIC, 1969).

1258. Gordon, S. E. "Instrument to Measure Attitudes' Toward Selected Fraternity Activities." Journal of College Student Personnel 13: 229-32 (May 1972).

1259. Green, Margaret E. Pre-school Kindergarten Readiness Inventory. Paper presented at the American Personnel and Guidance Association Convention, 1969. ED 032 599 (Arlington, VA: ERIC, 1969).

1260. Greene, Michael B. On Involvement. Paper presented at the annual meeting of the American Educational Research Association, 1973. ED 080 564 (Arlington, VA: ERIC, 1973).

1261. Grossman, Jack H. A Diagnostic Aid to Facilitate Counseling with Academic Underachievers. ED 032 575 (Arlington, VA: ERIC, 1969).

1262. Halasa, Ofelia. Construction of a Bilingual Attitude Rating Scale. Paper presented at the annual meeting of the American Educational Research Association, 1977. ED 140 663 (Arlington, VA: ERIC, 1977).

1263. Hambleton, Ronald K. "Testing and Decision-making Procedures for Selected Individualized Instructional Programs." Review of Educational Research (44): 371-400 (1974).

1264. Harper, Betty. The Construction of an Instrument to Measure Elementary Teachers' Knowledge of a Subskills Approach to Teaching Reading. Technical Report No. 501. ED 174 976 (Arlington, VA: ERIC, 1979).

1265. Helsel, A. Ray and Donald J. Willower. Toward Definition and Measurement of Pupil Control Behavior. Paper presented at the annual meeting of the American Educational Research Association, 1978. ED 074 073 (Arlington, VA: ERIC, 1973).

1266. Herr, Gregory and Peter A. Cohen. Improving College Instruction: The Formative Assessment of College Teaching (FACT). Paper presented at the annual meeting of the American Psychological Association, 1978. ED 163 049 (Arlington, VA: ERIC, 1978).

1267. Hines, Brainard. Attainment of Cognitive Objectives. Technical Report No. 3. ED 052 833 (Arlington, VA: ERIC, 1971).

1268. Homeratha, Linda and others. Screening and Identification Model for Title IV-C: Primary Gifted Education. Presentation on Identification Procedure, National Association for Gifted Children, 1978. ED 191 248 (Arlington, VA: ERIC, 1978).

1269. Horne, Marcia D. Assessment of Classroom Status: Using
      the Perception of Social Closeness Scale. Revised version
      of a paper presented at the annual meeting of the
      American Psychological Association, 1977. ED 200 616
      (Arlington, VA: ERIC, 1977).

1270. Hovey, Larry M. "Design of an Instrument to Measure
      Teacher's Attitudes Toward Experimenting." School Science
      and Mathematics 75(2): 175-84 (1975).

1271. How to Succeed as a New Teacher: A Handbook for Teaching
      Assistants. ED 157 438 (New Rochelle, NY: Change Magazine
      Press, 1978).

1272. Hsu, Yi-Ming and Owen Scott. An Inventory for Appraising
      Experimental Research Designed for Introductory Research
      Methods Classes. Paper presented at the annual meeting of
      the American Educational Research Association, 1977. ED
      141 384 (Arlington, VA: ERIC, 1977).

1273. Hulle, William. "A Model for an Occupational-based
      Competency Examination." Man/Society/Technology 33(5):
      147-50 (1974).

1274. Inglis, Sandra Cheldelin. The Development and Validation
      of an Instrument to Assess Teacher Invitations and
      Teacher Effectiveness as Reported by Students in a
      Technical and General Post-secondary Educational Setting.
      Paper presented at the annual meeting of the American
      Educational Research Association, 1978. ED 167 594
      (Arlington, VA: ERIC, 1978).

1275. Isakson, Richard L. and Randy Ellsworth. "The Measurement
      of Teacher Attitudes Toward Educational Research."
      Educational Research Quarterly 4(2): 12-18 (1979).

1276. Iverson, Barbara K. and Diane P. Schiller. Development of
      a Home Assessment Measure. Paper presented at the annual
      meeting of the American Educational Research Association,
      1980. ED 194 610 (Arlington, VA: ERIC, 1980).

1277. Iwanicki, Edward F. "Performance Standards: Toward
      Resolving the Controversy." Education and Urban Society
      12(1): 56-64 (1979).

1278. Jensen, Linda R. "Diagnosis and Evaluation of Creativity,
      Research and Thinking Skills of Academically Talented
      Elementary Students." Gifted Child Quarterly 22(1): 98-
      110 (1978).

1279. Jones, John A. Validation of the Curriculum Accommodation
      Questionnaire. Paper presented at the annual meeting of
      the American Educational Research Association, 1974. ED
      091 436 (Tallahassee, FL: Florida State Dept. of
      Education, 1974).

1280. Jordan, A. M. Measurement in Education: An Introduction.
      (New York: McGraw-Hill, 1953).

1281. Kahn, Paul and Sol Ribner. "A Brief Behavior Rating Scale
       for Children in a School Setting." Psychology in the
       Schools 19(1): 113-16 (1982).

1282. Kantor, Jeffrey E. and others. Development and Validaton
       of the Air Force Technical Training Student Survey:
       Attitudinal Correlates of Course Attrition Level and
       Student Gender. Final Report for Period March 1973--
       December 1978. ED 173 423 (Arlington, VA: ERIC, 1979).

1283. Karlitz, H. "Development of a New Teacher Attitudinal
       Militancy Scale (TAM)." College Student Journal 13: 306-9
       (Winter 1979).

1284. Kaufman, Barry A. and others. Standardization of a
       Piaget-based Pre-school Teachers' Beliefs Inventory. ED
       175 873 (Arlington, VA: ERIC, 1975).

1285. Keeves, J. P. Some Attitude Scales for Educational
       Research Purposes. Home Environment and School Study
       Report 1974:2. ED 121 913 (Mystic, CT: Laurence Verry,
       Inc., 1974).

1286. Kegan, Daniel L. "The Cycles Survey: Longitudinal
       Indictors of the Quality of Student Life and a Framework
       for Evaluation and Administrative Experimentation."
       Evaluation Quarterly 2(2): 293-314 (1978).

1287. Kerwin, Michael A. Development of an Instrument to
       Measure the Teaching Behavior of Adult Educators. Paper
       presented at the Lifelong Learning Research Conference,
       1980. ED 183 743 (Arlington, VA: ERIC, 1980).

1288. Krus, Patricia and John Maher. Assessing Teacher Skills
       Needed to Implement Objectives-based Intruction. ED 208
       031 (Arlington, VA: ERIC, 1979).

1289. Lapan, Stephen D. The Development and Validation of an
       Instrument that Measures Student Perceptions of Teacher
       Credibility. Paper presented at the annual meeting of the
       American Educational Research Association, 1976. ED 121
       820 (Arlington, VA: ERIC, 1976).

1290. Lapp, Diane. "Behavioral Objectives Writing Skills Test."
       Journal of Education 154(3): 13-24 (1972).

1291. Lawson, Anton E. "The Development and Validation of a
       Classroom Test of Formal Reasoning." Journal of Research
       in Science Teaching 15(1): 11-24 (1978).

1292. Leles, Sam and others. A Rationale and Related
       Exploratory Studies for Validating the Ohio State
       Instructional Preference Scale, Form I. Paper presented
       at the annual meeting of the American Educational
       Research Association, 1969. ED 028 129 (Arlington, VA:
       ERIC, 1968).

1293.   Lemke, Jay L. and others. Attitudes to Educational
        Issues: Development of an Instrument. Paper presented at
        the annual meeting of the American Educational Research
        Association, 1977. ED 161 877 (Arlington, VA: ERIC,
        1977).

1294.   Levin, Joel R. and others. "A Comparison of Sentence-
        learning Errors in Children of Different Achievement
        Levels." Contemporary Educational Psychology 3(4): 358-66
        (1978).

1295.   _____. "Individual Differences in Learning From Pictures
        and Words: The Development and Application of an
        Instrument." Journal of Educational Psychology 66(3):
        296-303 (1974).

1296.   Lichtenstein, Robert. Validity of Preschool Screening
        Procedures: Research With the Minneapolis Preschool
        Screening Instrument. Paper presented at the Annual
        International Convention of the Council for Exceptional
        Children, 1982. ED 218 898 (Arlington, VA: ERIC, 1982).

1297.   Lowery, Lawrence F. and William H. Leonard. "Development
        and Method for Use of an Instrument Designed to Assess
        Textbook Questioning Style." School Science and
        Mathematics 78(5): 393-400 (1978).

1298.   Lym, C. Lavor and Wayne R. Murray. Construction and
        Investigation of the Reliabilities of the School
        Perception Scales. ED 109 187 (Washington, DC: Public
        Television Library, 1975).

1299.   Lynch, P. P. and others. "Course Orientations of Staff
        and Students: A Procedure for Curriculum Evaluation."
        Higher Education 9(4): 409-17 (1980).

1300.   McBean, Edward A. and Sabah Al-Nassri. "Questionnaire
        Design for Student Measurement of Teaching
        Effectiveness." Higher Education 11(3): 273-88 (1982).

1301.   McDaniel, Ernest. An Observation Scale for Inquiry
        Teaching. Paper presented at the annual meeting of the
        American Educational Research Association, 1979. ED 175
        927 (Arlington, VA: ERIC, 1979).

1302.   McDavis, R. J. "Development and Field Testing of an
        Instrument to Evaluate Student Personnel Programs."
        Journal of College Student Personnel 17: 100-4 (March
        1976).

1303.   Marshall, Jon Clark. Course Evaluation Schedule, Form B.
        Manual. Paper presented at the American Educational
        Research Association Meeting, 1973. ED 076 615
        (Arlington, VA: ERIC, 1973).

1304.   Martin, Jack. "The Development and Use of Classroom
        Observation Instruments." Canadian Journal of Education
        2(3): 43-55 (1977).

1305. Masonis, Edward J. Problems and Procedures in Planning a
       Situation Based Video Test on Teaching. Paper presented
       at the annual meeting of the American Personnel and
       Guidance Association, 1971. ED 057 095 (Arlington, VA:
       ERIC, 1971).

1306. Masters, James R. and Waldo G. Weaver. The Development of
       a Student Observation of Teachers Instrument for Use in
       High Schools. Paper presented at the annual meeting of
       the National Council on Measurement in Education, 1977.
       ED 141 409 (Arlington, VA: ERIC, 1977).

1307. Mastery Learning Developer's Guide. How to Develop Tests
       and Teaching Materials for all Types of Mastery Learning
       Students. Especially for Teaching Consumer Education and
       Basic Competencies to Teenagers and Adults Who Are
       Deficient or Reluctant Readers. ED 214 866 (Arlington,
       VA: ERIC, 1982).

1308. Medley, Donald M. Specifications for a New Teacher
       Examination: A First Approximation. ED 055 094
       (Arlington, VA: ERIC, 1970).

1309. Meredith, Gerald M. and Todd H. Ogasawara. "Scale for
       Excellence in Teaching Award for Teaching Assistants."
       Perceptual and Motor Skills 53(2): 633-34 (1981).

1310. Merino de Manzano, Ana Maria and others. Feedback on
       Student Learning for Instructional Television in El
       Salvador. Research Report Number 6. ED 070 254
       (Arlington, VA: ERIC, 1971).

1311. Meyer, William J. The Adaptive Behavior Rating Scale. ED
       068 148 (Arlington, VA: ERIC, 1972).

1312. Michael, William B. and Robert A. Smith. "The Development
       and Preliminary Validity of Three Forms of a Self-concept
       Measure Emphasizing School-related Activities."
       Educational and Psychological Measurement 36(2): 521-8
       (1976).

1313. Millman, Jason. Task and Administrative Facets of
       Teaching Performance Tests. Paper presented at the annual
       meeting of the American Educational Research Association,
       1974. ED 090 300 (Arlington, VA: ERIC, 1974).

1314. Mink, Oscar G. and others. A Manual for the
       Individualized Instruction Inventory (III). ED 226 795
       (Arlington, VA: ERIC, 1983).

1315. Moen, Ross and Kenneth O. Doyle Jr. "Construction and
       Development of the Academic Motivations Inventory (AMI)."
       Educational and Psychological Measurement 37(2): 509-12
       (1977).

1316. Moore, K. D. "Development and Validation of a Science
       Teacher Needs-assessment Profile." Journal of Research in
       Science Teaching 14: 145-9 (March 1977).

1317. Morstain, Barry R. The Educational Attitudes and Learning
      Orientations of Undergraduates: A Pilot Study of Inter-
      institutional Differences. Paper presented at the annual
      forum of the Association for International Research,
      1973. ED 080 585 (Arlington, VA: ERIC, 1973).

1318. Multiple-choice Cloze Exercises: Handbook. SPPED Test
      Development Notebook, Form 86. Revised. ED 226 028
      (Arlington, VA: ERIC, 1977).

1319. Musgrove, Walter J. "A Scale to Measure Attitudes Toward
      Behavior Modification." Psychology in the Schools 11(4):
      392-96 (1974).

1320. Nash, Robert Terry. "A Special Education Research Test
      for the Assessment of Critical Reading Abilities." Ed.D.
      diss., Utah State University, 1973. ED 080 959. Available
      from University Microfilms, Ann Arbor, MI.

1321. Neuburger, Wayne F. A Computer Support System For a
      Teacher Evaluation Model. Paper presented at the National
      Association of Users of Computer Applications to Learning
      Conference, 1976. ED 131 839 (Arlington, VA: ERIC, 1976).

1322. Nickse, Ruth S. Development of a Performance Assessment
      System for the Central New York External High School
      Diploma Program: An Educational Alternative for Adults: A
      Progress Report. ED 110 740 (Arlington, VA: ERIC, 1975).

1323. Nottingham, B. "Measurement of Pupils' Attitudes."
      Educational Research 12: 247-49 (June 1970).

1324. Nyberg, V. R. and S. C. T. Clarke. Technical Report on
      the School Subjects Attitude Scales (and) Improving and
      Extending the School Subjects Attitude Scales (and)
      Manual for Administration, Scoring, and Interpretation of
      the School Subjects Attitude Scales. ED 179 575
      (Arlington, VA: ERIC, 1979).

1325. Okey, James R. and William Capie. "Assessing the
      Competence of Science Teachers." Science Education 64(3):
      279-87 (1980).

1326. O'Reilly, Patrick A. and others. Evaluating Performances.
      Implementing Competency Based Education in Community
      Colleges, 4. ED 195 302 (Arlington, VA: ERIC, 1980).

1327. Orientation to Instruction in the Community College: A
      Series of Ten Self-instructional Units for Part-time
      Faculty Members, and Other Instructors New to the
      Community College. ED 196 480 (Arlington, VA: ERIC,
      1979).

1328. Orton, Kenneth D. A New Approach to Curriculum
      Evaluation. ED 011 964 (Arlington, VA: ERIC, 1966).

1329. O'Triel, Frances S. and B. Diane Terry. A New Instrument
      for Measuring Teacher Effectiveness. Paper presented at
      the annual meeting of the Southeastern Psychological
      Association, 1978. ED 193 310 (Arlington, VA: ERIC,
      1978).

1330. Owens, L. and R. G. Straton. "The Development of a Co-operative Competitive, and Individualised Learning Preference Scale for Students." British Journal of Educational Psychology 50(2): 147-61 (1980).

1331. Panell, R. C. and G. J. Laabs. "Construction of a Criterion-referenced, Diagnostic Test for an Individualized Instruction Program." Journal of Applied Psychology 64(3): 255-61 (1979).

1332. Parent Opinion Inventory. Instructions for Use. Part A. Part B. ED 155 183 (Arlington, VA: ERIC, 1976).

1333. Park, James. The Use and Development of Videotape Tests to Assess Achievement of Educational Objectives: Application in Educational Psychology. Paper presented at the CAPE Conference, 1972. ED 069 754 (Arlington, VA: ERIC, 1972).

1334. Payne, D. A. and others. "Development and Validation of an Observation Instrument to Assess Competencies of School Principals." Educational and Psychological Measurement 36: 945-52 (Winter 1976).

1335. Peak, Laurie and James M. Brown. A Conceptual Framework and Process for Identifying the Inservice Needs of Vocational Educators Serving Special Needs Populations. Pilot Test Report. ED 198 288 (Arlington, VA: ERIC, 1980).

1336. Performance-based Certification in Georgia. Teaching Field Criterion-referenced Tests Development. On-the-job Assessment Development. Schedule for Implementation of Performance-based Certification. ED 179 605 (Arlington, VA: ERIC, 1979).

1337. Perney, Jan. "The Development and Validation of the Student Opinion Inventory Factor Scales." Educational and Psychological Measurement 35(4): 983-6 (1975).

1338. Pinsky, Paul D. Achievement Monitoring of Individually Paced Instruction. Final Report. ED 092 175 (Arlington, VA: ERIC, 1973).

1339. _____. A Mathematical Model of Testing for Instructional Management Purposes. From symposium "Designing Instructional Systems with Longitudinal Testing Using Item Sampling Techniques," annual meeting, American Educational Research Association, 1970. ED 041 937 (Arlington, VA: ERIC, 1970).

1340. Purkey, W. W. and others. "Florida Key: A Scale to Infer Learner Self-concept." Educational and Psychological Measurement 33: 979-84 (Winter 1973).

1341. Randhawa, Bikkar S. and Frank van Hesteren. The Development and Validation of a Hybrid Semantic Differential Measure of School Related Attitudes in Young Children. Paper presented at the annual meeting of the Canadian Psychological Association, 1982. ED 223 691 (Arlington, VA: ERIC, 1982).

1342. The Refinement and Modification of an Instrument for Assessing the Achievement of Interpersonal Skills of Social Work Students. Institutional Report No. 4. Wayne State University. ED 148 857 (Arlington, VA: ERIC, 1975).

1343. Resnick, Lauren B. and Margaret C. Wang. Approaches to the Validation of Learning Hierarchies. Preprint 50. Paper presented at the 18th Annual Western Regional Conference on Testing Problems, 1969. ED 035 943 (Arlington, VA: ERIC, 1969).

1344. Reynolds, William M. "Development and Validation of a Scale to Measure Learning-related Classroom Behaviors." Educational and Psychological Measurement 39(4): 1011-18 (1979).

1345. _____. "Development of a Scale to Measure Learning-related Behaviors." Paper presented at the annual meeting of the American Psychological Association, 1978. ED 173 366 (Arlington, VA: ERIC, 1978).

1346. Reynolds, William M. and others. "Initial Development and Validation of the Academic Self-concept Scale." Educational and Psychological Measurement 40(4): 1013-16 (1980).

1347. Richards, James M. Jr. Can Computers Write College Admissions Tests. Appears in ACT Research Reports No. 15, October 1966. ED 013 488. (Washington,D.C.: American Documentation Institute, No. 9174, Library of Congress, 1966).

1348. Riley, John F. The Development of an Instrument to Measure Creative Teaching Abilities. Paper presented at the annual meeting of the Southwest Educational Research Association, 1982. ED 220 521 (Arlington, VA: ERIC, 1982).

1349. Roberts, Joseph B. The Impact of Behavioral Modification Based Programs Versus Developmental Based Programs on Pupil Role Development. Paper presented at the annual meeting of the American Educational Research Association, 1973. ED 080 562 (Arlington, VA: ERIC, 1973).

1350. Robinson, Lora and Richard Seligman. "A Scale For Measuring Campus Morale." Journal of Educational Measurement 6(2): 109-10 (1969).

1351. Rosen, Jacqueline L. Perceptions of the Childhood Self and Teacher-child Relations. Final Report. ED 115 604 (Arlington, VA: ERIC, 1975).

1352. Russell, Earl B. "An Instrument to Measure the Change Orientation of Teachers." Illinois Career Education Journal 33(1): 42-4 (1975).

1353. Schmeck, Ronald Ray and others. "Development of a Self-report Inventory for Assessing Individual Differences in Learning Processes." Applied Psychological Measurement 1(3): 413-31 (1977).

1354.   Sciara, Frank J. and Richard K. Jantz. An Attempt to
        Measure Pre-service Teacher Attitude Utilizing an Empathy
        Towards Poverty Scale. ED 088 958 (Arlington, VA: ERIC,
        1973).

1355.   Seidman, Edward and others. "Assessment of Classroom
        Behavior: A Multiattribute, Multisource Approach to
        Instrument Development and Validation." Journal of
        Educational Psychology 71(4): 451-64 (1979).

1356.   Strom, Bruce and others. "The Course Structure Inventory:
        Discriminant and Construct Validity." Educational and
        Psychological Measurement 42(4): 1125-33 (1982).

1357.   Student Opinion Inventory. Instructions for Use. Part A.
        Part B. ED 155 184 (Arlington VA: ERIC, 1974).

1358.   Teacher Opinion Inventory. Instructions for Use. Part A.
        Part B. ED 155 185 (Arlington, VA: ERIC, 1975).

1359.   Thompson, Bruce. Refinement of the Administrator
        Professional Leadership Scale (APLS-II). Report 74-3. ED
        175 911 (Arlington, VA: ERIC, 1974).

1360.   Trickett, E. J. and R. H. Moos. "Social Environment of
        Junior High and High School Classrooms; Classroom
        Environment Scale." Journal of Educational Psychology 65:
        93-102 (1973).

1361.   Turner, Kenne G. "Competency Inventory on Vocational
        Education for the Handicapped (CIVEH): Development and
        Validation." Journal of Vocational Education Research
        6(2): 23-39 (1981).

1362.   Valentine, Jerry. "Audit of Administrator Communication:
        Instrumentation for Researcher and Practitioner." Peabody
        Journal of Education 59(1): 1-10 (1981).

1363.   Virbickis, Joseph A. The Classroom Adaptation Scale: A
        Behavior Rating Scale Designed to Screen Primary Grade
        Children for School Adaptation Problems. Paper presented
        at the annual International Convention of the Council for
        Exceptional Children, Session T-31, 1979. ED 171 018
        (Arlington, VA: ERIC, 1979).

1364.   Walker, Thomas J. "Assessing the Cognitive Base for
        Teacher Behavior: Formative Applications for Criterion-
        referenced Testing." Journal of Vocational Education
        Research 7(2): 44-51 (1982).

1365.   Walker, Wanda. Development of a Readiness Test for
        Disadvantaged Pre-school Children in the United States.
        Final Report. ED 037 253 (Arlington, VA: ERIC, 1969).

1366.   Weinhold, John Donald. "An Attempt to Measure the
        Scientific Attitudes of Elementary School Teachers."
        Ph.D. diss., Ball State University, 1970. ED 053 958.
        Available from University Microfilms, Ann Arbor, MI.

1367. Weinstein, Claire E. and others. Design and Development
of the Learning Activities Questionnaire. ED 206 661
(Arlington, VA: ERIC, 1980).

1368. Whale, W. B. and R. E. Brack. The Development of an
Instrument to Differentiate Students' Perceptions of
Teachers' Bases of Power. ED 062 633 (Arlington, VA:
ERIC, 1972).

1369. Woog, Pierre and Estelle Gellman. The Surveying of the
Level of Individualization in the Classroom. Paper
presented at the annual meeting of the American
Educational Research Association, 1974. ED 095 200
(Arlington, VA: ERIC, 1974).

1370. Wotruba, Thomas R. and Penny L. Wright. "Developing a
Teaching Effectiveness Assessment Instrument." ED 152 694
(Arlington, VA: ERIC, 1978).

1371. _____. "How to Develop a Teacher-rating Instrument: A
Research Approach." Journal of Higher Education 46: 653-
63 (November 1975).

1372. Wright, S. "Development and Use of a Liberal Studies
Attitude Scale." Vocational Aspects of Education 28:
105-10 (December 1976).

1373. Zeichner, Kenneth M. "The Development of an Instrument to
Measure Group Membership in Elementary School
Classrooms." Journal of Experimental Education 48(3):
237-44 (1980).

HEALTH AND PHYSICAL EDUCATION

1374. Althoff, Michael E. The Development of a Test to Assess
Drug Using Behavior. ED 092 850 (Arlington VA: ERIC
1972).

1375. Anderson, Barbara J. A Methodology for Observation of the
Childbirth Environment. Paper presented at the annual
meeting of the American Psychological Association, 1976.
ED 135 502 (Arlington, VA: ERIC, 1976).

1376. Archer, E. and R. Arundell. "Measuring Instrument for Use
in Drug Education Programs: Development of the McLeod
High Risk Inventory." Journal of Drug Education 8(4):
313-25 (1978).

1377. Austin, Dean A. and William Walker. "A Senior High
Preventive Health Waiver Test: Development and
Validation." Health Education 12(6): 43-5 (1981).

1378. Avery, C. A. and others. "Practical Tennis Serve Test:
Measurement of Skill Under Simulated Game Conditions."
Research Quarterly of the AAHPER 50: 554-64 (1979).

1379. Boldt, Robert F. and Nancy L. Gitomer. Editing and
Scaling of Instrument Packets for the Clinical Evaluation
of Narcotic Antagonists. Final Report. ED 115 684
(Arlington, VA: ERIC, 1975).

1380. Burkhardt, E. and others. "Statistical Comprehension for Graduate Students in Physical Education: Test and Norms." Research Quarterly of the AAHPER 42: 235-43 (1971).

1381. Bush, Patricia J. and others. Reliability of a Shortened Children's Health Locus of Control Scale. ED 223 354 (Arlington, VA: ERIC, 1982).

1382. Byrd-Bredbenner, Carol. "A Nutrition Knowledge Test for Nutrition Educators." Journal of Nutrition Education 13(3): 97-9 (1981).

1383. Clarke, H. Harrison. Application of Measurement to Health and Physical Education. Fifth Edition. ED 131 020 (Englewood Cliffs, NJ: Prentice-Hall, 1976).

1384. Cormier, Patricia and others. "Dental Health Knowledge Tests: Their Development, Implementation and Evaluation." Journal of School Health 48(10): 610-15 (1978).

1385. Cunningham, Jo Lynn and others. "Development of CANKAP -- A Multidimensional Measure of Nutritional Beliefs." Journal of Nutrition Education 13(3): 109-14 (1981).

1386. Davis, Gwendolyn C. An Annotated Bibliography on the Construction and the Development of a Basketball Skill Test. ED 190 514 (Arlington, VA: ERIC, 1978).

1387. Digennaro, Joseph. "Construction of Forehand Drive, Backhand Drive, and Service Tennis Tests." Research Quarterly of the AAHPER 40(3): 496-501 (1969).

1388. Disch, James G. and others. The Construction and Analysis of a Test Battery Related to Volleyball Playing Capacity in Females. ED 148 815 (Arlington, VA: ERIC, 1977).

1389. Dwyer, Johanna T. and others. "A Nutrition Knowledge Test for High School Students." Journal of Nutrition Education 13(3): 93-4 (1981).

1390. Edmonson, Barbara and others. Development of a Sex Knowledge and Attitude Test for the Moderately and Mildly Retarded. Final Report. ED 160 643 (Arlington, VA: ERIC, 1977).

1391. Fanslow, Alyce M. and others. "The NATS -- Nutrition Achievement Tests for the Elementary Grades." Journal of Nutrition Education 13(3): 90-92 (1981).

1392. Fox, Robert A. How to Design, Construct and Evaluate a Multiple-choice Examination in Health Education -- A Practical Approach. ED 190 489 (Arlington, VA: ERIC, 1979).

1393. Gesten, Ellis L. "A Health Resources Inventory: The Development of a Measure of the Personal and Social Competence of Primary-grade Children." Journal of Consulting and Clinical Psychology 44(5): 775-86 (1976).

1394.   Gliksman, L. and others. "Adolescent Alcohol
        Questionnaire: Its Development and Psychometric
        Evaluation." Journal of Drug Education 10(3): 209-27
        (1980).

1395.   Gough, Harrison G. "A 24-item Version of the Miller-Fisk
        Sexual Knowledge Questionnaire." Journal of Psychology
        87: 183-92 (1974).

1396.   Hensley, L.D. and others. "Racquetball Skills Test."
        Research Quarterly of the AAHPER 50: 114-18 (1979).

1397.   Jackson, Vicki D. and Eileen Zunich. "Self-reported Use
        of Health Products. Developing an Instrument for
        Assessment." Health Education 11(6): 24-7 (1980).

1398.   Janda, Louis H. and Kevin E. O'Grady. "Development of a
        Sex Anxiety Inventory." Journal of Consulting and
        Clinical Psychology 48(2): 169-75 (1980).

1399.   Johnson, Shirley M. and F. Snow-Loudell. "Assessment of
        Reproductive Knowledge in a Inner-city Clinic." Social
        Science & Medicine 16(19): 1657-62 (1982).

1400.   Kleinman, Susan P. "Development of Dental Health
        Knowledge Tests for the Primary Grades." Health Education
        12(6): 16-19 (1981).

1401.   Lackey, Carolyn J. and others. "Development of the NKT--A
        General Nutrition Knowledge Test for Teachers." Journal
        of Nutrition Education 13(3): 100-101 (1981).

1402.   Levitov, Justin E. and others. "Measuring Drug-related
        Attitudes." Educational and Psychological Measurement
        41(4): 1277-83 (1981).

1403.   Martens, Fred L. "A Scale for Measuring Attitude Toward
        Physical Education in the Elementary School." Journal of
        Experimental Education 47(3): 239-47 (1979).

1404.   Meyers, Carlton R. "In Quest of Sound Fitness Testing."
        Physical Educator 37(2): 69-75 (1980).

1405.   Mood, Dale. "Test of Physical Fitness Knowledge:
        Construction, Administration and Norms." Research
        Quarterly of the American Association for Health,
        Physical Education, and Recreation 42(4): 423-30 (1971).

1406.   Moskowitz, Joel M. and others. Psychometric Properties of
        the "Drug and Alcohol Survey". ED 212 678 (Arlington, VA:
        ERIC, 1981).

1407.   Murphy, Richard F. "An Attitude Scale for Dental Health."
        The Journal of School Health 40(5): 268-70 (1970).

1408.   Nehemkis, Alexis, ed. and others. Drug Abuse Instrument
        Handbook: Selected Items for Psychosocial Drug Research.
        Research Issues 12. ED 154 304 (Arlington, VA: ERIC,
        1977).

1409. Oacel, S. M., ed. "Perspectives on Nutrition Education Instrumentation (Symposium)." Journal of Nutrition Education 13: 83-114 (1981).

1410. Olsen, L. K. "Evaluation Instrument for Appraising the Health Related Attitudes of College Students." Journal of School Health 42: 408-11 (1972).

1411. Schmidt, Norma G. and others. "An Instrument to Evaluate the VD Knowledge of Elementary Teachers." Health Education 7(2): 30 (1976). For related information see ED 113 335.

1412. Schneider, R. J. and J. M. Rothberg. "Predicting Involvement with Illicit Drugs: Development of the Instrument." Educational and Psychological Measurement 36: 1055-62 (1976).

1413. Secarea, Rebecca V. and Larry K. Olsen. An Evaluation Instrument for Appraising the Health Knowledge of Seventh Grade Students Participating in a Special School Health Education Project. Paper presented at the annual meeting of the American School Health Association, 1974. ED 164 559 (Arlington, VA: ERIC, 1974).

1414. Shaw, Don. "Evaluation--The Classroom Dilemma." Health Education 8(2): 5-6 (1977).

1415. Shick, Jacqueline. "Written Test in Activity Classes." Journal of Physical Education and Recreation 52(4): 21-2,83 (1981).

1416. Shifflett, Bethany and Barbara J. Schuman. "A Criterion-referenced Test for Archery." Research Quarterly for Exercise and Sport 53(4): 330-35 (1982).

1417. Sullivan, Ann D. and Nancy E. Schwartz. "Assessment of Attitudes and Knowledge About Diet and Heart Disease." Journal of Nutrition Education 13(3): 106-8 (1981).

1418. Talmage, H. and S. P. Rasher. "Design Issues in Developing and Selecting Measurement Instruments [Nutrition Education]." Journal of Nutrition Education 14: 54-5 (1982).

1419. Thornburg, Hershel. "Developing a Secondary Health Needs Assessment." High School Journal 64(6): 243-48 (1981).

1420. Tinsley, Ann M. and others. "A Nutrition and Physical Fitness Test for Fifth and Sixth Graders." Journal of Nutrition Education 13(3): 95-6 (1981).

1421. White, Charles B. A Scale for the Assessment of Attitudes and Knowledge Regarding Sexuality in the Aged. Paper presented at the annual convention of the American Psychological Association, 1981. ED 210 566 (Arlington, VA: ERIC, 1981).

1422. Yu, J. M. and R. Mendell. "Development and Utility of a Leisure Behavior Index." Research Quarterly for Exercise and Sport 51: 553-8 (1980).

HOME ECONOMICS

1423. Brailsford, Amelia T. Development of a Criterion
       Referenced Test for Home Economics (Consumer Education),
       10/7/81-6/15/82. ED 217 218 (Arlington, VA: ERIC, 1982.

1424. The Certificate of Secondary Education: Trial
       Examinations--Home Economics. Examinations Bulletin No.
       9. ED 068 481 (London: Her Majesty's Stationery Office,
       S.O. Code No. 27-364-9, 1966).

1425. Evaluation in Home Economics. ED 109 334 (Arlington, VA:
       ERIC, 1974).

1426. Home Economics. Sample Test Items. Levels I and II. ED
       140 066(Arlington, VA: ERIC, 1976).

1427. Hunter, Betty A. Clothing Construction Performance
       Assessment. Final Report. ED 133 580 (Arlington, VA:
       ERIC, 1976).

1428. Measuring Student Achievement in Home Economics. ED 118
       588 (Arlington, VA: ERIC, 1975).

1429. Paciorek, Karen M. "Construction of an Assessment
       Instrument to Measure Adolescents' Knowledge of Child
       Development." Dissertation Abstracts International
       42(11-A): 4712 (1982).

1430. Pestle, Ruth E. and others. "Lifestyle Alternatives:
       Development and Evaluation of an Attitude Scale." Home
       Economics Research Journal 11(2): 175-82 (1982).

1431. Stanley, Thomas O. "The Development of the Test of
       Consumer Competencies." Business Education Forum 31(5):
       34-5 (1977).

1432. _____. "The Development of the Test of Consumer
       Competency." Delta Pi Epsilon Journal 19(3): 1-15 (1977).

INDUSTRIAL ARTS

1433. Achievement Test Program. ED 023 791 (Arlington, VA:
       ERIC, 1967).

1434. The Certificate of Secondary Education: Experimental
       Examinations--Technical Drawing. Examinations Bulletin
       No. 6. ED 068 478 (London: Her Majesty's Stationery
       Office, S.O. Code No. 27-364-6, 1965).

1435. Fortune, Jim C. Performance Test Development in Machine
       Shop: Appendix H. Final Report. ED 097 415 (Arlington,
       VA: ERIC, 1972).

1436. _____. Performance Test for Auto Mechanics: Appendix I.
       Final Report. ED 097 416 (Arlington, VA: ERIC, 1972).

1437. Hambleton, Ronald K. and Francis Olszewski. Woodworking
       Objective and Test Item Bank: Appendix J. Final Report.
       ED 097 417 (Arlington, VA: ERIC, 1972).

1438.   Hambleton, Ronald K. and Frank P. Stetz. "The Development
        of Objective-based Instructional Programs in Career
        Education." Journal of Career Education 5(3): 220-25
        (1979).

1439.   Hawkins, H.M. "Design a Test to Measure Performance."
        School Shop 36: 30-32 (1977).

1440.   Industrial Arts Test Development, Book III. Resource
        Items for Graphics Technology, Power Technology,
        Production Technology. ED 186 442 (Arlington, VA: ERIC,
        1979).

1441.   Larkin, John and Barry Martin. Testing and Evaluation
        Methods for the Maryland Plan Approach to Industrial
        Arts. ED 179 755 (Arlington, VA: ERIC, 1979).

1442.   Rosin, William John. A Comparison of Student Achievement
        Between Two- and Three-hour Public School Trade and
        Industrial Education Welding Classes. ED 034 859. Ed.D.
        diss., Texas A and M University, 1969. Available from
        University Microfilms, Ann Arbor, MI.

1443.   Shimberg, Benjamin. "An Evaluation Tool for IA." American
        Vocational Journal 46(2): 69-72 (1971).

LEARNING DISABILITIES

1444.   Aloia, G.F. and S. D. Aloia. "Teacher Expectation
        Questionnaire: A Scale to Help Determine the Most
        Appropriate Placement for the Mainstreamed Handicapped
        Student." Journal for Special Educators 19: 11-20 (Winter
        1983).

1445.   Balthazar, Earl E. Balthazar Scales of Adaptive Behavior
        for the Profoundly and Severely Mentally Retarded. A
        System for Program Evaluation and Development. Section I:
        The Scales of Functional Independence: Eating-drinking
        Scales, Dressing-undressing Scales, Toileting Scales.
        Part One: Handbook for the Professional Supervisor. ED
        069 721 (Champaign, IL: Research Press, 1971).

1446.   _____. Balthazar Scales of Adaptive Behavior for the
        Profoundly and Severely Mentally Retarded. A System for
        Program Evaluation and Development. Section 1: The Scales
        of Functional Independence. Part Two: Handbook for the
        Rater Technician. ED 069 720 (Champaign, IL: Research
        Press, 1971).

1447.   Brook, Mona Stephanie. "Competency Test Construction:
        Learning Disabilities Instructional Personnel." Ed.D.
        diss., University of Kansas, 1976. Dissertation Abstracts
        International 37(8-A): 5030 (1976).

1448.   Cawley, John F. and John O. Goodman. Arithmetical Problem
        Solving: A Program Demonstration by Teachers of the
        Mentally Handicapped. ED 031 823 (Arlington, VA: ERIC,
        1967).

1449. Christiansen, James. Criterion Referenced Assessment: A
       Mini-course. Trainer's Manual. ED 177 810 (Arlington, VA:
       ERIC, 1979).

1450. Dansereau, Donald F. and others. Learning Strategy
       Inventory Development and Assessment. Final Report for
       Period January 1974-May 1975. ED 111 741 (Arlington, VA:
       ERIC, 1975).

1451. DeJung, John E. and Daisy M. Reed. Measurement of
       Community Adjustment of Mildly Retarded Young Adults.
       Final Report. ED 196 221 (Arlington, VA: ERIC, 1978).

1452. DeRosa, Steve. The Parent Needs Inventory. Paper
       presented at the Annual International Convention of
       Council for Exceptional Children, 1982. ED 219 906
       (Arlington, VA: ERIC, 1982).

1453. Dunlap, W. P. and A. H. Brennan. "Diagnosing Learning
       Difficulties via IAI; Informal Arithmetic Inventory."
       Academic Therapy 12: 389-97 (Summer 1977).

1454. Eggert, Dietrich. "Psychological Diagnosis of Mental
       Retardation in West Germany." Exceptional Child 29(1):
       31-42 (1982).

1455. Fedje, Cheryl G. and others. Impact Research Focusing on
       Mildly Mentally Handicapped Students in Secondary
       Vocational Consumer and Homemaking Programs in Minnesota.
       ED 206 899 (Arlington, VA: ERIC, 1982).

1456. Feffer, Melvin. Role-taking Behavior in the Mentally
       Retarded. Final Report. ED 039 681 (Arlington, VA: ERIC,
       1970).

1457. Goodman, Marvin and Elias Mina. Toward Objectivity in
       Diagnosing Learning Disabilities: Refinement of
       Established Procedures. ED 175 912 (Arlington, VA: ERIC,
       1977).

1458. Grise, Philip and others. "Assessment of Minimum
       Competency in Fifth Grade Learning Disabled Students:
       Test Modifications Make a Difference." Journal of
       Educational Research 76(1): 35-40 (1982).

1459. Hall, James W. and others. Further Development and
       Refinement of DIAL: State of Illinois Contract L171.
       Final Report. ED 117 200 (Arlington, VA: ERIC, 1976).

1460. Halpern, Andrew S. and others. "Measuring Social and
       Prevocational Awareness in Mildly Retarded Adolescents:
       Social and Prevocational Information Battery." American
       Journal of Mental Deficiency 80(1): 81-9 (1975).

1461. Hively, Wells and Maynard C. Reynolds, ed. Domain-
       referenced Testing in Special Education. ED 108 410
       (Reston, VA: Council for Exceptional Children, 1975).

1462. Hofmann, Richard J. Illustrative Examples of the
       Development and Interpretation of Hierarchial Tests in
       the Field of Learning Disabilities. Paper presented at
       the International Scientific Conference of IFLD, 1976. ED
       135 145 (Arlington, VA: ERIC, 1976).

1463. Irvin, Larry K. and others. "Assessment of Retarded
       Student Achievement with Standardized True/false and
       Multiple-choice Tests." Journal of Educational
       Measurement 17(1): 51-8 (1980).

1464. Jarvis, Gilbert A. "Systematic Preparation of the
       Multiple-choice Listening Test." NALLD Journal 5(2): 18-
       25 (1970).

1465. Jordan, John E. "Construction of a Guttman Facet Designed
       Cross-cultural Attitude-behavior Scale Toward Mental
       Retardation." American Journal of Mental Deficiency
       76(2): 201-19 (1971).

1466. Mardell, C. G. and D. S. Goldenberg. Learning
       Disabilities/Early Childhood Research Project. Annual
       Report August 31, 1972. ED 082 408 (Arlington, VA: ERIC,
       1972).

1467. Merbler, John B. The Development of the Revised Peabody
       Mobility Scale. Paper presented at the Annual
       International Convention of the Council for Exceptional
       Children, 1976. ED 122 535 (Arlington, VA: ERIC, 1976).

1468. Mercer, Jane R. Cultural Diversity, Mental Retardation,
       and Assessment: The Case for Nonlabeling. Paper presented
       at the Fourth International Congress for the
       International Association for the Scientific Study of
       Mental Deficiency, 1976. ED 133 404 (Arlington, VA: ERIC,
       1976).

1469. Novack, H.S. and others. "Scale for Early Detection of
       Children with Learning Problems." Exceptional Child 40:
       98-105 (1973).

1470. Phillips, Phyllis P. and Gerald Halpin. The Development
       of More Efficient Measures for Evaluating Language
       Impairments in Aphasic Patients. ED 185 082 (Arlington,
       VA: ERIC, 1975).

1471. Proger, Barton B. and Lester Mann. "Criterion-referenced
       Measurement: The World of Gray Versus Black and White."
       Journal of Learning Disabilities 6(2): 72-84 (1973).

1472. Proger, Barton B. and others. Adapting Criterion-
       referenced Measurement to Individualization of
       Instruction for Handicapped Children: Some Issues and a
       First Attempt. Paper presented at the annual meeting of
       the American Educational Research Association, 1972. ED
       064 354 (Arlington, VA: ERIC, 1972).

1473. Reynolds, William M. "The Utility of Multiple-choice Test
       Formats with Mildly Retarded Adolescents." Educational
       and Psychological Measurement 39(2): 325-31 (1979).

1474.   Reynolds, William M. and Victor T. Greco. "The
        Reliability and Factorial Validity of a Scale for
        Measuring Teachers' Attitudes Towards Mainstreaming."
        Educational and Psychological Measurement 40(2): 463-68
        (1980).

1475.   Rie, Ellen D. and others. "A Parent-teacher Behavior
        Rating Scale for Underachieving Children." Journal of
        Learning Disabilities 11(10): 661-63 (1978).

1476.   Riegel, R. Hunt. Measuring Educationally Handicapped
        Children's Organizational Strategies by Sampling Overt
        Groupings. Research Report No. 37. ED 104 049 (Arlington,
        VA: ERIC, 1972).

1477.   Rosner, Jerome and Dorothea P. Simon. "The Auditory
        Analysis Test: An Initial Report." Journal of Learning
        Disabilities 4(7): 384-92 (1971).

1478.   Rosner, Jerome and others. The Identification of Children
        with Perceptual-motor Dysfunction: A Study of
        Perceptual-motor Dysfunction Among Emotionally Disturbed,
        Educable Mentally Retarded and Normal Children in the
        Pittsburgh Public Schools. ED 037 837 (Arlington, VA:
        ERIC, 1969).

1479.   Shapiro, Alvin H. "A New Brief Dyslexia Test." Reading
        Improvement 20(1): 45-9 (1983).

1480.   Skill Analysis as a Technique for Predicting Vocational
        Success of the Mentally Retarded. ED 043 902 (Arlington,
        VA: ERIC, 1970).

1481.   Steinkamp, Marjorie W. and Stephen P. Quigley. "Assessing
        Deaf Children's Written Language; Test of Syntactical
        Abilities." Volta Review 79(1): 10-18 (1977).

1482.   Taylor, Arthur and others. Applications of Ordering
        Theory Analysis in the Formative Evaluation of
        Instruction for Retarded Children. Paper presented at the
        annual meeting of the American Educational Research
        Association, 1974. ED 091 440 (Arlington, VA: ERIC,
        1974).

1483.   Thurman, Richard L. and others. The Peabody Mathematics
        Readiness Test: Rationale and Philosophy, Historical
        Development and Utility with Mentally Retarded Children.
        Paper presented at the Annual International Convention of
        the Council for Exceptional Children, 1976. ED 122 524
        (Arlington, VA: ERIC, 1976).

1484.   Travis, George Y. and others. "The London Procedure: A
        Screening Diagnostic and Teaching Guide for Adult
        Learning Problems." Adult Literacy and Basic Education
        2(3): 165-74 (1978).

1485.   Vaillancourt, Beverly. A Special Project for the
        Development of Assessment and Educational Programming
        Techniques Serving the Adult Basic Education Student with
        Learning Disabilities. Final Report. ED 193 433
        (Arlington, VA: ERIC, 1979).

1486.   Vocational Rehabilitation of the Hearing Impaired
        Mentally Retarded. Final Report, 10/1/76 to 12/31/77.
        Paper presented at the annual meeting of the Conference
        on College Composition and Communication, 1979. ED 177
        294 (Arlington, VA: ERIC, 1977).

1487.   Wright, William H. Jr. and William B. Michael. "The
        Development and Validation of a Scale for School
        Observation of Characteristics Associated with Learning
        Disabilities and Minimal Brain Dysfunction in Elementary
        School Boys." Educational and Psychological Measurement
        37(4): 917-28 (1977).

LISTENING COMPREHENSION

1488.   Brassard, Mary B. Direct Comparisons Between Listening
        and Reading as Language Comprehension Abilities in the
        Intermediate Grades. Paper presented at the Conference of
        the American Educational Research Association, 1970. ED
        040 824 (Arlington, VA: ERIC, 1970).

1489.   Chastain, Kenneth D. "Testing Listening Comprehension
        Tests." TESOL Quarterly 13(1): 81-8 (1979).

1490.   Cosgrave, Desmond P. "Aural Comprehension Tests and How
        to Prepare Them." ED 036 805. The Modern English Journal
        1(1): 5-16 (1970).

1491.   Hackett, Marie Gannon. A Hierarchy of Skills in Listening
        Comprehension and Reading Comprehension. ED 041 701
        (Arlington, VA: ERIC, 1970).

1492.   Smith, Raymond G. Development and Possibilities of
        Message Measurement Inventories. Paper presented at the
        annual meeting of the Central States Speech Association,
        1977. ED 136 316 (Arlington, VA: ERIC, 1977).

1493.   Steen, Arleen Mollie. The Effectiveness of Listening
        Lessons in the Kindergarten as Determined by the
        Listening Response Test. ED 060 012 (Ann Arbor, MI:
        University Microfilms, 1972).

1494.   Wallner, Nancy Kubin. "The Development of a Listening
        Comprehension Test for Kindergarten and Beginning First
        Grade." Educational and Psychological Measurement 34(2):
        391-6 (1974).

PSYCHOLOGY

1495.   Als, Heidelise and others. "The Brazelton Neonatal
        Behavioral Assessment Scale (BNBAS)." Journal of Abnormal
        Child Psychology 5(3): 215-31 (1977).

1496.   Barak, Azy. The Development of the Counselor Rating Form
        and its Cross-cultural Adaptation. Paper presented at the
        Annual Scientific Meeting of the Gerontological Society,
        1979. ED 184 022 (Arlington, VA: ERIC, 1979).

1497.   Bebeau, E. Charles. Development and Validation of a Scale
        to Measure Treatment Effectiveness in Psychotherapy.
        Paper presented at the Rocky Mountain Psychological
        Association, 1971. ED 056 093 (Arlington, VA: ERIC,
        1971).

1498.   Bellucci, Jo-ann Elizabeth and Michael K. Altekruse. The
        Development and Validaton of a Semantic Measure of
        Counselor Empathy. ED 138 866 (Arlington, VA: ERIC,
        1973).

1499.   Bersoff, Donald N. Alternates to Psychological Testing or
        How We've Turned a Silk Purse into a Sow's Ear. Paper
        presented at Session II of Southeastern Invitational
        Conference on Measurement in Education, 1972. ED 075 469
        (Arlington, VA: ERIC, 1972). Available as part of ED 075
        464.

1500.   Brazee, Edward N. "Student Responses to a Language Arts
        Test of Cognitive Functioning." Journal of Early
        Adolescence 1(4): 373-84 (1981).

1501.   Braziel, M. E. "College Freshman Adjustment Scale."
        Journal of the National Association for Women Deans,
        Administrators and Counselors 45: 27-33 (Winter 1982).

1502.   Brogan, Donna and Nancy G. Kutner. "Measuring Sex-role
        Orientation: A Normative Approach." Journal of Marriage
        and the Family 38(1): 31-9 (1976).

1503.   Buckwalter, Joseph A. and others. "Use of an Educational
        Taxonomy for Evaluation of Cognitive Performance."
        Journal of Medical Education 56(2): 115-21 (1981).

1504.   Bukacek, Susan E. Expectancy for Problem Solving. ED 188
        037 (Arlington, VA: ERIC, 1980).

1505.   Cairns, Ed and Tommy Commock. "Development of a More
        Reliable Version of the Matching Familiar Figures Test."
        Developmental Psychology 14(5): 555-60 (1978).

1506.   Campbell, Paul B. and Joan S. Beers. Definition and
        Measurement in the Affective Domain: Appreciation of
        Human Accomplishments. Paper presented at the annual
        meeting of the American Educational Research Association,
        1971. ED 050 173 (Arlington, VA: ERIC, 1971).

1507.   Cassidy, Phil. North York Self Concept Inventory: Junior
        High Level. Research Report. ED 226 025 (Arlington, VA:
        ERIC, 1982).

1508.   Cassidy, Phil and Gloria Broks. North York Self Concept
        Inventory: Secondary School Norms. Research Report. ED
        226 024 (Arlington, VA: ERIC, 1978).

1509.   Cooper, Shawn. "The Post-Wechsler Memory Scale." Journal
        of Clinical Psychology 38(2): 380-87 (1982).

1510.   Crawford, Patricia. Norms for the North York Self Concept
        Inventory: Intermediate and Primary Levels. Research
        Report. ED 226 023 (Arlington, VA: ERIC, 1977).

1511. Cromwell, Rue L. The Development of Behavior Dimensions
       for Emotionally Disturbed Children--A Study of Relevant
       Indicators for Classroom Techniques, Therapies Methods,
       and Prognosis. Interim Report. ED 019 783 (Arlington, VA:
       ERIC, 1967).

1512. Deci, Edward L. and others. "An Instrument to Assess
       Adults' Orientations Toward Control Versus Autonomy with
       Children: Reflections on Intrinsic Motivation and
       Perceived Competence." Journal of Educational Psychology
       73(5): 642-50 (1981).

1513. Diluzio, Geneva J. and others. Technical Manual for the
       Conceptual Learning and Development Assessment Series II:
       Cutting Tool. Technical Report No. 435. Reprinted
       December 1977. ED 154 011 (Arlington, VA: ERIC, 1975).

1514. _____. Technical Manual for the Conceptual Learning and
       Development Assessment Series II: Equilateral Triangle.
       Technical Report No. 434. Reprinted December 1977. ED 154
       009 (Arlington, VA: ERIC, 1975).

1515. _____. Technical Manual for the Conceptual Learning and
       Development Assessment Series III: Noun. Technical Report
       No. 436. Reprinted December 1977. ED 154 013 (Arlington,
       VA: ERIC, 1975).

1516. _____. Technical Manual for the Conceptual Learning and
       Development Assessment Series IV: Tree. Technical Report
       No. 437. Reprinted December 1977. ED 154 015 (Arlington,
       VA: ERIC, 1975).

1517. Duke, Marshall and Gayle Lewis. "The Measurement of Locus
       of Control in Black Preschool and Primary School
       Children." Journal of Personality Assessment 43(5): 479-
       80 (1979).

1518. Dunn, James A. The OST: Theory, Instrument and Norms.
       Paper presented at the American Psychological Association
       Convention, 1969. ED 036 808 (Arlington, VA: ERIC, 1969).

1519. Dusewicz, Russell A. "A Scale for Assessing Knowledge of
       Child Development." Education 93(3): 252-3 (1973).

1520. Edelbrock, Craig S. and Thomas N. Achenbach. Child
       Behavior Profile Patterns of Children Referred for
       Clinical Services. Paper presented at the annual meeting
       of the American Psychological Association, 1978. ED 168
       259 (Arlington, VA: ERIC, 1978).

1521. Ekstrom, Ruth B. and others. An Attempt to Confirm Five
       Recently Identified Cognitive Factors. Technical Report
       No. 8. ED 113 386 (Arlington, VA: ERIC, 1975).

1522. _____. "Cognitive Factors: Their Identification and
       Replication." Multivariate Behavioral Research Monographs
       79(2): 3-84 (1979).

1523. Elithorn, Alick, Sue Mornington and Andreas Stavrou.
"Automated Psychological Testing: Some Principles and
Practice." International Journal of Man-machine Studies
17(3): 247-63 (1982).

1524. Erwin, T. Dary. "The Scale of Intellectual Development:
Measuring Perry's Scheme." Journal of College Student
Personnel 24(1): 6-12 (1983).

1525. Espinosa, Renato and John Pierce-Jones. A Report on the
Results of the Administration of the Gumpcookies Test to
the Texas Evaluation Sample. Part of the Final Report on
Head Start Evaluation and Research: 1968-69 to the Office
of Economic Opportunity. ED 039 033 (Arlington, VA: ERIC,
1969).

1526. Fenigstein, Allen and others. "Public and Private Self-
consciousness: Assessment and Theory." Journal of
Consulting and Clinical Psychology 43(4): 522-27 (1975).

1527. Fisher-Beckfield, Denise and Richard M. McFall.
"Development of a Competence Inventory for College Men
and Evaluation of Relationships between Competence and
Depression." Journal of Consulting and Clinical
Psychology 50(5): 697-705 (1982).

1528. Form, A. L. "The Construction of a Scale on Attitudes
Toward Counseling." Journal of Counseling Psychology 2:
96-102 (1955).

1529. Freeman, B. J. and others. "Behavior Observation Scale
for Autism." Journal of the American Academy of Child
Psychology 17: 576-88 (Autumn 1978).

1530. Galejs, Irma and Dahlia F. Stockdale. "Cooperative-
competitive Preferences and Locus of Control of School-
age Children." Home Economics Research Journal 8(6):
386-93 (1980).

1531. Gheorghiu, V. A. and others. "Attempt to Construct a
Scale for the Measurement of the Effect of Suggestion on
Perception." Educational and Psychological Measurement
35(2): 341-52 (1975).

1532. Gibbs, John C., Keith F. Widaman and Anne Colby.
"Construction and Validation of a Simplified, Group-
administerable Equivalent to the Moral Judgment
Interview." Child Development 53(4): 895-910 (1982).

1533. Gioe, Adrienne. "The Construction and Validation of a
Scale to Measure Temporal Orientation." Dissertation
Abstracts International 43(1-A): 115 (1982).

1534. Gitter, A. George. Head Start Evaluation and Research
Center, Boston University. Report C-I, Perception of
Emotion Among Children: Race and Sex Differences. ED 022
561 (Arlington, VA: ERIC, 1967).

1535. Gleser, G. and others. "Adolescents View Their Mental
Health; Adolescent Life Assessment Checklist." Journal of
Youth and Adolescence 6: 249-63 (September 1977).

1536. Greeson, Richard J. "Development of a Psycholinguistic Index to Assess Self-esteem in the Counseling Session." Dissertation Abstracts International 43(2-B): 556 (1982).

1537. Grosek, Robert J. Problem Behavior Rating Scale. Technical Report 78-01. ED 166 915 (Arlington, VA: ERIC, 1979).

1538. Gross, Ruth B. and Marion Marsh. "An Instrument for Measuring Creativity in Young Children: The Gross Geometric Forms." Developmental Psychology 3(2): 267 (1970).

1539. Guion, Robert M. and Gail H. Ironson. Principles of Work Sample Testing. Volume I: A Non-empirical Taxonomy of Test Uses; Volume II: Evaluation of Personnel Testing Programs; Volume III: Construction and Evaluation of Work Sample Tests; Volume IV: Generalizability. ED 193 241 (Arlington, VA: ERIC, 1979).

1540. Hart, Joseph T. Remembering--Memory Searching and Memory Checking. Final Report. ED 054 234 (Arlington, VA: ERIC, 1971).

1541. Jackson, Linda J. and Raymond C. Hawkins. Stress Related Overeating Among College Students: Development of a Mood Eating Scale. Paper presented at the annual meeting of the Midwestern Psychological Association, 1980. ED 188 087 (Arlington, VA: ERIC, 1980).

1542. Jones, Kenneth Melvin and Daniel Lee Randolph. "Construction and Validation of a Scale to Measure Maslow's Concept of Self-actualization." Southern Journal of Educational Research 12(2): 97-110 (1978).

1543. Kapur, Malavika. "A Short Screening Battery of Tests to Detect Organic Brain Dysfunction." Journal of Clinical Psychology 34(1): 104-11 (1978).

1544. Khatena, J. "Something About Myself: A Brief Screening Device for Identifying Creatively Gifted Children and Adults." Gifted Child Quarterly 15: 262-6 (1971).

1545. Kifer, Edward. "An Approach to the Construction of Affective Evaluation Instruments." Journal of Youth and Adolescence 6(3): 205-14 (1977).

1546. Kilmann, R. H. and K. W. Thomas. "Developing a Forced-choice Measure of Conflict-handling Behavior: The MODE Instrument." Educational and Psychological Measurement 37: 309-25 (1977).

1547. Kinnane, John F. and Antanas Suziedelis. Sources of Interpersonal Anxiety in the Physically Handicapped. ED 010 896 (Arlington, VA: ERIC, 1964).

1548. _____. Work Values of the Handicapped. ED 016 110 (Arlington, VA: ERIC, 1966).

1549. Kinzie, J. David et al. "Development and Validation of a
Vietnamese-language Depression Rating Scale." American
Journal of Psychiatry 139(10): 1276-81 (1982).

1550. Klinedinst, James K. "Multiphasic Measurement of Child
Personality: Construction of Content Scales Using the
Personality Inventory for Children." Journal of
Consulting and Clinical Psychology 43(5): 708-15 (1975).

1551. Kogan, Nathan and others. "Understanding Visual Metaphor:
Developmental and Individual Differences." Monographs of
the Society for Research in Child Development 45(1): 1-78
(1980).

1552. LaCrosse, E. Robert Jr. Primary Influences on the
Development of Competence: The Development of a Maternal
Behavior Scale. Progress Report. Paper presented at the
Society for Research in Child Development Biennial
Meeting, 1969. ED 032 127 (Arlington, VA: ERIC, 1969).

1553. Ladewig, D., P. Graw, P. C. Miest, V. Hobi and E.
Schwarz. "Basler Drug-questionnaire and Alcohol-
questionnaire - 1st Experiences in Construction of a Test
Instrument for Evaluation of Dependency of Drug-consumers
and-or Alcohol-consumers." Pharmakopsychiatrie Neuro
Psychopharmakologie 9(6): 305-12 (1976).

1554. Lanyon, Richard I. "Development and Validation of a
Psychological Screening Inventory." Journal of Consulting
and Clinical Psychology 35(1, pt. 2): 1-23 (1970).

1555. Lanzo, Mary A. "The Construction of an Instrument to
Assess Primary School Children's Knowledge of Positional
Concepts." Dissertation Abstracts International 42(12-A):
5095 (1982).

1556. Lawrence, D. "The Development of a Self-esteem
Questionnaire." British Journal of Educational Psychology
51(2): 245-51 (1981).

1557. Lawson, J. S. and others. "The Social Self-esteem
Inventory." Educational and Psychological Measurement
39(4): 803-11 (1979).

1558. Lee, Dong Yul and others. "Development and Validation of
a Microcounseling Skill Discrimination Scale." Journal of
Counseling Psychology 23(5): 468-72 (1976).

1559. Lefcourt, Herbert M. and others. The Multidimensional-
multiattributional Causality Scale: The Development of a
Goal Specific Locus of Control Scale. ED 171 737
(Arlington, VA: ERIC, 1978).

1560. Lefkovitz, Paul M., Dennis P. Morrison, and Jeffrey H.
Davis. "The Assessment of Current Functioning Scale
(ACFS)." Journal of Psychiatric Treatment & Evaluation
4(3): 297-305 (1982).

1561. Leibowitz, Gerald and Sherwood Chorost. Development of an Institutional Behavior Rating Scale. Paper presented at the annual meeting of the Eastern Psychological Association, 1970. ED 058 265 (Arlington, VA: ERIC, 1970).

1562. Leitner, L. M. and Suzana Cado. "Personal Constructs and Homosexual Stress." Journal of Personality & Social Psychology 43(4): 869-72 (1982).

1563. Lessing, Elise E. and others. "Parallel Forms of the IJR Behavior Checklist for Parents, Teachers, and Clinicians." Journal of Consulting and Clinical Psychology 49(1): 34-50 (1981).

1564. Lynch, Mervin and Teresa Cochran. Development and Validation of a Set of Semantic Differential Scales for Children. ED 064 341 (Arlington, VA: ERIC, 1972).

1565. McCroskey, J. C. and D. W. Wright. "Development of an Instrument for Measuring Interaction Behavior in Small Groups." Speech Monographs 38: 335-40 (1971).

1566. McQuitty, Louis L. "An Analysis of Additive Variance in Relation to a Theory of Types." Educational and Psychological Measurement 33(1): 19-41 (1973).

1567. Madaus, George F. and others. A Causal Model Analysis Suggests Modification of the Cumulative Hierarchical Structure Assumed in Bloom's Taxonomy of the Cognitive Domain. Paper presented at the annual meeting of the American Educational Research Association, 1971. ED 054 203 (Arlington, VA: ERIC, 1971).

1568. Mathes, Eugene W., Michael A. Zevon, Petra M. Roter and Steven M. Joerger. "Peak Experience Tendencies: Scale Development and Theory Testing." Journal of Humanistic Psychology 22(3): 92-108 (1982).

1569. May, Harold J. and Frederick J. Breme. "SIDS Family Adjustment Scale: A Method of Assessing Family Adjustment to Sudden Infant Death Syndrome." Omega: Journal of Death & Dying 13(1): 59-74 (1982-1983).

1570. Meagher, Robert B. Jr. and others. "The Development of a Scale Assessing Self-discontent in an Adolescent Psychological Inventory (MMAI)." Measurement and Evaluation in Guidance 11(3): 136-42 (1978).

1571. Meehan, Kenneth A. and others. Manual for the Early School Self Concept Inventory. Grades 1-3 (6 to 8 years of age). Elementary Form, 1977 Edition. Department of Research and Evaluation Report. ED 154 028 (Arlington, VA: ERIC, 1977).

1572. Mehrabian, A. "Development and Validation of Measures of Affiliative Tendency and Sensitivity to Rejection." Educational and Psychological Measurement 30: 417-28 (Summer 1970).

1573.   Mendelsohn, Mark and James Linden. (Development of an
        Atypical Response Scale.). Paper presented at the annual
        meeting of the Midwestern Psychological Association,
        1971. ED 059 244 (Arlington, VA: ERIC, 1971).

1574.   Metcalf, David R. An Investigation of Cerebral Lateral
        Functioning and the EEG. Final Report. ED 147 319
        (Arlington, VA: ERIC, 1975).

1575.   Meyer, Roger A. Development of a Committed-nominal
        Religious Attitude Scale. Paper presented at the annual
        meeting of the Southeastern Psychological Association,
        1976. ED 166 201 (Arlington, VA: ERIC, 1976).

1576.   Meyerstein, Israela. "The Family Behavioral Snapshot: A
        Tool for Teaching Family Assessment." American Journal of
        Family Therapy 7(1): 48-56 (1979).

1577.   Miles, David T. Development of a Test for an Experimental
        Research Program in Creative Problem Solving. Final
        Report. ED 024 208 (Arlington, VA: ERIC, 1968).

1578.   Milliones, Jake. The Pittsburgh Project - Part II:
        Construction of a Black Consciousness Measure. ED 148 945
        contained in ED 148 939. (Arlington, VA: ERIC, 1977).

1579.   Milner, Joel S. "Development of a Lie Scale for the Child
        Abuse Potential Inventory." Psychological Reports 50(3,
        Pt. 1): 871-74 (1982).

1580.   Motowidlo, Stephan J. "Development of a Measure of
        Generalized Expectancy of Task Success." Educational and
        Psychological Measurement 39(1): 69-80 (1979).

1581.   Mould, Douglas E. "Differentiation Between Depression and
        Anxiety: A New Scale." Journal of Consulting and Clinical
        Psychology 43(4): 592 (1975).

1582.   Muller, Douglas G. and Robert Leonetti. Primary Self-
        concept Scale: Test Manual. ED 062 847 (Arlington, VA:
        ERIC, 1972).

1583.   Murillo, N. and others. "Development and Validation of a
        Preliminary Measure for Student Evaluation of Group
        Counseling Experiences." Educational and Psychological
        Measurement 41: 463-72 (Summer 1981).

1584.   Neman, Janice and others. Language and Adjustment Scales
        for the Thematic Apperception Test for Children 6-11
        Years. ED 090 295 (Arlington, VA: ERIC, 1973).

1585.   Nitzberg, Mildred. "Development of Likert Scale to
        Measure Salience of Need for Interpersonal Relationships
        with Parents and Friends." Adolescence 15(60): 871-77
        (1980).

1586.   Nitzberg, Mildred C. "Development of Modified Q-sort
        Instrument to Measure Priorities Adolescent Places on
        Developmental Tasks." Adolescence 15(59): 501-08 (1980).

1587. Norem-Hebeisen, Ardyth A. Multi-dimensional Construct of Self-esteem: Tools for Developmental Counseling. Paper presented at the annual meeting of the American Psychological Association, 1975. ED 120 629 (Arlington VA: ERIC, 1975).

1588. Northrop, Lois C. Experimental Item Types to Measure Judgment. ED 150 176 (Arlington, VA: ERIC, 1977).

1589. Obayuwana, Alphonsus O. et al. "Hope Index Scale: An Instrument for the Objective Assessment of Hope." Journal of the National Medical Association 74(8): 761-65 (1982).

1590. Orlofsky, Jacob L., Mark W. Ramsden and Ralph S. Cohen. "Development of the Revised Sex-role Behavior Scale." Journal of Personality Assessment 46(6): 632-38 (1982).

1591. O'Sullivan, Maureen and others. Measurement of Social Intelligence. ED 010 278 (Arlington, VA: ERIC, 1965).

1592. Owens, Douglas T. and Leslie P. Steffe. Differential Performance of Kindergarten Children on Transitivity of Three Matching Relations. Paper presented at the annual meeting of the American Educational Research Association, 1971. ED 049 942 (Arlington, VA: ERIC, 1971).

1593. Paul, Gordon L. and others. "The Inpatient Scale of Minimal Functioning: A Revision of the Social Breakdown Syndrome Gradient Index." Journal of Consulting and Clinical Psychology 44(6): 1021-22 (1976).

1594. Pearson, Lea and Colin Elliott. "The Development of a Social Reasoning Scale in the New British Ability Scales." Journal of Moral Education 10(1): 40-48 (1980).

1595. Pittel, Stephen M. and Gerald A. Mendelsohn. "Situational Appraisal Inventory: Development and Validation of a Measure of Evaluative Attitudes." Journal of Consulting Clinical Psychology 33(4): 396-405 (1969).

1596. Prager, Edward and Arthur Blum. "A Client-developed Self-assessment Measure." Rehabilitation Counseling Bulletin 23(3): 227-29 (1980).

1597. Pryor, R. G. L. "Psychological Test-construction -- Some Lessons Learnt." Australian Psychologist 15(2): 273 (1980).

1598. "Psychological Testing." Exceptional Parent 1(4): 15-17 (1972).

1599. Randolph, E. M. and C. A. Dye. "Peter Pan Profile: Development of a Scale to Measure Reluctance to Grow Up." Adolescence 16: 841-50 (1981).

1600. Reading, A. E., B. S. Everitt, and C. M. Sledmere. "The McGill Pain Questionnaire: A Replication of its Construction." British Journal of Clinical Psychology 21(4): 339-49 (1982).

1601. Rest, James R. New Options in Assessing Moral Judgment and Criteria for Evaluating Validity. Paper presented at the biennial meeting of the Society for Research in Child Development, 1975. ED 113 017 (Arlington, VA: ERIC, 1975).

1602. Rest, James R. and others. "Judging the Important Issues in Moral Dilemmas -- An Objective Measure of Development." Developmental Psychology 10(4): 491-501 (1974).

1603. Reynolds, William M. "Development of Reliable and Valid Short Forms of the Marlowe-Crowne Social Desirability Scale." Journal of Clinical Psychology 38(1): 119-25 (1982).

1604. Ribner, S. and I. Chein. "Anti-social Activities Attitude Scale." Adolescence 14: 421-6 (1976).

1605. Richman, N. and P. J. Graham. "Behavioral Screening Questionnaire for Use with Three-year-old Children; Preliminary Findings." Journal of Child Psychology and Psychiatry 12: 5-33 (1971).

1606. Riechmann, Sheryl Wetter and Anthony F. Grasha. "A Rational Approach to Developing and Assessing the Construct Validity of a Student Learning Style Scales Instrument." Journal of Psychology 87: 213-23 (1974).

1607. Roberson, Don R. Assessment Techniques in the Affective Domain. ED 125 096 (Austin, TX: Educational Systems Associates, 1974).

1608. Russell, Dan. "The Causal Dimension Scale: A Measure of How Individuals Perceive Causes." Journal of Personality & Social Psychology 42(6): 1137-45 (1982).

1609. Russell, Elbert W. Memory Testing: The Next Step. Paper presented at the annual meeting of the American Psychological Association, 1980. ED 209 254 (Arlington, VA: ERIC, 1980).

1610. Ruznisky, Sonja A. and Patrick C. Thauberger. "Incidents of Reality: Sources of Ontological Stress and Concern." Social Science & Medicine 16(9): 1005-11 (1982).

1611. Sheehan, Mary A. and Frank J. Kobler. The Loyola Sentence Completion Blank for Clergymen: Construction and Validation. Paper presented at the Midwestern Psychological Association Meeting, 1972. ED 069 714 (Arlington, VA: ERIC, 1972).

1612. Sherer, Mark and others. "The Self-efficacy Scale: Construction and Validation." Psychological Reports 51(2): 663-71 (1982).

1613. Shorkey, Clayton T. and Victor L. Whiteman. "Development of the Rational Behavior Inventory: Initial Validity and Reliability." Educational and Psychological Measurement 37(2): 527-34 (1977).

1614. Sieburg, Evelyn Ratchford. <u>Dysfunctional Communication and Interpersonal Responsiveness in Small Groups</u>. Ph.D. diss., University of Denver, 1969. ED 042 781. Available from University Microfilms, Ann Arbor, MI.

1615. Silbergeld, Sam and others. "Assessment of Environment-therapy Systems: The Group Atmosphere Scale." <u>Journal of Consulting and Clinical Psychology</u> 43(4): 460-68 (1975).

1616. Silverstein, A. B. and others. "Identity Conservation and Equivalence Conservation: A Question of Developmental Priority." <u>Child Development</u> 53(3): 819-21 (1982).

1617. Stokes, J. and G. Lautenschlager. "Development and Validation of the Counselor Response Questionnaire." <u>Journal of Counseling Psychology</u> 25: 157-63 (1978).

1618. Stokes, J. P. and R. C. Tait. "Group Incidents Questionnaire: A Measure of Skill in Group Facilitation." <u>Journal of Counseling Psychology</u> 25: 250-4 (1979).

1619. Stoltman, Joseph P. <u>Manual -- Territorial Decentration Test (Revised Edition)</u>. ED 065 512 (Arlington, VA: ERIC, 1971).

1620. Strupp, Hans H. and others. <u>Toward the Measurement of Negative Effects in Psychotherapy</u>. Paper presented at the Conference of the Society for Psychotherapy Research, 1980. ED 189 530 (Arlington, VA: ERIC, 1980).

1621. Thorne, Frederick C. "Methodological Advances in the Validation of Inventory Items, Scales, Profiles and Interpretations." <u>Journal of Clinical Psychology</u> 34(2): 283-301 (1978).

1622. _____. "Technical Problems in Inventory Construction for the Objectification of Psychological States." <u>Journal of Clinical Psychology</u> 36(1): 127-36 (1980).

1623. Tobin, Kenneth G. and William Capie. "The Development and Validation of a Group Test of Logical Thinking." <u>Educational and Psychological Measurement</u> 41(2): 413-23 (1981). For related information see ED 191 885.

1624. _____. <u>The Test of Logical Thinking: Development and Applications</u>. Paper presented at the annual meeting of the National Association for Research in Science Teaching, 1980. ED 188 891 (Arlington, VA: ERIC, 1980).

1625. Tomko, Thomas N. and Robert H. Ennis. <u>Evaluation of Informal Logic Competence. Rational Thinking Reports Number 3</u>. ED 183 589 (Arlington, VA: ERIC, 1979).

1626. Vacc, Nicholas A. "Development of a Nonsexist-language Form of the Adapted Modified Role Repertory Test for Children." <u>Perceptual and Motor Skills</u> 55(1): 338 (1982).

1627. Vacc, Nicholas A. and others. "Further Development of the Adapted Modified Role Repertory Test." <u>Measurement and Evaluation in Guidance</u> 12(4): 216-22 (1980).

1628. Wagner, Betty S. Developmental Assessment of Infants and Toddlers in Child Care Programs. Paper presented at the annual meeting of the Texas Association for the Education of Young Children, 1982. ED 223 656 (Arlington, VA: ERIC, 1982).

1629. Walker, Hill M. Assessment and Treatment of Deviant Behavior in Children - Section Two: Construction and Validation of a Three Stage Model for Identifying and Assessing Deviant Behavior in Children. Final Report. ED 049 590 (Arlington, VA: ERIC, 1967).

1630. Walker, Hill M. and Robert H. Mattson. Identification and Treatment of Social-emotional Problems. Interim Report. ED 022 286 (Arlington, VA: ERIC, 1967).

1631. Wallston, Barbara Strudler and others. "Development and Validation of the Health Locus of Control (HLC) Scale." Journal of Consulting and Clinical Psychology 44(4): 580-84 (1976).

1632. Weir, Kirk and Gerard Duveen. "Further Development and Validation of the Prosocial Behavior Questionnaire for Use by Teachers." Journal of Child Psychology and Psychiatry and Allied Disciplines 22(4): 357-74 (1981).

1633. Weissman, Arlene N. and Aaron T. Beck. Development and Validation of the Dysfunctional Attitude Scale: A Preliminary Investigation. Paper presented at the annual meeting of the American Educational Research Association, 1978. ED 167 619 (Arlington, VA: ERIC, 1978).

1634. Westbrook, Mary T. and Linda L. Viney. "Scales Measuring People's Perception of Themselves as Origins and Pawns." Journal of Personality Assessment 44(2): 167-74 (1980).

1635. Wheatley, Grayson H. The Development of a Group Film Test of Certain Piagetian Conservations. Paper presented at the annual meeting of the American Educational Research Association, 1972. ED 064 315 (Arlington, VA: ERIC, 1972).

1636. Williams, Carolyn L. and Anthony R. Ciminero. "Development and Validation of a Heterosocial Skills Inventory: The Survey of Heterosexual Interactions for Females." Journal of Consulting and Clinical Psychology 46(6): 1547-48 (1978).

1637. Willner, Allen E. "Abstraction, Associative Focusing, and Similarities Tests: Towards More Clinically Sensitive and Better Understood Tests." Psychological Reports 29(3): 683-731 (1971).

1638. Yearworth, R. C. "Development of an Adolescent Life Change Event Scale." Adolescence 15: 91-8 (1980).

1639. Zuckerman, Marvin. "Development of a Situation-specific Trait-state Test for the Prediction and Measurement of Affective Responses." Journal of Consulting and Clinical Psychology 45(4): 513-23 (1977).

RELIGIOUS EDUCATION

1640. Davies, Richard E. Approaches to Measurement in Religious Education. Paper presented at the International Convention of the Religious Education Association, 1977. ED 170 300 (Arlington, VA: ERIC, 1977).

1641. Kanoti, G. A. and E. Laverdiere. "Criterion for the Measurement of Theological Awareness in College Students." Religious Education 67: 476-7 (1972).

SOCIOECONOMIC STATUS

1642. Dellas, M. and L. P. Jernigan. "Development of an Objective Instrument to Measure Identity Status in Terms of Occupation Crisis and Commitment." Educational and Psychological Measurement 41: 1039-50 (1981).

1643. Ellison, Robert L. and others. The Identification of Talent Among Negro and White Students from Biographical Data. ED 047 011 (Arlington, VA: ERIC, 1970).

1644. Frech, William P. Jr. "Construction of a Scale to Measure Children's Ethnocentric Attitudes." Journal of Social Studies Research 3(1): 16-23 (1979).

1645. Gies, Frederick John and John W. Alspaugh. "The Measurement of Teacher Values Concerning Disadvantaged Pupils: VDPQ." Journal of Negro Education 42(1): 39-43 (1973).

1646. Gilbert, Lucia A. and Gary R. Hanson. "Perceptions of Parental Role Responsibilities Among Working People: Development of a Comprehensive Measure." Journal of Marriage and the Family 45(1): 203-12 (1983).

1647. Kelley, Marjorie G. The Value Orientation Test: An Exploration of the Culture of Poverty Thesis Using a New Projective Instrument. Center Research and Development Report No. 15. ED 080 723 (Arlington, VA: ERIC, 1972).

1648. Moore, Allen B. "An Instrument to Measure Anomia." Adult Education 30(2): 82-91 (1980).

1649. Moore, Shirley G. A Sociometric Status Test for Young Children: Manual of Instructions. ED 103 490 (Arlington, VA: ERIC, 1973).

1650. Olson, Mary and others. The Measurement of Political and Income Aspirations and Expections. Paper presented at the annual meeting of the Rural Sociological Society, 1979. ED 176 929 (Arlington, VA: ERIC, 1979).

1651. Roberts, William B. Identifying a Power Elite in a Microcosmic Adult Community. ED 092 797 (Arlington, VA: ERIC, 1974).

1652. Robinson, Mildred Blackwell. Developing a Cultural
      Awareness Scale: An Assessment of Sensitivity to Cultural
      Differences in Children From the "Culture of Poverty." ED
      124 655 (1974). Available from University Microfilms, Ann
      Arbor, MI.

TEST PROGRAMS

1653. Allen, Russell and Vicki Fredrick. Testing Services
      Manual. ED 190 667 (Arlington, VA: ERIC, 1979).

1654. Campbell, Jeff H. "CLEP Changes Teachers, Too. A
      Professor Works on Test Development." College Board
      Review 108: 20-4 (1978).

1655. The Canadian Awareness Project. ED 209 295 (Arlington,
      VA: ERIC, 1981).

1656. The Certificate of Secondary Education: Some Suggestions
      for Teachers and Examiners. Examinations Bulletin No. 1.
      ED 068 473 (London: Her Majesty's Stationery Office, S.O.
      Code 27-364, 1963).

1657. Christiansen, Peter. Curriculum-related Testing: An
      Improvement Program. Symposium paper presented at the
      annual meeting of the American Educational Research
      Association, 1972. ED 064 338 (Arlington, VA: ERIC,
      1972).

1658. College Outcome Measures Project. COMP Annual Report
      1978. ED 173 396 (Arlington, VA: ERIC, 1978).

1659. The Colorado Evaluation Project (Common Status Measures).
      Progress Report. ED 079 383 (Arlington, VA: ERIC, 1970).

1660. Cooper, Mildred P. Criterion-referenced Test Development
      - A Contractual Agreement Between the Public Schools of
      the District of Columbia and a Commercial Test Publisher.
      ED 078 047 (Arlington, VA: ERIC, 1973). Available as part
      of ED 078 046.

1661. Development and Analysis of 18 Experimental Objectives-
      based Measures Administered in 1972. ED 079 397
      (Arlington, VA: ERIC, 1972).

1662. Doherty, Victor. Developments in Goal Based Measurement
      in the Portland Public Schools. Paper presented at the
      annual meeting of the American Educational Research
      Association, 1976. ED 126 566 (Arlington, VA: ERIC,
      1976).

1663. Forster, Fred and Victor Doherty. Using the Rasch
      Approach to Measurement to Solve Practical School Testing
      Problems. Paper presented at the annual meeting of the
      American Educational Research Association, 1978. ED 164
      580 (Arlington, VA: ERIC, 1978).

1664. Fremer, John. Developing Tests for Assessment Programs:
      Issues and Suggested Procedures. ED 093 990 (Arlington,
      VA: ERIC, 1974).

1665.   _____. Impact of Test Disclosure Legislation on Test
Development. Paper presented at the annual meeting of the
American Educational Research Association, 1981. ED 206
690 (Arlington, VA: ERIC, 1981).

1666.   Gartland, Michael J. "Joint Development of Mathematics
and Language Arts Criterion-referenced Item Pools."
Illinois School Research and Development 16(3): 99-103
(1980).

1667.   Gorth, William P. and others. "Massachusetts Statewide
Education Assessment 1977-78. Summary and
Interpretations. Career and Occupational Development." ED
164 868 (Arlington, VA: ERIC, 1978).

1668.   _____. Massachusetts Statewide Educational Assessment
1977-78. Technical Report. Career and Occupational
Development. ED 164 869 (Arlington, VA: ERIC, 1978).

1669.   Greaney, Vincent. "Developing National Attainment
Measures: A Study of Irish Experience." International
Review of Education 26(1): 3-16 (1980).

1670.   Greenberg, Lydia. Test Development Procedures for
Including Handicapped-Students in New Jersey's State
Assessment Program. ED 187 767 (Arlington, VA: ERIC,
1980).

1671.   Guide for an Assessment of Basic Life Skills. ED 139 819
(Arlington, VA: ERIC, 1977).

1672.   A Guide For Local District Testing Programs. Occasional
Papers in Education. ED 194 604 (Arlington, VA: ERIC,
1980).

1673.   Hardy, Roy. From Circus to El Circo: Issues in Instrument
Development for Young Spanish-speaking Children. Paper
presented at the National Conference on Multicultural
Curriculum Materials, 1976. ED 150 185 (Arlington, VA:
ERIC, 1978).

1674.   Hines, Everett B. A Testing Program for Introductory
Accounting. ED 078 009 (Arlington, VA: ERIC, 1973).

1675.   Hively, Wells and others. Domain-referenced Curriculum
Evaluation: A Technical Handbook and a Case Study from
the Minnemast Project. CSE Monograph Series in
Evaluation, 1. ED 177 226 (Arlington, VA: ERIC, 1973).

1676.   Hood, Paul D. and Laird Blackwell. An Assessment System
for Competence Based Education: The Educational
Development, Dissemination, and Evaluation Training
Program. ED 126 142 (Arlington, VA: ERIC, 1975).

1677.   Instruction Manual: Career and Occupational Development
Kit. ED 171 997 (Arlington, VA: ERIC, 1971).

1678.   Johnson, Carl I. The New Jersey Minimum Basic Skills
Testing Program: From A to Z. Occasional Papers in
Education. ED 194 606 (Arlington, VA: ERIC, 1980).

1679. Johnson, Richard T. Conducting Large-scale Examinations:
      A Handbook. ED 128 433 (Arlington, VA: ERIC, 1971).

1680. Justiz, Thomas B. Evaluating Career, Economic, and
      Community Education Programs. Final Report, July 16,
      1974, to June 30, 1976 (and) Appendices to Final Report.
      ED 171 886 (Arlington, VA: ERIC, 1979).

1681. _____. "Involving Business, Labor and Professional
      Leaders in Career Education Through Instrument
      Development." Journal of Career Education 5(4): 286-99
      (1979).

1682. Katzenmeyer, Conrad G. and others. A Model for the
      Development and Evaluation of Placement Tests for
      Objective Based Curriculum Management Systems. ED 091 412
      (Arlington, VA: ERIC, 1974).

1683. Kohr, Richard L. and others. Getting Inside the EQA
      Inventory: Grades 5, 8, and 11. Revised 1978. ED 178 591
      (Arlington, VA: ERIC, 1979).

1684. Kriewall, Thomas E. "Design of a Standard Testing,
      Scoring and Analysis System." Illinois School Research
      8(3): 5-16 (1972).

1685. McNeil, Judy T. and others. National Evaluation of Head
      Start Educational Services and Basic Education Skills
      Initiative Programs. Project Report 11: The First Cohort
      of Children. Final Project Report. ED 210 297 (Arlington,
      VA: ERIC, 1981).

1686. Masters, James R. and James P. Dorwart. The Development
      and Validation of a Decision-making Skills Test. Paper
      presented at the annual meeting of the National Council
      on Measurement in Education, 1980. ED 189 110 (Arlington,
      VA: ERIC, 1980).

1687. Mathews, Walter M. An Alternative to a Standardized
      Testing Program. ED 064 334 (Arlington, VA: ERIC, 1972).

1688. Mathis, William J. Large-scale Objective Referenced
      Testing: Some Practical Problems and Concerns. Paper
      presented at the annual meeting of the National Council
      on Measurement in Education, 1975. ED 117 145 (Arlington,
      VA: ERIC, 1975).

1689. National Assessment's Consumer Skills Assessments. ED 155
      116 (Arlington, VA: ERIC, 1978).

1690. Otey, John W. A K-2 Screening Instrument. Paper presented
      at the annual meeting of the Southwestern Educational
      Research Association, 1980. ED 187 462 (Arlington, VA:
      ERIC, 1980).

1691. Peterson, Joseph L. and others. Crime Laboratory
      Proficiency Testing Research Program. ED 166 242
      (Arlington, VA: ERIC, 1978).

1692. _Profiles of School District Performance 1976-77. A Guide to Interpretation._ ED 161 881 (Arlington, VA: ERIC, 1977).

1693. Rentz, R. Robert. "Innovations in the Practice of Measurement." _New Directions for Testing and Measurement_ 10: 91-8 (1981).

1694. Rickard, Patricia L. and others. _California Adult Student Assessment System (CASAS) Project. Final Report: July 1, 1980-June 30, 1981._ ED 212 326 (Arlington, VA: ERIC, 1981).

1695. Rodel, Lee J. _CAM Coordinator's Manual._ ED 183 580 (Arlington, VA: ERIC, 1979).

1696. Rubinstein, Sherry Ann and Paula Nassif-Royer. _The Outcomes of Statewide Assessment: Implicatons for Curriculum Evaluation._ Paper presented at the annual meeting of the American Educational Research Association, 1977. ED 141 394 (Arlington, VA: ERIC, 1977).

1697. Rueve, Mary H. and John H. Grate. _Revisions and Research Design for a Computer-based Criterion-referenced Testing Program, Model for Improving Basic Skills._ Paper presented at the annual meeting of the American Educational Research Association, 1975. ED 108 932 (Arlington, VA: ERIC, 1975).

1698. Russell, Dale and John Plakos. _Developing a Pupil Assessment System for Proficiency-based Instructional Programs._ ED 179 564 (Arlington, VA: ERIC, 1977).

1699. Ryan, S. K. "CAM Challenges Students to Perform Better; Comprehensive Achievement Monitoring Program." _Educational Leadership_ 37: 590-3 (1980).

1700. Sapone, Carmelo V. _An Administrative View._ Paper presented at the annual meeting of the American Educational Research Association, 1972. ED 064 333 (Arlington, VA: ERIC, 1972).

1701. _Technical Report of Selected Aspects of the 1969-70 Michigan Educational Assessment Program._ ED 064 286 (Arlington, VA: ERIC, 1971).

1702. _Technical Report of the California Assessment Program._ ED 161 882 (Arlington, VA: ERIC, 1977).

1703. _Technical Report: Tests of General Ability and Tests of Reading, Inter-American Series, Forms CE, DE, CES, DES._ Paper presented at the lecture series on Chicago Research Perspectives (Indiana University, Bloomington, 1975). ED 107 133 (Arlington, VA: ERIC, 1967).

1704. Tuckman, Bruce W. and Alberto P. S. Montare. _Psychometrics and Behavior: The New Jersey Scales of School-based Goal Attainment._ Paper presented at the annual meeting of the American Psychological Association, 1974. ED 104 913 (Arlington, VA: ERIC, 1974).

1705. Ward, Barbara. <u>The National Assessment Approach to
       Objectives and Exercise Development</u>. ED 194 577
       (Arlington, VA: ERIC, 1980).

1706. Zavarella, Joseph A. "How to Develop a Testing Program
       That Reflects--Not Dictates--Your Curriculum." <u>National
       Elementary Principal</u> 59(3): 58-60 (1980).

Multi-Aptitude Batteries

1707. Alvir, Howard P. Performance Tests: Their Conception, Elaboration, and Formulation. Second Edition. ED 095 222 (Arlington, VA: ERIC, 1974).

1708. Bayroff, Abram G. and Edmund F. Fuchs. The Armed Services Vocational Aptitude Battery. ED 042 128 (Springfield, VA: NTIS, AO 706832, 1970).

1709. Bernal, Ernest M. Jr. Gifted Mexican American Children: An Ethnico-Scientific Perspective. Paper presented at the American Educational Research Association, 1974. ED 091 411 (Arlington, VA: ERIC, 1974).

1710. Blanchard, B. Evarard. "The Blanchard Index of Scholastic Aptitude." Illinois School Research 6(1): 43-6 (1969).

1711. Boldt, R. F. and others. Sociolinguistic and Measurement Considerations for Construction of Armed Services Selection Batteries. Final Report for Period October 1975-June 1977. ED 151 405 (Arlington, VA: ERIC, 1977).

1712. Droege, Robert C. and others. "Development of a Nonreading Edition of the General Aptitude Test Battery." Evaluation and Guidance 3(1): 45-53 (1970).

1713. Haynes, Judith M. Educational Assessment of Immigrant Pupils. ED 064 293 (New York: Fernhill House, 1971).

1714. Herman, David O. Reducing Sex Bias in Ability Tests. Paper presented at the annual meeting of the American Psychological Association, 1981. ED 208 057 (Arlington, VA: ERIC, 1981).

1715. Lennon, Roger T. "The Anatomy of a Scholastic Aptitude Test." NCME Measurement in Education 11(2): (1980). Also available as ED 196 931.

Personality

1716. Abrahamson, R.E. "Development of an Instrument for
Measuring the Degrees of Divergent Responses Revealed in
Clay Images Formed by First Grade School Children."
Studies in Art Education 14: 47-58 (Fall 1972).

1717. Adkins, Dorothy C. Exploratory Work on an Objective-
Projective Test of Factors of Moral Development in Young
Children. Paper presented at the annual convention of the
American Psychological Association, 1973. ED 086 353
(Arlington, VA: ERIC, 1973).

1718. Adkins, Dorothy C. and Bonnie L. Ballif. Factors of
Motivation in Young Children: Theoretical and Empirical.
Paper presented at American Psychological Association
Convention, 1970. ED 043 900 (Arlington, VA: ERIC, 1970).

1719. Alban-Metcalfe, Robert J. and others. "The Construction,
Reliability and Validity of a Stress Inventory for
Children." Educational Psychology 2(1): 59-71 (1982).

1720. Allen, Jon G. and J. Herbert Hamsher. "The Development
and Validation of a Test of Emotional Styles." Journal of
Consulting and Clinical Psychology 42(5): 663-68 (1974).

1721. Almgren, Eva and Evy Gustafsson. "World Citizen
Responsibility: Assessment Techniques, Developmental
Studies, Material Construction, and Experimental
Teaching." Educational and Psychological Interactions 48
(April 1974). Also available as ED 110 373.

1722. Alper, T. G. "Relationship Between Role Orientation and
Achievement Motivation in College Women; Wellesley Role-
Orientation Scale." Journal of Personality 41: 9-31
(March 1973).

1723. Ames, Russell and Terry Lied. Measuring Teacher Value
Systems. Paper presented at the annual meeting of the
National Council on Measurement in Education, 1975. ED
104 956 (Arlington, VA: ERIC, 1975).

1724. Anderson, L. W. "Measuring Change in Academic Self-concept Resulting from Curricular and Instructional Innovations." Journal of Youth and Adolescence 6: 215-28 (1977).

1725. Anderson, Ora S. "The Development and Validation of Two Attitude Scales and an Investigation of the Relationships Among Selected Attitude and Reading Achievement Variables." Dissertation Abstracts International 43(5-A): 1416 (1982).

1726. Andrews, Frank M. and Stephen B. Withey. Developing Measures of Perceived Life Quality: Results from Several National Surveys. ED 081 887 (Arlington, VA: ERIC, 1973).

1727. Antonak, Richard F. and Patricia R. Rankin. "Measurement and Analysis of Knowledge and Attitudes Toward Epilepsy and Persons With Epilepsy." Social Science & Medicine 16(17): 1591-93 (1982).

1728. Ard, Nicholas and Stuart W. Cook. "A Short Scale for the Measurement of Change in Verbal Racial Attitude." Educational and Psychological Measurement 37(3): 741-4 (1977).

1729. Ayers, Jerry B. "Elementary School Teachers' Attitudes Toward Instructional Television." Journal of Experimental Education 41(1): 1-4 (1972).

1730. Bagley, Christopher and Kanka Mallick. "Development of a Short Form of the Piers-Harris Self-concept Scale." Educational Review 30(3): 265-68 (1978).

1731. Bailey, Bruce E. and John W. Butler. An MMPI Derived Child Abuser Scale: An Area in Need of Future Research. Paper presented at the annual convention of the American Psychological Association, 1979. ED 188 038 (Arlington, VA: ERIC, 1980).

1732. Baker, Robert P. and Ralph Mason Dreger. "The Preschool Behavioral Classification Project: A Follow-up Report." Journal of Abnormal Child Psychology 5(3): 241-8 (1977).

1733. Ball, Ruby C. Testing for Creative Traits of College Students. ED 010 414 (Arlington, VA: ERIC, 1967).

1734. Barber, Lucie W. and John H. Peatling. A Manual for the Barber Scales of Self-regard: Preschool Form. ED 152 821 (Schenectady, N.Y.: Character Research Press, 1977).

1735. Barnes, Gordon E. and Brent A. Vulcano. "Measuring Rationality Independent of Social Desirability." Personality & Individual Differences 3(3): 303-9 (1982).

1736. Bavolek, Stephen J. and others. The Development of the Adolescent Parenting Inventory (API): Identification of High Risk Adolescents Prior to Parenthood. ED 159 860 (Arlington, VA: ERIC, 1977).

1737. Beardsley, Donna A. Children's Social Attitudes Inventory: A Specialized Instrument for the Study of Attitudes Toward the Handicapped. ED 216 493 (Arlington, VA: ERIC, 1982).

1738. Beere, Carole A. "Development of a Group Instrument to Measure Young Children's Attitudes Toward School." Psychology in the Schools 10(3): 308-15 (1973).

1739. Benson, Jeri and Stuart Wilcox. The Effect of Positive and Negative Item Phrasing on the Measurement of Attitudes. Paper presented at the annual meeting of the National Council on Measurement in Education, 1981. ED 204 404 (Arlington, VA: ERIC, 1981).

1740. Benson, Peter L. and Steven Vincent. "Development and Validation of the Sexist Attitudes Toward Women Scale (SATWS)." Psychology of Women Quarterly 5(2): 276-91 (1980).

1741. Berger, Wallace G. "Note on Emotionality of Item Wording as a Variable in a Personality Scale." Perceptual and Motor Skills 32(2): 415-18 (1971).

1742. Berryman, J. D. and others. "Validation of a Scale to Measure Attitudes Toward the Classroom Integration of Disabled Students." Journal of Educational Research 73: 199-203 (1980).

1743. Billeh, V. Y. and G. A. Zakhariades. "Development and Application of a Scale for Measuring Scientific Attitudes." Science Education 59: 155-65 (1975).

1744. Billman, Jean. The Preschool Temperament Inventory: Construction and Standardization of a Teacher-rated Instrument for Assessing Temperament of Three- to Six-year-old Children. ED 224 592 (Arlington, VA: ERIC, 1981).

1745. Bingham, William C. and Carol J. Turner. "Modified Questionnaire on the Occupational Status of Women." Educational and Psychological Measurement 41(3): 909-15 (1981).

1746. Bjerstedt, Ake. Explorations in Creativity. ED 141 397 (Arlington, VA: ERIC, 1976).

1747. Blair, Mark W. and others. Development of the Tredyffrin/Easttown Sex Fairness Survey. Paper presented at the annual meeting of the American Educational Research Association, 1978. ED 164 552 (Arlington, VA: ERIC, 1978).

1748. Blakely, Craig H. and others. "Self-reported Delinquency as an Evaluation Measure: Comparative Reliability and Validity of Alternative Weighting Schemes." Criminal Justice and Behavior 7(4): 369-83 (1980).

1749. Blumenfeld, Phyllis. The Development of Materialistic Values During Middle Childhood. ED 080 575 (Arlington, VA: ERIC, 1972).

1750. Bogacki, David F. "Attitudes Toward Corporal Punishment: Authoritarian Personality and Pupil Control Ideology of School Personnel." <u>Dissertation Abstracts International</u> 42(12-B, Pt. 1): 4925 (1982).

1751. Bogardus, E. S. "A Social-Distance Scale." <u>Sociological and Social Research</u> 17: 265-71 (1933).

1752. Bolea, A. S. and others. "Pictorial Self-concept Scale for Children in K-4." <u>Journal of Educational Measurement</u> 8: 223-4 (1971). For related information see ED 037 780.

1753. Breckler, Steven J. and Anthony G. Greenwald. <u>Charting Coordinates for the Self-concept in Multidimensional Trait Space</u>. Paper presented at the annual convention of the American Psychological Association, 1982. ED 226 297 (Arlington, VA: ERIC, 1982).

1754. Bridges, K. Robert. <u>The Development of an Instrument to Measure Attitudes Toward Education for Parenthood and the Responses of Working- and Middle-class Students to the Instrument</u>. Paper presented at the annual meeting of the Eastern Psychological Association, 1980. ED 192 174 (Arlington, VA: ERIC, 1980).

1755. Brodsky, Annette M. and others. "Development of the Attitudes Toward Feminist Issues Scale." <u>Measurement and Evaluation in Guidance</u> 9(3): 140-45 (1976).

1756. Brown, Les and others. "A Humor Index: A Report on the Preliminary Development of an Instrument to Measure Children's Humor." <u>Illinois School Research and Development</u> 18(2): 13-17 (1982).

1757. Burgoon, J. K. "Unwillingness-to-Communicate Scale: Development and Validation." <u>Communication Monographs</u> 43: 60-9 (March 1976).

1758. Burisch, Matthias. "Construction Strategies for Multiscale Personality Inventories." <u>Applied Psychological Measurement</u> 2(1): 97-111 (1978).

1759. Burrello, Leonard C. and Daniel D. Sage. "A Behavior Preference Inventory for Special Education Administrators." <u>Exceptional Children</u> 37(5): 365-9 (1971).

1760. Butzow, J. W. and A. Davis. "Development of a Semantic Differential Test of Teachers' Attitudes Toward Teaching Elementary School Science." <u>Science Education</u> 59: 211-20 (1975).

1761. Callahan, Joseph P. <u>Evaluating Indian Education Programs: Development of Instruments in the Affective Domain</u>. Paper presented at the Annual Montana Indian Education Conference, 1980. ED 195 568 (Arlington, VA: ERIC, 1980).

1762. Campbell, Donald T. "The Indirect Assessment of Social Attitudes." <u>Psychological Bulletin</u> 47(1): 15-38 (1950).

1763. Campbell, Noma Jo and Stephen Grissom. Influence of Item Direction on Student Responses in Attitude Assessment. Paper presented at the annual meeting of the American Educational Research Association, 1979. ED 170 366 (Arlington, VA: ERIC, 1979).

1764. Campbell, R. J. and others. "Development and Validation of a Scale to Measure Affective Sensitivity (Empathy)." Journal of Counseling Psychology 18: 407-12 (September 1971).

1765. Carlson, Alfred B. and others. The Development and Pilot Testing of Criterion Rating Scales. GRE Board Professional Report GREB No. 73-1P. ED 163 089 (Arlington, VA: ERIC, 1976).

1766. Cassel, Russell N. Development of a Semantic Differential to Assess the Attitude of Secondary School and College Students. ED 039 553 (Arlington, VA: ERIC, 1970).

1767. Caughren, Harry J. Jr. "An Experimental Measure of Motivation for Community College Students." Journal of College Student Personnel 16(3): 232-37 (1975).

1768. Chapman, J. L. "Development and Validation of a Scale to Measure Empathy." Journal of Counseling Psychology 18: 281-2 (May 1971).

1769. Ciccone, Beverlee S. "The Development of an Instrument to Study Attitudes Towards Incest." Dissertation Abstracts International 42(12-B, Pt. 1): 4743 (1982).

1770. Cleminshaw, Helen and John Guidubaldi. Assessing Parent Satisfaction. Paper presented at the annual meeting of the National Council on Family Relations, 1980. ED 200 858 (Arlington, VA: ERIC, 1980).

1771. Click, Eulalia Tate and Judith A. Powell. Preschool Children's Perceptions of the Aged. ED 149 849 (Arlington, VA: ERIC, 1976).

1772. Cohen, A. D. and E. Olshtain. "Developing a Measure of Sociocultural Competence: The Case of Apology." Language Learning 31: 113-34 (June 1981).

1773. Connor, Jane M. and others. "A Self-report Measure of Assertiveness in Young Adolescents." Journal of Clinical Psychology 38(1): 101-6 (1982).

1774. Conte, Hope R., Marcella B. Weiner and Robert Plutchik. "Measuring Death Anxiety: Conceptual, Psychometric, and Factor-analytic Aspects." Journal of Personality & Social Psychology 43(4): 775-85 (1982).

1775. Conte, Vincent A. and Michael J. Salamon. "An Objective Approach to the Measurement and Use of Life Satisfaction with Older Persons." Measurement & Evaluation in Guidance 15(3): 194-200 (1982).

1776. Cook, Stuart W. Studies of Attitude and Attitude
       Measurement. Progress Report. ED 017 010 (Arlington, VA:
       ERIC, 1966).

1777. Cottle, William C. Predicting Potential Delinquents in
       Junior High School. Final Report. ED 044 733 (Arlington,
       VA: ERIC, 1969).

1778. Dager, Edward Z. and B. Claire McCullough. Family
       Integration: A Multi-dimensional Concept. ED 184 029
       (Arlington, VA: ERIC, 1976).

1779. Damico, Sandra B. and others. The Measurement of Pupils'
       Attitudes Toward School: A Handbook for Teachers.
       Resource Monograph No. 15. ED 159 193 (Arlington, VA:
       ERIC, 1975).

1780. Day, H. I. A Progress Report on the Development of a Test
       of Curiosity. Paper presented at the National Seminar on
       Adult Education Research, 1969. ED 026 610 (Arlington,
       VA: ERIC, 1969).

1781. Deitz, Sheila R., Karen T. Blackwell, Paul C. Daley, and
       Brenda J. Bentley. "Measurement of Empathy Toward Rape
       Victims and Rapists." Journal of Personality & Social
       Psychology 43(2): 372-84 (1982).

1782. Delys, Pamela. Rationale, Method, and Validity of the
       SDRCI IE Measure for Preschool Children. Paper presented
       at the 79th annual convention of the American
       Psychological Association, 1971. ED 057 893 (Arlington,
       VA: ERIC, 1971).

1783. Downs, Gary E. Affective Domain Measuring Scale (ADMS).
       ED 184 879 (Arlington, VA: ERIC, 1980).

1784. Duke, Marshall P. and Stephen Nowicki Jr. "A New Measure
       and Social-learning Model for Interpersonal Distance."
       Journal of Experimental Research in Personality 6(2-3):
       119-32 (1972).

1785. Dyer, Prudence. A Preliminary Report of Expressed Values
       of Students. ED 038 688 (Arlington, VA: ERIC, 1969).

1786. Eber, Herbert W. "Comparative Validity vs. Utility as
       Considerations in Personality Scale Construction."
       Multivariate Behavioral Research 12(3): 331-3 (1977).

1787. _____. Personality Measurement with Mentally Retarded and
       Other Sub-cultural Adults. Final Report. ED 025 080
       (Arlington, VA: ERIC, 1965).

1788. Edgerton, H. A. and others. "Performance Index: A Measure
       of Maturity of Young Adult Males." Measurement and
       Evaluation in Guidance 3: 213-19 (Winter 1971).

1789. Edwards, A. L. "Correlations Between Scores on
       Personality Scales When Items are Stated in the First and
       Third Person Form: Edwards Personality Inventory."
       Educational and Psychological Measurement 29: 561-63
       (Autumn 1969).

1790.   Edwards, Allen L. Techniques of Attitude Scale
        Construction. (New York: Appleton-Century-Crofts, 1957).

1791.   Edwards, Allen L. and F. P. Kilpatrick. "A Technique for
        the Construction of Attitude Scales." Journal of Applied
        Psychology 32: 374-84 (1948).

1792.   Edwards, Allen L. and K. C. Kenney. "A Comparison of the
        Thurstone and Likert Techniques of Attitude Scale
        Construction." Journal of Applied Psychology 30: 72-83
        (1946).

1793.   Elias, Maurice J. and others. An Innovative Measure of
        Children's Cognitions in Problematic Interpersonal
        Situations. Paper presented at the annual meeting of the
        American Psychological Association, 1978. ED 178 181
        (Arlington, VA: ERIC, 1978).

1794.   Epp, Carl C. "The Measurement of Self-esteem and other
        Self-concept Dimensions." Dissertation Abstracts
        International 42(10-B): 4241 (April 1982).

1795.   Erwin, T. Dary and Ursula Delworth. "An Instrument to
        Measure Chickering's Vector of Identity." NASPA Journal
        17(3): 19-24 (1980).

1796.   Evans, David R. and Mel Stangland. "Development of the
        Reaction Inventory to Measure Anger." Psychological
        Reports 29(2): 412-14 (1971).

1797.   Faschingbauer, Thomas R. "A 166-item Written Short Form
        of the Group MMPI: The FAM." Journal of Consulting and
        Clinical Psychology 42(5): 645-55 (1974).

1798.   Feingold, Alan. "Measuring Humor: A Pilot Study."
        Perceptual & Motor Skills 54(3, Pt. 1): 986 (1982).

1799.   Ferguson, L. W. "The Influence of Individual Attitudes on
        Construction of an Attitude Scale." Journal of Social
        Psychology 6: 115-17 (1935).

1800.   _____. "A Study of the Likert Technique of Attitude Scale
        Construction." Journal of Social Psychology 13: 51-7
        (1941).

1801.   Ferguson, Leonard W. Personality Measurement. (New York:
        McGraw-Hill, 1952).

1802.   Final Report--Vernon Non-verbal Personality Test. (SRS
        70-28). ED 059 245. (Arlington, VA: ERIC, 1971).

1803.   Finnerty-Fried, Pamela. "Instruments for the Assessment
        of Attitudes Toward Older Persons." Measurement &
        Evaluation in Guidance 15(3): 201-9 (1982).

1804.   Friedman, Howard S. and others. "Understanding and
        Assessing Nonverbal Expressiveness: The Affective
        Communication Test." Journal of Personality and Social
        Psychology 39(2): 333-51 (1980).

1805.   Frymier, Jack R. "Development and Validation of a
        Motivation Index: Junior Index of Motivation." Theory
        Into Practice 9(1): 56-88 (1970).

1806.   Gable, Robert K. and Robert M. Pruzek. Methodology For
        Instrument Validation: An Application to Attitude
        Measurement. Paper presented at the annual meeting of the
        American Educational Research Association, 1972. ED 064
        401 (Arlington, VA: ERIC, 1972).

1807.   Gardner, Eric F. and George G. Thompson. Investigation
        and Measurement of the Social Values Governing
        Interpersonal Relations Among Adolescent Youth and Their
        Teachers. Summary. ED 029 076 (Arlington, VA: ERIC,
        1962).

1808.   Gardner, R. C. and P. C. Smythe. "On the Development of
        the Attitude/Motivation Test Battery." Canadian Modern
        Language Review 37(3): 510-25 (1981).

1809.   George, Archie. Development and Validation of a Concerns
        Questionnaire. Paper presented at the annual meeting of
        the American Educational Research Association, 1977. ED
        147 314 (Arlington, VA: ERIC, 1977).

1810.   George, Carolyn S. and others. The Development of a
        Measure of Complex Concepts. Paper presented at the
        annual meeting of the National Council on Measurement in
        Education, 1974. ED 109 208 (Arlington, VA: ERIC, 1974).

1811.   Gibbs, J. C. and others. "Construction and Validation of
        a Simplified, Group-administerable Equivalent to the
        Moral Judgment Interview." Child Development 53: 895-910
        (August 1982).

1812.   Gibson, James L. and Richard D. Bingham. "On the
        Conceptualization and Measurement of Political
        Tolerance." American Political Science Review 76(3):
        603-20 (1982).

1813.   Giguere, Constance L. and Eva L. Baker. The Development
        of Criterion-referenced Tests of Self-concept and
        Attitude Toward School. ED 054 192 (Arlington, VA: ERIC,
        1971).

1814.   Goldberg, Carlos. Women's Liberation Scale (WLS): A
        Measure of Attitudes Toward Positions Advocated by
        Women's Groups. ED 132 475. JSAS MS 1187 (Washington,
        D.C.: American Psychological Association, 1976).

1815.   Golden, Charles J. "A Group Version of the Stroop Color
        and Word Test." Journal of Personality Assessment 39(4):
        386-8 (1975).

1816.   Gordon, Leonard V. "Weber in the Classroom." Journal of
        Educational Psychology 62(1): 60-6 (1971).

1817.   Gray, David B. "Measuring Attitudes Toward the Church."
        Journal for the Scientific Study of Religion 9(4): 293-7
        (1970).

1818. Greenberg, H. M. "The Development of an Integration
       Attitude Scale." Journal of Social Psychology 54: 103-9
       (1964).

1819. Greenberger, Ellen and others. "The Measurement and
       Structure of Psychosocial Maturity." Journal of Youth and
       Adolescence 4(2): 127-43 (1975). For related information
       see ED 096 359 and ED 052 262.

1820. Greene, John F. and Perry A. Zirkel. The Validation of a
       Scale Designed to Measure Cultural Attitudes. ED 117 246
       (Arlington, VA: ERIC, 1975).

1821. Grice, H. H. "The Construction and Validation of a
       Generalized Scale Designed to Measure Attitudes Toward
       Defined Groups." Bulletin of Purdue University 25: 37-46
       (1934).

1822. Gristle, M. "The Construction of a Scale for Measuring
       Attitude Toward Militarism-pacifism." Journal of Social
       Psychology 11: 383-91 (1940).

1823. Guilford, Joan S. and others. Development of a Values
       Inventory for Grades 1 through 3 in Five Ethnic Groups.
       Final Report. ED 050 178 (Arlington, VA: ERIC, 1971). For
       related information see ED 050 179 and ED 050 180.

1824. Haley, Elizabeth G. and Norejane J. Hendrickson.
       "Children's Preferences for Clothing and Hair Styles."
       Home Economics Research Journal 2(3): 176-93 (1974).

1825. Hall, Cleo A. The Motivational Patterns of Women Engaged
       in Educational Activities of Voluntary Organizations. ED
       010 244 (Arlington, VA: ERIC, 1965).

1826. Hall, Gene E. and Archie A. George. Stages of Concern
       About the Innovation: The Concept, Initial Verification
       and Some Implications. 1st Draft. ED 187 716 (Arlington,
       VA: ERIC, 1979).

1827. Hall, Gene E. and others. Measuring Stages of Concern
       About the Innovation: A Manual for the Use of the SOC
       Questionnaire. ED 147 342 (Arlington, VA: ERIC, 1977).

1828. Hallinan, Maureen and Diane Felmlee. "An Analysis of
       Intransitivity in Sociometric Data." Sociometry 38(2):
       195-212 (1975).

1829. Hamersma, R. J. and others. "Construction of a Guttman
       Facet Designed Cross-cultural Attitude-behavior Scale
       Toward Racial-ethnic Interaction." Educational and
       Psychological Measurement 33: 565-76 (1973).

1830. Hansen, Gary L. "Measuring Prejudice Against
       Homosexuality (Homosexism) Among College Students: A New
       Scale." Journal of Social Psychology 117(2): 233-6
       (1982).

1831. Hardy, K. R. "Construction and Validation of a Scale
       Measuring Attitudes Toward the L.D.S. Church." Master's
       thesis, University of Utah, 1949.

1832. Harrell, Thomas H. and Diane L. Chambless. The
      Situational Self-statement and Affective State Inventory:
      A Research Scale to Assess Cognitions and Affects. ED 190
      938 (Arlington, VA: ERIC, 1979).

1833. Hart, R. P. and others. "Attitudes Toward Communication
      and the Assessment of Rhetorical Sensitivity."
      Communication Monographs 47: 1-22 (1980).

1834. Harter, Susan and Edward Zigler. "The Assessment of
      Effectance Motivation in Normal and Retarded Children."
      Developmental Psychology 10(2): 169-80 (1974).

1835. Hartke, Alan R. "The Development of Conceptually
      Independent Sub-scales in the Measurement of Attitudes."
      Educational and Psychological Measurement 39(3): 585-92
      (1979).

1836. Hartmann, Paul and Charles Husband. "A British Scale for
      Measuring White Attitudes to Coloured People." Race
      14(2): 195-204 (1972).

1837. Head, Mary K. and others. "A Scale for Measuring Student
      Attitudes Toward Selected School Factors." Educational
      and Psychological Measurement 34(4): 971-6 (1974).

1838. Hecht, Michael L. "The Conceptualization and Measurement
      of Interpersonal Communication Satisfaction." Human
      Communication Research 4(3): 253-64 (1978).

1839. Henderson, James E. and Wayne K. Hoy. Leader
      Authenticity: The Development and Test of an Operational
      Measure. Paper presented at the annual meeting of the
      American Educational Research Association, 1982. ED 219
      408 (Arlington, VA: ERIC, 1982).

1840. Henerson, Marlene E. and others. How to Measure
      Attitudes. Program Evaluation Kit, 5. ED 175 894 (Beverly
      Hills, CA: Sage, 1978).

1841. Hepburn, Mary A. and John D. Napier. "Development and
      Initial Validation of an Instrument to Measure Political
      Attitudes." Educational and Psychological Measurement 40:
      1131-39 (1980).

1842. _____. Validation of an Instrument to Measure Political
      Attitudes. Paper presented at the annual meeting of the
      American Educational Research Association, 1980. ED 186
      491 (Arlington, VA: ERIC, 1980).

1843. Heppner, P. Paul and Chris H. Petersen. "The Development
      and Implications of a Personal Problem-solving
      Inventory." Journal of Counseling Psychology 29(1): 66-75
      (1982).

1844. _____. A Personal Problem Solving Inventory. Paper
      presented at the annual convention of the American
      Psychological Association, 1981. ED 210 585 (Arlington,
      VA: ERIC, 1981).

1845.   Hermans, Hubert J. M. "A Questionnaire Measure of
        Achievement Motivation." Journal of Applied Psychology
        54(4): 353-63 (1970).

1846.   Hiett, Robert L. and others. The Racial Attitudes and
        Perceptions Survey (RAPS). Final Report (Mar 73-Mar 74).
        Technical Paper 338. ED 169 098 (Arlington, VA: ERIC,
        1978).

1847.   Hinckley, E. D. "A Follow-up Study on the Influence of
        Individual Opinion on the Construction of an Attitude
        Scale." Journal of Abnormal Social Psychology 67: 290-92
        (1963).

1848.   _____. The Influence of Individual Opinion on
        Construction of an Attitude Scale. (Chicago: University
        of Chicago Library, 1932).

1849.   _____. The Influence of Individual Opinion on
        Construction of an Attitude Scale." Journal of Social
        Psychology 3: 283-96 (1932).

1850.   Hocevar, Dennis. The Development of the Creative Behavior
        Inventory (CBI). Paper presented at the annual meeting of
        the Rocky Mountain Psychological Association, 1979. ED
        170 350 (Arlington, VA: ERIC, 1979).

1851.   Hoepfner, Ralph. The Validity of Tests of Social
        Intelligence. Address presented to the German Congress of
        Psychology, Saarbrucken, Germany, 1972. ED 081 803
        (Arlington, VA: ERIC, 1973).

1852.   Hogan, H. Wayne. "A Symbolic Measure of Authoritarianism:
        An Exploratory Study." Journal of Social Psychology
        82(2): 215-19 (1970).

1853.   Hogan, Robert and Ellen Greenberger. Development of a
        Curiosity Scale. Report No. 32. ED 030 154 (Arlington,
        VA: ERIC, 1969).

1854.   Holden, Ronald R. and Douglas N. Jackson. "Item Subtlety
        and Face Validity in Personality Assessment." Journal of
        Consulting and Clinical Psychology 47(3): 459-68 (1979).

1855.   Hopple, Gerald W. "A New Scale for Measuring College
        Student Attitudes Toward Protest." Journal of College
        Student Personnel 17(3): 211-14 (1976).

1856.   Hoshaw, L. D. "The Construction and Evaluation of a Scale
        for Measuring Attitude Toward any Teacher." Bulletin of
        Purdue University 37: 238-51 (1936).

1857.   Humphrey, Laura Lynn. "Children's and Teachers'
        Perspectives on Children's Self-control: The Development
        of Two Rating Scales." Journal of Consulting and Clinical
        Psychology 50(5): 624-33 (1982).

1858.   Iazzo, Anthony N. "The Attitudes Toward Men Scale."
        Dissertation Abstracts International 43(3-B): 853 (1982).

1859. Jackson, Douglas N. "The Relative Validity of Scales
       Prepared by Naive Item Writers and Those Based on
       Empirical Methods of Personality Scale Construction."
       Educational and Psychological Measurement 35(2): 361-70
       (1975).

1860. Jackson, Steve and Ron Klinger. Cross Cultural Attitude
       Inventory (and) Test Manual. ED 083 310 (Arlington, VA:
       ERIC, 1974).

1861. Jacobson, Michael and Stuart Palonsky. Guttman-Jordan
       Facet Design and the Study of Law-related Attitudes.
       Paper presented at the annual meeting of the American
       Educational Research Association, 1980. ED 194 625
       (Arlington, VA: ERIC, 1980).

1862. Jenkins, W. O. and others. The Weekly Activity Record
       (WAR): A Measure of Time Allocation in the Analysis and
       Prediction of Criminal Behavior and Recidivism. ED 096
       319 (Arlington, VA: ERIC, 1974).

1863. Johnson, Marion Lee. "Construction of Sportsmanship
       Attitude Scales." Research Quarterly of the American
       Association for Health, Physical Education, and
       Recreation 40(2): 312-16 (1969).

1864. Johnson, Richard P. "Assessing Retirement Maturity."
       Measurement & Evaluation in Guidance 15(3): 221-7 (1982).

1865. Jones, Warren H. and Dan Russell. "The Social Reticence
       Scale: An Objective Instrument to Measure Shyness."
       Journal of Personality Assessment 46(6): 629-31 (1982).

1866. Jordan, John E. Facet Theory and Non-metric Methods. The
       Quantification of the Qualitative. Paper presented at the
       annual meeting of the American Educational Research
       Association, 1976. ED 164 558 (Arlington, VA: ERIC,
       1976).

1867. Jordan, John E. and J. Paul Maierle. Guttman Facet Theory
       Analysis of Attitudes Toward Mental Illness, Mental
       Retardation, and Racial Interaction. Paper presented at
       the World Mental Health Assembly, 1969. ED 037 750
       (Arlington, VA: ERIC, 1969).

1868. Kafer, Rudolph A. and others. "Aging Opinion Survey: A
       Report on Instrument Development." International Journal
       of Aging and Human Development 11(4): 319-33 (1980).

1869. Karlins, M. "Note on a New Test of Creativity: PUN Test."
       Journal of Creative Behavior 6(2): 95-101 (1972).

1870. Karmos, A. H. "Development and Validation of a Nonverbal
       Measure of Self-esteem: The Sliding Person Test."
       Educational and Psychological Measurement 39: 479-84
       (1979).

1871. Kay, William. "The Self-concept as a Moral Control."
       Journal of Moral Education 2(1): 63-7 (1972).

1872.   Kerlinger, Fred N. "The Structure and Content of Social
        Attitude Referents: A Preliminary Study." Educational and
        Psychological Measurement 32(3): 613-30 (1972).

1873.   Kilmann, Ralph H. and Kenneth W. Thomas. "Developing a
        Forced-choice Measure of Conflict-handling Behavior: The
        'Mode' Instrument." Educational and Psychological
        Measurement 37(2): 309-25 (1977).

1874.   King, Lynda A. and others. A New Measure of Sex-role
        Attitudes. Paper presented at the annual meeting of the
        Midwestern Psychological Association, 1981. ED 205 863
        (Arlington, VA: ERIC, 1981).

1875.   Kirkpatrick, C. "The Construction of a Belief Pattern
        Scale for Measuring Attitudes Toward Feminism." Journal
        of Social Psychology 7: 421-27 (1936).

1876.   Klein, Ronald and others. The Development of the Alpha-
        Omega Completed Sentence Form (AOCSF): An Instrument to
        Aid in the Measurement, Identification, and Assessment of
        an Individual's "Adaptational Approach(es)" to the
        Stressful Event of Death and Related Issues. Paper
        presented at the annual meeting of the American
        Educational Research Association, 1978. ED 167 618
        (Arlington, VA: ERIC, 1978).

1877.   Kogan, N. "Attitudes Toward Old People: The Development
        of a Scale and an Examination of Correlates." Journal of
        Abnormal Social Psychology 62: 44-54 (1961).

1878.   Krus, David J. and others. ECHO: A Computer Based Test
        for the Measurement of Individualistic, Cooperative,
        Defensive, and Aggressive Models of Behavior. Occasional
        Paper No. 30. ED 105 337 (Arlington, VA: ERIC, 1974).

1879.   Kulp, Daniel H. "The Forms of Statements in Attitude
        Tests." Sociology and Social Research 18: 18-25 (1933).

1880.   Lerner, Richard M. and others. "Assessing the Dimensions
        of Temperamental Individuality Across the Life Span: The
        Dimensions of Temperament Survey (DOTS)." Child
        Development 53(1): 149-59 (1982).

1881.   Levine, Samuel and Freeman F. Elzey. Development of a
        Social Competency Scale for Preschool Children. Final
        Report. ED 020 004 (Arlington, VA: ERIC, 1968).

1882.   Likert, Rensis. "A Technique for the Measurement of
        Attitudes." Archives of Psychology 140: 1932.

1883.   Lind, Gunter. "Microevaluation of Subject-matter-directed
        Motivation." Studies in Educational Evaluation 2(2):
        103-20 (1976).

1884.   Lowney, Frank. "Construct Validity in Self-concept
        Measures." Journal of the Association for the Study of
        Perception 10(2): 15-19 (1975).

1885. Lynch, Mervin D. and others. Development of the Minimood and Some Evidence of its Validity and Stability. Paper presented at the annual meeting of the American Educational Research Association, 1974. ED 093 999 (Arlington, VA: ERIC, 1974).

1886. McCue, B. F. "Constructing an Instrument for Evaluating Attitudes Toward Intensive Competition in Team Games." Research Quarterly 24: 205-9 (1953).

1887. McDevitt, Sean C. and William B. Carey. "The Measurement of Temperament in 3-7 Year Old Children." Journal of Child Psychology and Psychiatry and Allied Disciplines 19(3): 245-53 (1978).

1888. McNemar, Quinn. "Opinion-attitude Methodology." Psychological Bulletin 43(4): 289-374 (1946).

1889. Maguire, T. O. and others. "Development and Validation of an Instrument to Assess Student Attitudes Towards Work." Educational and Psychological Measurement 42: 643-9 (Summer 1982).

1890. Marshall, Nancy J. "Dimensions of Privacy Preferences." Multivariate Behavioral Research 9(3): 255-71 (1974).

1891. Meitus, W. S. "Development of an Instrument Measuring Values Associated with Work." Journal of Industrial Teacher Education 14: 63-72 (Summer 1977).

1892. Milner, Joel S. and Ronald C. Wimberley. "An Inventory for the Identification of Child Abusers." Journal of Clinical Psychology 35(1): 95-100 (1979).

1893. Neill, John A. and Douglas N. Jackson. "An Evaluation of Item Selection Strategies in Personality Scale Construction." Educational and Psychological Measurement 30(3): 647-61 (1970).

1894. Newman, Robert C. II. "Development and Standardization of Instruments Measuring Four Aspects of Sex-roles in Primary Grade Children." Journal of Personality Assessment 41(2): 164-9 (1977).

1895. Norman, Warren T. 2800 Personality Trait Descriptors-- Normative Operating Characteristics for a University Population. ED 014 738 (Arlington, VA: ERIC, 1967).

1896. Ory, John C. and John P. Poggio. The Development and Empirical Validation of a Measure of Achievement Motivation. Paper presented at the annual meeting of the American Educational Research Association, 1975. ED 124 567 (Arlington, VA: ERIC, 1975).

1897. _____. "Empirical Development of a Measure of Achievement Motivation." Journal of Educational Measurement 13: 157-9 (1976).

1898. Ostrom, Thomas M. "Item Construction in Attitude Measurement." Public Opinion Quarterly 35(4): 593-600 (1972).

1899.   Page, R. and others. "Attitude Scale for Technology."
        Research in Education 26: 55-63 (November 1981).

1900.   Page, Roger and James Bode. "Comparison of Measures of
        Moral Reasoning and Development of a New Objective
        Measure." Educational and Psychological Measurement
        40(2): 317-29 (1980).

1901.   Page, William Thomas. "The Development of a Test to
        Measure Anticipated Communicative Anxiety." Ph.D. diss.,
        University of Illinois at Urbana-Champaign, 1970. ED 070
        117. Available from University Microfilms, Ann Arbor, MI.

1902.   Parker, George V. C. "Prediction of Individual
        Stability." Educational and Psychological Measurement
        31(4): 875-86 (1971).

1903.   Payne, Frank D. Assessment of Altruism in Children. Final
        Report. ED 146 191 (Arlington, VA: ERIC, 1975).

1904.   Pease, Damaris and others. "The Social Competency Scale
        for Preschool-age Children: Its Development and Factorial
        Validity." Educational and Psychological Measurement
        41(3): 851-61 (1981).

1905.   Peck, Robert F. Coping Styles and Achievement: A Cross-
        National Study of School Children. Volume I of V Volumes:
        The Theory, Design, and Validation Results. ED 206 716
        (Arlington, VA: ERIC, 1981).

1906.   Peeler, E. and S. M. Rimmer. "Assertiveness Scale for
        Children." Elementary School Guidance and Counseling 16:
        43-6 (October 1981).

1907.   Perkes, A. C. "Development and Field Testing of an
        Instrument to Measure Apprehension Toward Animals."
        School Science and Mathematics 82: 157-62 (February
        1982).

1908.   Perricone, P. J. "Doctor-patient Interaction: Formulation
        of a Hypothesis and Development of a Test for Measuring
        Attitudes Toward Physicians." Master's thesis, University
        of Florida, 1964.

1909.   Powell, J. P. and Margot Pearson. "A Procedure for
        Testing Students' Interpersonal Skills." Studies in
        Educational Evaluation 6(2): 209-10 (1980).

1910.   Ragheb, Mounir G. and Jacob G. Beard. "Measuring Leisure
        Attitude." Journal of Leisure Research 14(2): 155-67
        (1982).

1911.   Reece, Mary J. and Robert K. Gable. "The Development and
        Validation of a Measure of General Attitudes Toward
        Computers." Educational and Psychological Measurement
        42(3): 913-16 (1982).

1912.   Rigby, K. "A Concise Scale for the Assessment of
        Attitudes Towards Institutional Authority." Australian
        Journal of Psychology 34(2): 195-204 (1982).

1913. Ritt, L. W. "The Development of a Scale for Measuring Attitudes Toward Negroes, Based on a Stochastic Model." Master's thesis, University of Florida, 1964.

1914. Roberts, Dennis M. and Edward W. Bilderback. "Reliability and Validity of a Statistics Attitude Survey." Educational and Psychological Measurement 40(1): 235-8 (1980).

1915. Roecks, Alan L. and others. The Development of an Instrument for Assessing Young Children's Perceptions of Individual Differences. Paper presented at the annual meeting of the Wisconsin Educational Research Association, 1975. ED 129 442 (Arlington, VA: ERIC, 1975).

1916. Rohner, Ronald P. and others. Development and Validation of the Personality Assessment Questionnaire: Test Manual. ED 159 502 (Arlington, VA: ERIC, 1978).

1917. Rookey, T. Jerome. Pennsylvania Assessment of Creative Tendency: Norms-technical Manual. ED 054 224 (Arlington, VA: ERIC, 1971).

1918. Ross, Alan O. and others. "The Development of a Behavior Checklist for Boys." Child Development 36(4): 1013-27 (1965).

1919. Ross, Shirley and James Walters. "Perceptions of a Sample of University Men Concerning Women." Journal of Genetic Psychology 112(2): 329-36 (1973).

1920. Rowe, David C. and Robert Plomin. "Temperament in Early Childhood." Journal of Personality Assessment 41(2): 150-6 (1977).

1921. Saltzer, Eleanor B. "The Weight Locus of Control (WLOC) Scale: A Specific Measure for Obesity Research." Journal of Personality Assessment 46(6): 620-28 (1982).

1922. Schack, David W. and Charles D. Helper. "Modification of Hall's Professionalism Scale for Use With Pharmacists." American Journal of Pharmaceutical Education 43(2): 98-104 (1979).

1923. Schaefer, E. S. and R. Q. Bell. "Development of a Parental Attitude Research Instrument." Child Development 29: 339-62 (1958).

1924. Schaefer, Earl S. and Marianna Edgerton. Parental Modernity in Childrearing and Educational Attitudes and Beliefs. ED 202 605 (Arlington, VA: ERIC, 1981).

1925. Schaffner, Paul E. and Richard B. Darlington. A New Technique for Personality Scale Construction. Preliminary Findings. ED 151 689 (Arlington, VA: ERIC, 1977).

1926. Schoenfeld, Lawrence S. "Construction of a Personality Inventory Through Thurstone Scaling of Daydreams." Perceptual and Motor Skills 31(2): 678 (1970).

1927. Severy, Lawrence J. "Individual Differences in Helping Dispositions." Journal of Personality Assessment 39(3): 282-92 (1975).

1928. Simonson, Michael. "Attitude Measurement: Why and How." Educational Technology 19(9): 34-8 (1979).

1929. Simpson, Ronald D. and others. "Influence of Instrument Characteristics on Student Responses in Attitude Assessment." Journal of Research in Science Teaching 13(3): 275-81 (1976).

1930. Smith, Charles A. The Effects of an On-site and Community Outdoor Education Program on Selected Attitudes Toward School of Sixth Grade Students. ED 182 067 (Arlington, VA: ERIC, 1979).

1931. Snyder, C. R. and Howard L. Fromkin. "Abnormality as a Positive Characteristic: The Development and Validation of a Scale Measuring Need for Uniqueness." Journal of Abnormal Psychology 86(5): 518-27 (1977).

1932. Soto-Padin, Jose L. Dependency and Social Performance: The Development of a Scale to Measure Level of Independence in Small Children. Part of the Final Report. ED 026 129 (Arlington, VA: ERIC, 1968).

1933. Spitzer, D. R. and J. M. Keller. "Developing an Objective Measure of Academic Motivation." Educational Technology 18: 26-30 (June 1978).

1934. Spivack, George and Marshall Swift. "The Hahnemann High School Behavior (HHSB) Rating Scale." Journal of Abnormal Child Psychology 5(3): 299-307 (1977).

1935. Stanback, Bessie Alsop. Student Behaviors in Desegrated Junior High School Science Classrooms. Paper presented at the annual meeting of the National Association for Research in Science Teaching, 1981. ED 202 734 (Arlington, VA: ERIC, 1981).

1936. Starkweather, Elizabeth K. Preschool Children's Willingness to Try Difficult Tasks. ED 010 286 (Arlington, VA: ERIC, 1966).

1937. Starr, Ann M. and others. College Student Satisfaction Questionnaire (CSSQ) Manual. ED 058 268 (Arlington, VA: ERIC, 1971).

1938. Stauffer, A. J. "An Investigation of Procedures for Developing and Validating the Classroom Attitude Measure Toward Educational Inquiry." Educational and Psychological Measurement 34(4): 893-8 (1974).

1939. Steers, Richard M. and Daniel N. Braunstein. "A Behaviorally-based Measure of Manifest Needs in Work Settings." Journal of Vocational Behavior 9(2): 251-65 (1976).

1940.   Stein, Judy B. "The Development of a New Work Construct:
        Work Conscientiousness." Ph.D. diss., Iowa State
        University, 1982. Dissertation Abstracts International
        43(4-B): 1291 (1982).

1941.   Stein, Kenneth B. and others. "Interpersonal Trust and
        Disaffected High School Youth." Journal of Youth and
        Adolescence 3(4): 281-92 (1974).

1942.   Stein, Kenneth B. and Peter Lenrow. "Expressive Styles
        and Their Measurement." Journal of Personality and Social
        Psychology 16(4): 656-64 (1970).

1943.   Steiner, R. L. and R. B. Barnhart. "The Development of an
        Instrument to Assess Environmental Attitudes Utilizing
        Factor Analytic Techniques: Inventory of Societal
        Issues." Science Education 56(3): 427-32 (1972).

1944.   Stenner, A. Jackson and W. G. Katzenmeyer. Structural
        Integrity in Measures of Self Concept. ED 141 378
        (Arlington, VA: ERIC, 1977).

1945.   Stern, Carolyn and others. Teachers Expectations for
        Achievement of Children in Head Start (TEACH). ED 045 735
        (Arlington, VA: ERIC, 1971).

1946.   Stevenson, Joanne S. "Construction of a Scale to Measure
        Load, Power, and Margin in Life." Nursing Research 31(4):
        222-5 (1982).

1947.   Stolman, Cynthia J. and Rodney L. Doran. "Development and
        Validation of a Test Instrument for Assessing Value
        Preferences in Medical Ethics." Journal of Medical
        Education 57(3): 170-79 (1982).

1948.   Strickland, Guy. Development of a School Attitude
        Questionnaire for Young Children. ED 043 919 (Arlington,
        VA: ERIC, 1970).

1949.   Strom, R. and H. Slaughter. "Measurement of Childrearing
        Expectations Using the Parent as a Teacher Inventory."
        Journal of Experimental Education 46: 44-53 (1978).

1950.   Strumpfer, D. J. W. Construction of a Personal Autonomy
        Inventory. ED 138 905. JSAS MS. 1278 (Washington, D.C.:
        American Psychological Association, 1976).

1951.   Sudweeks, Richard R. and others. Development of the
        Syracuse Mathematics Anxiety Scale. Paper presented at
        the annual meeting of the American Educational Research
        Association, 1980. ED 186 266 (Arlington, VA: ERIC,
        1980).

1952.   Taylor, P. L. and others. "Daydreaming in the Adolescent
        Years: Instrument Development, Factor Analysis, and Sex
        Differences." Adolescence 13: 735-50 (1978).

1953.   Technical Recommendations for Psychological Tests and
        Diagnostic Techniques. Prepared by a Joint Committee of
        the American Psychological Association, American

Educational Research Association, and National Council on Measurements Used in Education. Supplement to the Psychological Bulletin 51(2) Part 2, (1954).

1954. Teglasi, Hedwig. "First and Third Person Pronouns in Sex Role Questionnaires." Psychology of Women Quarterly 5(5): 785-9 (1981).

1955. Terrell, Francis and Sandra Terrell. "An Inventory to Measure Cultural Mistrust Among Blacks." Western Journal of Black Studies 5(3): 180-85 (1981).

1956. Thomas, A. and others. "Temperament Questionnaire for Early Adult Life." Educational and Psychological Measurement 42: 593-600 (1982).

1957. Thomas, Charles W. and J. Sherwood Williams. "The Construction of Likert-type Attitude Scales: An Examination of Alternative Techniques of Item Selection." International Journal of Contemporary Sociology 14(1-2): 45-60 (1977).

1958. Thomas, L. E. "I-E Scale, Ideological Bias, and Political Participation." Journal of Personality 38: 273-86 (1970).

1959. Thomas, Sandra P. and others. The Development of a Naturalistic Self-management Inventory. Paper presented at the annual meeting of the American Educational Research Association, 1982. ED 219 657 (Arlington, VA: ERIC, 1982).

1960. Thomas, Walter L. Manual for the Differential Value Profile. Form A. ED 041 335 (Grand Rapids, MI: Educational Service Co., P. O. Box 1882, 1969).

1961. _____. The Thomas Self-concept Values Test. ED 027 068 (Grand Rapids, MI: Educational Service Co., P. O. Box 1882, 1967).

1962. Thweatt, Roger C. Development of a K Scale for a Motivational Test Battery. ED 003 289 (Arlington, VA: ERIC, 1965).

1963. Torshen, Kay Pomerance and others. "Self-concept Assessment for Young Children: Development of a Self-report, Peer Comparison Measure." Contemporary Educational Psychology 2: 325-31 (1977).

1964. _____. A Self-Concept Inventory for the Primary Grades. Paper presented at the annual meeting of the American Educational Research Association, 1974. ED 092 582 (Arlington, VA: ERIC, 1974).

1965. Trosky, Odarka S. Individualizing Through a Self-concept Inventory at the Primary Levels. Paper presented at the annual meeting of the International Reading Association, 1974. ED 092 886 (Arlington, VA: ERIC, 1974).

1966. Tziner, A. E. and T. Cheatham. "Attitude Measurement Through Use of Computer Constructed Questionnaires." _Educational and Psychological Measurement_ 37: 241-3 (1977).

1967. Venkataiah, N. "Construction of Attitude Scales." _Indian Journal of Adult Education_ 40(2): 27-40 (1979).

1968. Vockell, Edward L. "Assessing Attitudes Toward Animal Life Among Elementary School Pupils." _Science Education_ 66(5): 783-88 (1982).

1969. Vondracek, Sarah I. and Fred Vondracek. "The Manipulation and Measurement of Self-disclosure in Preadolescents." _Merrill-Palmer Quarterly of Behavior and Development_ 17(1): 51-8 (1971).

1970. Walther, Regis H. _The Measurement of Work-relevant Attitudes, A Report on the Development of a Measuring Instrument. Final Report_. ED 052 366. Available from NTIS, PB 195 986 (1970).

1971. Williams, John E. "Preschool Racial Attitude Measure II (PRAM II): General Information and Manual of Directions." ED 055 660 (Arlington, VA: ERIC, 1971).

1972. Woelfel, John C. and others. _A Preliminary Version of a Scale to Measure Sex-role Attitudes in the Army. Research Memorandum 76-3_. ED 178 549 (Arlington, VA: ERIC, 1976).

1973. Wollack, S. "Development of the Survey of Work Values; Dimensions of Protestant Ethic." _Journal of Applied Psychology_ 55: 331-8 (1971).

1974. Yamauchi, Kent T. and Donald I. Templer. "The Development of a Money Attitude Scale." _Journal of Personality Assessment_ 46(5): 522-28 (1982).

1975. Yonker, Robert J. and others. _A Methodological Investigation of the Development of a Semantic Differential to Assess Self-concept_. Paper presented at the National Council on Measurement in Education Annual Meeting, 1974. ED 090 264 (Arlington, VA: ERIC, 1974).

1976. Zirkel, Perry Alan and John F. Greene. _Cultural Attitude Scale(s): Anglo American; Black American; Mexican American; Puerto Rican; (and) Technical Report_. ED 187 763 (Arlington, VA: ERIC, 1974).

Reading

1977.   Aaron, Robert L. Using the Cloze and Sight Vocabulary to
        Develop a Group Informal Reading Inventory. Paper
        presented at the annual meeting of the International
        Reading Association, 1975. ED 109 627 (Arlington, VA:
        ERIC, 1975).

1978.   Anderson, Thomas H. and others. Development and Trial of
        a Model for Developing Domain Referenced Tests of Reading
        Comprehension. Technical Report No. 86. ED 157 036
        (Arlington, VA: ERIC, 1978).

1979.   Askov, Eunice N. Development of an Instrument Measuring
        Attitudes Toward Reading in Primary Pupils. Paper
        presented at the American Educational Research
        Association meeting, 1979. ED 027 164 (Arlington, VA:
        ERIC, 1969).

1980.   Axelrod, Jerome. "Reading and Extraneous-free Tests."
        Reading Horizons 14(3): 118-20 (1974).

1981.   Bennett, Dale E. and Alton L. Raygor. A Guide to High
        School and College Reading Tests. ED 013 702 (Arlington,
        VA: ERIC, 1965).

1982.   Berk, Ronald A. "Estimation of Test Length for Domain-
        referenced Reading Comprehension Tests." Journal of
        Experimental Education 48(3): 188-93 (1980).

1983.   _____. Item Sampling From Finite Domains of Written
        Discourse. Paper presented at the annual meeting of the
        American Educational Research Association, 1978. ED 161
        934 (Arlington, VA: ERIC, 1978).

1984.   Besel, Ronald and Masahito Okada. The Development of
        Domain-referenced Tests for an Objectives-based Reading
        Program. Paper presented at the California Association of
        Teachers of English to Speakers of Other Languages, 1974.
        ED 093 918 (Arlington, VA: ERIC, 1974).

1985.   Bezdek, Anna Miars. "The Assessment of Fundamental Skills
        Involved in Reading Comprehension." Ph.D. diss.,

University of Illinois, 1973. ED 083 577. Available from University Microfilms, Ann Arbor, MI.

1986. Bradley, Michael. "Adjectives as Information Sources for Reading-comprehension Test Items." Perceptual and Motor Skills 33(2, pt. 2): 1205-6 (1971).

1987. Brown, Barbara E. Identifying Inservice Topics for Volunteer Literacy Tutors. ED 209 506 (Arlington, VA: ERIC, 1981).

1988. Brunner, Regina Baron. "Construction and Construct-validation of a Reading Comprehension Test of Mathematical Exposition." Journal of Structural Learning 4(4): 349-63 (1977).

1989. Calfee, Robert C. and Priscilla A. Drum. How the Researcher Can Help the Reading Teacher With Classroom Assessment. ED 155 638 (Arlington, VA: ERIC, 1976).

1990. Cardish, Edna Catherine. The Relationship Between Reading Content and Reading Comprehension Among Ninth Grade Pupils in an Urban Area--Population 114,973. ED 177 478 (Arlington, VA: ERIC, 1971).

1991. Carver, Ronald P. The Criterion-referenced Aspects of the Carver-Darby Chunked Reading Test. Paper presented at the National Reading Conference, 1970. ED 047 911 (Arlington, VA: ERIC, 1970).

1992. Carver, Ronald P. and Charles A. Darby Jr. "Development and Evaluation of a Test of Information Storage During Reading." Journal of Educational Measurement 8(1): 33-44 (1971).

1993. Comerford, James P. and James E. Scheib. The Construction of a Machine-scored Reading Inventory for Use in Secondary Compensatory Reading Programs, and an Investigation into its Sensitivity to Instruction. Paper presented at the annual meeting of the American Educational Research Association, 1978. ED 164 551 (Arlington, VA: ERIC, 1978).

1994. Converse, Jerry. What is So Difficult About Measuring Flexibility. Paper presented at the annual meeting of the International Reading Association, 1978. ED 163 417 (Arlington, VA: ERIC, 1978).

1995. Corman, Louise and others. More Effective Reading Tests of Comprehension and Rate. ED 085 682 (Arlington, VA: ERIC, 1975).

1996. Cranney, A. Garr. "The Construction of Two Types of Cloze Reading Tests for College Students." Journal of Reading Behavior 5(1): 60-64 (1973).

1997. Deck, Dennis and J. Jackson Barnette. Measuring Attitudes Toward Reading in Large Scale Assessment. Paper presented at the annual meeting of the American Educational Research Association, 1976. ED 128 407 (Arlington, VA: ERIC, 1976).

1998. Degrees of Reading Power: Description of a New Kind of
       Reading Test and its Related Technology. ED 170 712
       (Arlington, VA: ERIC, 1977).

1999. Dryden, Beverly J. "The Development of a Diagnostic
       Reading Attitude Assessment for Grades Two Through Five."
       Reading Improvement 19(3): 173-82 (1982).

2000. Duffy, Gerald G. and William Metheny. The Development of
       an Instrument to Measure Teacher Beliefs About Reading.
       Paper presented at the annual meeting of the National
       Reading Conference, 1978. ED 163 433 (Arlington, VA:
       ERIC, 1978).

2001. _____. Measuring Teachers' Beliefs About Reading.
       Research Series No. 41. ED 174 954 (Arlington, VA: ERIC,
       1979).

2002. Elementary Reading Inventory. ED 038 248 (Arlington, VA:
       ERIC, 1969).

2003. Ellinger, Bernice D. and others. Development and
       Refinement of a Test of Critical Reading Ability of
       Elementary School Children. ED 018 335 (Arlington, VA:
       ERIC, 1967).

2004. Estes, Thomas H. Assessing Attitudes Toward Reading.
       Paper presented at the meeting of the International
       Reading Association, 1972. ED 063 077 (Arlington, VA:
       ERIC, 1972).

2005. _____. "A Scale to Measure Attitudes Toward Reading."
       Journal of Reading 15(2): 135-38 (1971).

2006. Farr, Roger. The Fallacies of Testing. Paper presented at
       the Conference on Reading and the National Interest,
       1970. ED 040 020 (Arlington, VA: ERIC, 1970).

2007. Feldmann, Shirley and May Weiner. Measurement of Reading
       Skills in Lower Socioeconomic Status Children. ED 002 599
       (Arlington, VA: ERIC, 1963).

2008. Fetler, Mark. Text Structure, Processing and the Design
       of Reading Achievement Tests. Paper presented at the
       annual meeting of the American Educational Research
       Association, 1982. ED 218 335 (Arlington, VA: ERIC,
       1982).

2009. Ganopole, Selina. The Fundamental Reading Competencies
       Test. 1. Supporting Technical Information. 2. Forms A and
       B of the Test. 3. Test Specifications For Each Subtest.
       ED 182 318 (Arlington, VA: ERIC, 1977).

2010. Glover, Michael. Quickie Tests for Reading: Fast, Simple
       Tests to Determine Reading Level. ED 101 286 (Arlington,
       VA: ERIC, 1974).

2011. Gordon, Belita. Item Specifications for a College Level
       Basic Skills Reading Test. ED 205 893 (Arlington, VA:
       ERIC, 1981).

2012.   Griffin, Peg, ed. Assessing Comprehension in a School
        Setting. Linguistics and Reading, Series: 3. Papers in
        Applied Linguistics. ED 183 003 (Arlington, VA: ERIC,
        1978).

2013.   Hahn, Christine T. Measuring Attitudes Toward Reading. An
        Annotated ERIC Bibliography. ED 151 423 (Arlington, VA:
        ERIC, 1977).

2014.   Hammond, Bill. Georgia's Criterion-referenced Reading
        Test--New Help for Teachers. ED 133 685 (Arlington, VA:
        ERIC, 1976).

2015.   Hanna, Gerald S. and Thomas R. Oaster. "How Important is
        Passage Dependence in Reading Comprehension." Journal of
        Educational Research 71(6): 345-48 (1978).

2016.   _____. "Toward a Unified Theory of Context Dependence."
        Reading Research Quarterly 14(2): 226-43 (1978).

2017.   Hansen, Lee H. and Karl D. Hesse. An Interim Report of
        Results of the Pilot Assessment of Reading Literacy. ED
        079 704 (Arlington, VA: ERIC, 1972).

2018.   Hayford, Paul D. A Basic Program Analysis and Monitoring
        System in Reading: Alternative Monitoring Devices. Paper
        presented at the annual meeting of the American
        Educational Research Association, 1979. ED 200 899
        (Arlington, VA: ERIC, 1979).

2019.   Hayford, Paul D. and Ruth Salter. Rule-based Measures of
        Literal Comprehension. Paper presented at the annual
        meeting of the American Educational Research Association,
        1978. ED 200 906 (Arlington, VA: ERIC, 1978).

2020.   Jackson, Rex. Development of a Collection of Adult Tasks
        for Assessment of Literacy. Paper presented at the
        meeting of the American Educational Research Association,
        1972. ED 061 023 (Arlington, VA: ERIC, 1972).

2021.   Johnson, Marjorie Seddon and Roy A. Kress. Informal
        Reading Inventories. Reading Aids Series No. 2. ED 072
        437 (Arlington, VA: ERIC, 1965).

2022.   _____. "Task Analysis for Criterion-referenced Tests."
        Reading Teacher 24(4): 355-59 (1971).

2023.   Kemp, Max. "Innovations and Practice: Standardised Tests
        and the Clerical Mentality." Australian Journal of
        Reading 3(2): 95-101 (1980).

2024.   Kennedy, L. D. and R. S. Halinski. "Measuring Attitudes:
        An Extra Dimension: Attitude Towards Reading." Journal of
        Reading 18: 518-22 (1975).

2025.   Kibby, Michael W. "Test Review: The Degrees of Reading
        Power." Journal of Reading 24(5): 416-27 (1981).

2026.   Klopp, Pamela M. and others. Technical Manual for Forms P
        and Q of the Wisconsin Tests of Reading Skill
        Development: Comprehension. Technical Report No. 465. ED

162 279 (Arlington, VA: ERIC, 1978).

2027. Kossack, Sharon Wall. "A Mathematical Reading Inventory."
       Ph.D. diss., University of Georgia, 1976. ED 141 768 (Ann
       Arbor, MI: University Microfilms, 1976).

2028. Kurak, Alex. Developing a Junior College Reading Test. ED
       018 186 (Arlington, VA: ERIC, 1967).

2029. Leibert, Robert E. The Development of Informal Tests of
       Reading and the Analysis of the Reading Performance of
       Adults Attending Basic Education Classes. Final Report.
       ED 034 963 (Arlington, VA: ERIC, 1969).

2030. Lewis, John. "A Reading Attitude Inventory for Elementary
       School Pupils." Educational and Psychological Measurement
       39(2): 511-13 (1979).

2031. Lichtman, Marilyn. "The Development and Validation of
       REAL, an Instrument to Assess Functional Literacy."
       Journal of Reading Behavior 6(2): 167-82 (1974). For
       related information see ED 081 811.

2032. McKenna, Michael C. "Informal Reading Inventories: A
       Review of the Issues." Reading Teacher 36(7): 670-79
       (1983).

2033. McLeod, John and Jonathan Anderson. Development of a
       Standard Reading Test Designed to Discriminate
       Effectively at the Adolescent Level. ED 155 602
       (Arlington, VA: ERIC, 1977).

2034. Martin, Wanda and others. A Methodology for Reading Skill
       Improvement in Vocational Secondary Programs. ED 209 499
       (Arlington, VA: ERIC, 1981).

2035. Mason, Jana and Christine McCormick. Testing the
       Development of Reading and Linguistic Awareness.
       Technical Report No. 126. ED 170 735 (Arlington, VA:
       ERIC, 1979).

2036. Mikulecky, Larry Joseph. "The Developing, Field Testing,
       and Initial Norming of a Secondary/Adult Level Reading
       Attitude Measure that is Behaviorally Oriented and Based
       on Krathwohl's Taxonomy of the Affective Domain." Ph.D.
       diss., University of Wisconsin, 1976. ED 146 550.
       Available from University Microfilms, Ann Arbor, MI.

2037. Moore, Samuel C. and Robert Lemons. "Measuring Reading
       Attitudes: Three Dimensions." Reading World 22(1): 48-57
       (1982).

2038. Moskowitz, S. "Building Your Own Reading Tests."
       Instructor 80: 52 (March 1971).

2039. Murphy, R. T. "Assessment of Adult Reading Competence."
       International Reading Association Conference Papers
       (Perspectives in Reading Series) 19: 50-61 (1974).

2040. Narang, Harbans Lal. "The Development and Validation of a
       Test of Teacher Knowledge of Reading at the Secondary

Level." Ph.D. diss., University of Oregon, 1976. ED 147 770. Available from University Microfilms, Ann Arbor, MI.

2041. Niedermeyer, Fred C. and Howard Sullivan. Development of Teacher-administered Tests for the SWRL Reading Programs. ED 110 513 (Arlington, VA: ERIC, 1975).

2042. Nystrand, Martin. Ontological Aspects of Validity Concerns in Language Arts Assessment. ED 133 733 (Arlington, VA: ERIC, 1976).

2043. O'Brien, Michael L. Developing a Word Analysis Skill Inventory for Diagnosing and Evaluating Reading Problems of Middle School Students. ED 215 429 (Fairborn, OH: National Middle Schools Association, 1981).

2044. Olson, Margot A. "Criterion-referenced Reading Assessment in a Large City School District." Journal of Reading Behavior 8(4): 387-96 (1976).

2045. _____. Criterion-referenced Reading Assessment in a Large City School District. Paper presented at the annual meeting of the American Educational Research Association, 1975. ED 109 239 (Arlington, VA: ERIC, 1975).

2046. O'Reilly, Robert P. and others. Validation of a Multiple-choice Cloze Test of Literal Comprehension: Summary Report. Paper presented at the annual meeting of the National Council on Measurement in Education, 1976. ED 120 265 (Arlington, VA: ERIC, 1976).

2047. Otto, Wayne and Betty Harper. Constructing a Test of Teacher's Knowledge of Reading. Paper presented at the annual meeting of the National Reading Conference, 1977. ED 151 744 (Arlington, VA: ERIC, 1977).

2048. Ozete, Oscar. Assessing Reading Comprehension in Spanish for Bilingual Children. Bulletin No. 9533. ED 157 667 (Arlington, VA: ERIC, 1978).

2049. Panackal, Abraham A. and Carl S. Heft. "Cloze Technique and Multiple Choice Technique: Reliability and Validity." Educational and Psychological Measurement 38(4): 917-32 (1978).

2050. Piontkowski, Dorothy. Clinical Assessment of Beginning Reading Skills. Paper presented at the annual meeting of the International Reading Association, 1976. ED 126 490 (Arlington, VA: ERIC, 1976).

2051. Potter, Thomas C. A Taxonomy of Cloze Research, Part I: Readability and Reading Comprehension. ED 035 514 (Arlington, VA: ERIC, 1968).

2052. Powers, W. G. and others. "The Development of a Reading Avoidance Measure." Reading Improvement 18(4): 321-28 (1981).

2053. Pyrczak, Fred. "Passage-dependence of Reading Comprehension Questions: Examples." Journal of Reading 18(4): 308-11 (1975).

2054.   Ratekin, Ned H. The Adequacy of the Cloze in Measuring
        Comprehension of Different Logical Patterns. Paper
        presented at the National Reading Conference, 1971. ED
        061 012 (Arlington, VA: ERIC, 1971).

2055.   Reading Resource Items for Minimal Competency Testing. A
        Collection of Reading Items for State and Local Education
        Agencies to Draw Upon in Custom-building Their Own
        Minimal Competency Instruments. ED 173 394 (Arlington,
        VA: ERIC, 1977).

2056.   Redelheim, Paul S. "The Construction of an Instrument to
        Measure the Attitude of Young Children Toward Reading."
        Ed.D. diss., University of Georgia, 1975. ED 123 618.
        Available from University Microfilms, Ann Arbor, MI.

2057.   _____. "Multidimensional Test of Reading Attitude for
        Children; Children's Attitude Toward Reading Test." The
        Reading Teacher 30: 181-6 (1976).

2058.   Ribovich, Jerilyn K. Comprehension of Syntactic
        Structures in Oral Language and its Relationship to
        Reading Comprehension in First-Grade Children. ED 144 103
        (Arlington, VA: ERIC, 1976).

2059.   Richardson, Ellis and others. The Use of the Decoding
        Skills Test in the Measurement of Auditory and Visual
        Word Recognition Skills. Paper presented at the annual
        convention of the International Reading Association,
        1979. ED 185 072 (Arlington, VA: ERIC, 1979).

2060.   Rowell, E. H. and Florence G. Hennen. The Interaction
        Between Sex Referents in Test Items and Reading
        Performance on Individualized Reading Tests. ED 191 009
        (Arlington, VA: ERIC, 1978).

2061.   Royal, M. "Performance Objectives and C-R Tests: We Wrote
        Our Own! Bangor, Mich." Reading Teacher 27: 701-3 (1974).

2062.   Rude, Robert R. "A Knowledge Test of Reading for
        Elementary School Teaching." Journal of Educational
        Research 74(6): 411-18 (1981).

2063.   Salter, Ruth. Resources for the Implementation of a
        Productivity Analysis in Education. Paper presented at
        the annual meeting of the American Educational Research
        Association, 1975. ED 111 874 (Arlington, VA: ERIC,
        1975).

2064.   Schlesinger, I. M. and Zehavit Weiser. "A Facet Design
        for Tests of Reading Comprehension." Reading Research
        Quarterly 5(4): 566-80 (1970).

2065.   Schoenfeldt, L. F., B. B. Schoenfeldt, S. R. Acker and M.
        R. Perlson. "Content Validity Revisited: The Development
        of a Content-oriented Test of Industrial Reading."
        Journal of Applied Psychology 61: 581-88 (1976).

2066.   Schreiner, Robert, ed. Reading Tests and Teachers: A
        Practical Guide. ED 178 871 (Arlington, VA: ERIC, 1979).

2067. Schwartz, Judy I. "Standardizing a Reading Test." Reading Teacher 30(4): 364-68 (1977).

2068. Smith, Kenneth and others. The KEEP Phone Discrimination Test. Technical Report No. 64. ED 153 445 (Arlington, VA: ERIC, 1977).

2069. Smithies, Michael. "Two Methods of Testing Comprehension." English Language Teaching Journal 30(2): 144-50 (1976).

2070. Sopher, E. "Multiple-choice Comprehension Tests." English Language Teaching 27(3): 281-88 (1973).

2071. Spearritt, D. and others. Measuring Reading Comprehension in the Upper Primary School. EDRC Report No. 11. ED 155 609 (Arlington, VA: ERIC, 1977).

2072. Sticht, Thomas G. and John S. Caylor. Development and Evaluation of Job Reading Task Tests. ED 064 683 (Arlington, VA: ERIC, 1972).

2073. Sticht, Thomas G. and Lawrence J. Beck. Development of an Experimental Literacy Assessment Battery. Final Report. ED 129 900 (Arlington, VA: ERIC, 1976).

2074. Summers, Edward G. A Review of Research and Bibliography on Published Attitudinal Instruments in Reading. Paper presented at the annual meeting of the American Educational Research Association, 1976. ED 123 558 (Arlington, VA: ERIC, 1976).

2075. Summers, Edward G. and Peter Edwards. Developing a Canadian Criterion Referenced Core Reading Vocabulary Test for Junior Secondary Grades. ED 122 229 (Arlington, VA: ERIC, 1975).

2076. Tuinman, J. Jaap. "Asking Reading-dependent Questions." Journal of Reading 14(5): 289-92 (1971).

2077. _____. Passage-related Reading Comprehension Questions. Paper presented at the annual meeting of the American Educational Research Association, 1971. ED 047 919 (Arlington, VA: ERIC, 1971).

2078. Valmont, William J. "Creating Questions for Informal Reading Inventories." Reading Teacher 25(6): 509-12 (1972).

2079. Venezky, Richard L. and Dale Johnson. "Development of Two Letter-sound Patterns in Grades One Through Three." Journal of Educational Psychology 64(1) 109-15 (1973).

2080. Wark, David M. "The Measurement of Test Anxiety in a Reading Class." Reading World 20(3): 215-22 (1981).

2081. Williams, Robert T. and Mitchell A. Kaman. A Model for the Development of a Reading and Study Skills Inventory for Every Content Area. Paper presented at the annual meeting of the Western College Reading Association, 1975. ED 108 115 (Arlington, VA: ERIC, 1975).

2082. Worden, Thomas W. "Critical Reading: Can the Skills be
       Measured." Reading Improvement 18(4): 278-86 (1981).

DIAGNOSTIC

2083. Anderson, Carolyn C. and Karl Koenke. An Informal Reading
       Readiness Inventory: A Diagnostic Method of Predicting
       First Grade Reading Achievement. Paper presented at the
       annual meeting of the International Reading Association,
       1980. ED 184 068 (Arlington, VA: ERIC, 1980).

2084. Athey, Irene and Robert P. O'Reilly. A Criterion-
       referenced Testing Model for Assessing Growth in Reading.
       Paper presented at the annual meeting of the National
       Council for Measurement in Education, 1975. ED 105 422
       (Arlington, VA: ERIC, 1975).

2085. Auerbach, Irma-Theresa. An Analysis of Reading
       Comprehension Tests. Final Report. ED 052 914 (Arlington,
       VA: ERIC, 1971).

2086. Avant, Glen R. and Michael L. O'Brien. Developing, Field
       Testing and Calibrating a Word Analysis Skill Inventory.
       Paper presented at the annual meeting of the Eastern
       Educational Research Association, 1980. ED 193 296
       (Arlington, VA: ERIC, 1980).

2087. Ayrer, James E. "Problems in the Development of a Test of
       Functional Literacy." Journal of Reading 20(8): 697-705
       (1977).

2088. Bullen, Gertrude F. Bullen Reading Attitude Measure. ED
       109 212. Contained in ED 109 211 (Arlington, VA: ERIC,
       1972).

2089. Forgione, Roberta Walsh. "Construction of a Diagnostic
       Reading Instrument for Secondary Students. (Volumes I and
       II)." Ed.D. diss., Boston University, 1976. ED 127 587.
       Available from University Microfilms, Ann Arbor, MI.

2090. Henry, G. and A. Grisay. Methodological Aspects of
       Evaluation in Primary Reading. ED 145 367 (Arlington, VA:
       ERIC, 1970).

2091. Marcus, A. D. "Development of a Diagnostic Test of
       Syntactic Meaning Clues in Reading." International
       Reading Association Conference Papers (Diagnostic
       Viewpoints in Reading) 15: 48-63 (1971).

2092. The Pre-reading Skills Battery; and Rationale for and
       Description of the Pre-reading Skills Battery. ED 096 637
       (Arlington, VA: ERIC, 1971).

2093. Skellings, Louise Noah. "The Development of a Criterion-
       referenced Functional Literacy Test for Miami-Dade
       Students." Ed.D. diss., Nova University, 1977. ED 142 256
       (Arlington, VA: ERIC, 1977).

2094. Smith, Cyrus F. Jr. and Richard D. Western. Reading
       Proficiency and Standardized Tests: Another Objection.

Paper presented at the annual meeting of the National
Reading Conference, 1978. ED 165 125 (Arlington, VA:
ERIC, 1978).

READINESS

2095.   Ollila, Lloyd and others. The New Canadian Reading
Readiness Test Research. ED 062 104 (Arlington, VA: ERIC,
1972).

2096.   Osborn, Julia B. Children's Prereading Skills and
Strategies: Development of an Assessment Inventory. Paper
presented at the annual meeting of the American
Psychological Association, 1979. ED 178 873 (Arlington,
VA: ERIC, 1979).

2097.   Special Project in Urban Reading Tests, Component I:
Pre-reading Skills Battery. ED 096 638 (Arlington, VA:
ERIC, 1971).

2098.   Stern, Carolyn. Echoic Response Inventory for Children
(ERIC). ED 039 931 (Arlington, VA: ERIC, 1969).

Science

2099. Anderson, Elaine J. and Deyanira Barnett Herrera. "Development of a Science Attitude Scale for Spanish-speaking Populations." Journal of Research in Science Teaching 13(1): 45-8 (1976).

2100. Bauman, Daniel Joseph. "Measurements and Analyses of Science Interest in a School District." Ph.D. diss., University of Colorado, 1970. ED 079 034. Available from University Microfilms, Ann Arbor, MI.

2101. Beard, Jean. "The Development of Group Achievement Tests for Two Basic Processes of AAAS Science--A Process Approach." Journal of Research in Science Teaching 8(2): 179-83 (1971).

2102. _____. Group Achievement Tests Developed for Two Basic Processes of AAAS Science--A Process Approach. Paper presented at the annual meeting of the National Association for Research in Science Teaching, 1970. ED 038 281 (Arlington, VA: ERIC, 1970).

2103. Billeh, Victor Y. and Muhammad H. Malik. "Development and Application of a Test on Understanding the Nature of Science." Science Education 61(4): 559-71 (1977).

2104. Bowyer, Jane B. and Marcia C. Linn. "Effectiveness of the Science Curriculum Improvement Study in Teaching Scientific Literacy." Journal of Research in Science Teaching 15(3): 209-19 (1978).

2105. Bratt, M. and A. DeVito. "Development and Field Testing of an Inventory of Humanistic Attitudes Towards Science Teaching." Journal of Research in Science Teaching 15: 551-7 (1978).

2106. Carlson, G. R. and E. Streitberger. "Construction and Comparison of Three Related Tests of Formal Reasoning." Science Education 67: 133-40 (January 1983).

2107. The Certificate of Secondary Education: Experimental Examinations--Science. Examinations Bulletin No. 8. ED

068 480 (London: Her Majesty's Stationery Office, S. O.
No. 27-390-9, 1965).

2108. Champlin, Robert Francis. The Development and Field
Testing of an Instrument to Assess Student Beliefs About
and Attitudes Toward Science and Scientists. Ph.D. diss.,
Ohio State University, 1970. ED 071 849. Available from
University Microfilms, Ann Arbor, MI.

2109. Cotham, J. C. and E. L. Smith. "Development and
Validation of the Conceptions of Scientific Theories
Test." Journal of Research in Science Teaching 18: 387-96
(September 1981).

2110. Cotham, Joseph C. and Edward L. Smith. "Development and
Validation of the Conceptions of Scientific Theories
Test." Journal of Research in Science Teaching 18(5):
387-96 (1981).

2111. Cropley, Murray C. and Peter P. Thomson. "The Australian
Item Bank Program Revisited." Australian Science Teachers
Journal 23(3): 43-5 (1977).

2112. Davis, Frederick B. and Gerald S. Lesser. Identification
of Gifted Elementary School Children With Exceptional
Scientific Talent. ED 002 864 (Arlington, VA: ERIC,
1960).

2113. Dietz, Maureen A. An Investigation to Develop an
Instrument to Determine the Problem-solving Skills in
Science of Children in Grades One, Two, and Three. ED 053
906 (Ann Arbor: University Microfilms, 1969).

2114. Dillashaw, F. Gerald and James R. Okey. "Test of the
Integrated Science Process Skills for Secondary Science
Students." Science Education 64(5): 601-8 (1980). For
related information see ED 184 867.

2115. Dressel, Paul L. and Clarence H. Nelson. Questions and
Problems in Science. ED 054 231 (Arlington, VA: ERIC,
1956).

2116. Duszynska, Anna. Reasoning Level Test. Application of
Piaget's Theoretical Model to the Construction of a
Science Test for Elementary School. ED 144 988
(Arlington, VA: ERIC, 1978).

2117. Finkelstein, Leonard Bernard. The Development of a
"Reading Free" Testing Procedure for the Evaluation of
Knowledge and Understandings in Elementary School
Science. ED 024 563 (Ann Arbor, MI: University
Microfilms, 1967).

2118. Fisher, Thomas H. "The Development of an Attitude Survey
for Junior High Science." School Science and Mathematics
73(8): 647-52 (1973).

2119. Fleetwood, George R. and Paul B. Hounshell. "Assessing
Cognitive and Affective Outcomes of Environmental
Education." Journal of Research in Science Teaching
13(1): 29-35 (1976).

2120.   Fraser, Barry J. "Developing Subscales for a Measure of
        Student Understanding of Science." Journal of Research in
        Science Teaching 15(1): 79-84 (1978).

2121.   _____. "Development of a Test of Science-related
        Attitudes." Science Education 62: 509-15 (O/D 1978).

2122.   _____. "Some Attitude Scales for Ninth Grade Science."
        School Science and Mathematics 78(5): 379-84 (1978).

2123.   Funk, Harold James. "Test-construction Behavior of Pre-
        service Secondary Science Teachers." Ed.D. diss., Indiana
        University, 1971. Dissertation Abstracts International
        32(8-A): 4465 (1971).

2124.   _____. Test Construction Behavior of Pre-service
        Secondary Science Teachers. Paper presented at the
        National Association for Research in Science Teaching
        annual meeting, 1972. ED 068 333 (Arlington, VA: ERIC,
        1972).

2125.   Fyffe, Darrel Wayne. "The Development of Test Items for
        the Integrated Science Processes: Formulating Hypotheses
        and Defining Operationally." Ed.D. diss., Wayne State
        University, 1971. ED 070 585. Available from University
        Microfilms, Ann Arbor, MI.

2126.   Hayward, Robert R. The Developing and Field Testing of an
        Instrument Using the Planetarium to Evaluate the
        Attainment of the Concept of Annual Motion. Paper
        presented at the annual meeting of the National
        Association for Research in Science Teaching, 1976. ED
        130 839 (Arlington, VA: ERIC, 1976).

2127.   Hedges, William D. Testing and Evaluation for the
        Sciences in the Secondary School. ED 013 761 (Belmont,
        California: Wadsworth, 1966).

2128.   Hofstein, A. and others. "Measurement of the Interest in,
        and Attitudes to, Laboratory Work Amongst Israeli High
        School Chemistry Students." Science Education 60: 401-11
        (1976).

2129.   Hungerford, Harold Ralph. "The Development and Validation
        of Test Instruments to Measure Observation and Comparison
        in Junior High School Science." Ph.D. diss., Southern
        Illinois University, 1970. ED 077 647 (Ann Arbor, MI:
        University Microfilms, 1970).

2130.   Jenkins, E. W. Objective Testing: A Guide for Science
        Teachers. ED 079 033 (Leeds, England: Centre for Studies
        in Science Education, Leeds University, 1972).

2131.   Johnson, Sandra and Brian Mahar. "Monitoring Science
        Performance Using a Computerized Question Banking
        System." British Journal of Educational Technology 13(2):
        97-106 (1982).

2132.   Jones, Howard Leon. The Development of a Test of
        Scientific Inquiry, Using the Tab Format, and an Analysis
        of its Relationship to Selected Student Behaviors and

Abilities. ED 013 212 (Ann Arbor, MI: University Microfilms, 1966).

2133. Kings, Clive B. and Murray C. Cropley. "The Australian Science Item Bank Project." Australian Science Teachers Journal 20(2): 69-73 (1974).

2134. Klopfer, Leopold E. "Evaluation of Science Achievement and Science Test Development in an International Context: The IEA Study in Science." Science Education 57(3): 387-403 (1973).

2135. Koballa, Thomas Jr. Designing a Likert-type Scale to Assess Attitude Toward Energy Conservation. Paper presented at the annual meeting of the National Association for Research in Science Teaching, 1981. ED 201 489 (Arlington, VA: ERIC, 1981).

2136. Kozlow, M. James and Marshall A. Nay. "An Approach to Measuring Scientific Attitudes." Science Education 60(2): 147-72 (1976).

2137. Krajkovich, Joseph G. and Jeffrey K. Smith. "The Development of the Image of Science and Scientists Scale." Journal of Research in Science Teaching 19(1): 39-44 (1982).

2138. Labinowich, Edward Peter. "A Study in Summative Evaluation of Elementary School Science Curricula." Ph.D. diss., Florida State University, 1970. ED 053 970. Available from University Microfilms, Ann Arbor, MI.

2139. Lee, Addison E. Testing and Evaluating Student Success with Laboratory Blocks, A Resource Book for Teachers. ED 038 319 (Lexington, MA: D. C. Heath, 1969).

2140. Lehmann, P. "Science Questions -- Item Bank." South Australian Science Teachers Journal 744: 52-3 (1974).

2141. Ludeman, Robert R. Development of the Science Processes Test. Paper presented at the annual meeting of the National Association for Research in Science Teaching, 1975. ED 108 898 (Arlington, VA: ERIC, 1975).

2142. McIntyre, P. J. "The Model Identification Test: A Limited Verbal Science Test." Science Education 56(3): 345-57 (1972).

2143. McLeod, Richard J. and others. "The Development of Criterion-validated Test Items for Four Integrated Science Processes." Journal of Research in Science Teaching 12(4): 415-21 (1975).

2144. Maddock, M. N. "An Attitude Scale for Papua New Guinea." Australian Science Teachers Journal 20(2): 83-9 (1974).

2145. Mandelare, John James. An Analysis of Expressed Cognitive Preferences on Forced-choice, Multiple-option and Rating Instruments. ED 114 248 (Ann Arbor, Michigan: University Microfilms, 1973).

2146.   Molitor, L. L. and K. D. George. "Development of a Test of Science Process Skills." <u>Journal of Research in Science Teaching</u> 13: 405-12 (September 1976).

2147.   Moore, Richard W. "The Development, Field Test, and Validation of Scales to Assess Teachers' Attitudes Toward Teaching Elementary School Science." <u>Science Education</u> 57(3): 271-78 (1973).

2148.   Moore, Richard W. and Frank X. Sutman. "The Development, Field Test and Validaton of Inventory of Scientific Attitudes." <u>Journal of Research in Science Teaching</u> 7(2): 85-94 (1970).

2149.   Morgan, David A. "STEPS -- A Science Test for Evaluation of Process Skills." <u>Science Teacher</u> 38(8): 77-9 (1971).

2150.   Nasca, Donald. <u>Effect of Varied Presentations of Laboratory Exercises Within Programed Materials on Specific Intellectual Factors of Science Problem Solving Behavior</u>. ED 010 292 (Arlington, VA: ERIC, 1965).

2151.   Nelson, Clarence H. <u>Improving Objective Tests in Science</u>. ED 017 467 (Arlington, VA: ERIC, 1967).

2152.   Nelson, Miles A. and Eugene C. Abraham. "Inquiry Skill Measures." <u>Journal of Research in Science Teaching</u> 10(4): 291-97 (1973).

2153.   Novick, Shimshon and Joseph Nussbaum. "Pupils' Understanding of the Particulate Nature of Matter: A Cross-age Study." <u>Science Education</u> 65(2): 187-96 (1981).

2154.   Page, R. L. and others. "Attitude Assessment in Science and Technology." <u>Core</u> 3(3): 9 (1979).

2155.   _____ . <u>Attitude Assessment in Science and Technology. Occasional Paper</u>. ED 179 385 (Arlington, VA: ERIC, 1979).

2156.   Raven, Ronald J. "The Development of a Test of Piaget's Logical Operations." <u>Science Education</u> 57(3): 377-85 (1973).

2157.   _____ . "The Development of a Test of Piaget's Operative Comprehension." <u>Science Education</u> 61(3): 377-85 (1973).

2158.   Ross, John A. and Florence J. Maynes. "Development of a Test of Experimental Problem-solving Skills." <u>Journal of Research in Science Teaching</u> 20(1): 63-75 (1983).

2159.   Rubba, P. A. and H. O. Andersen. "Development of an Instrument to Assess Secondary School Students' Understanding of the Nature of Scientific Knowledge." <u>Science Education</u> 62: 449-58 (1978).

2160.   Shayer, Michael and Hugh Wylam. "The Development of the Concepts of Heat and Temperature in 10-13 Year-olds." <u>Journal of Research in Science Teaching</u> 18(5): 419-34 (1981).

2161.   Smith, Richard B. "An Approach to Measurement in the New

Science Curriculum." Science Education 53(5): 411-15
(1969).

2162.   Stauss, Nyles G. "Testing and Evaluating in Science in
the Elementary School." Science Education 54(3): 247-52
(1970).

2163.   Steele, Joe M. The Relationship of Developmental Level
With Science Performance: A Case for an Alternative to IQ
Grouping of Mildly Retarded Children. Paper presented at
the annual meeting of the American Educational Research
Association, 1974. ED 091 876 (Arlington, VA: ERIC,
1974).

2164.   Stickney, Roland Francis. The Construction of a Science
Test for Ninth-grade Alaska Natives. ED 023 573 (Ann
Arbor, MI: University Microfilms, 1966).

2165.   Stillman, A. B. "The Rationale for Abilities Testing and
Specifically the Development of a Scientific Ability
Test." School Science Review 63(224): 423-33 (1982).

2166.   Tannenbaum, Harold E. and others. Evaluation in
Elementary School Science. ED 011 841 (Arlington, VA:
ERIC, 1964).

2167.   Tannenbaum, Robert S. The Development of the Test of
Science Processes. Paper presented at the meeting of the
National Association for Research in Science Teaching,
1969. ED 027 222 (Arlington, VA: ERIC, 1969).

2168.   Turner, Lawrence E. Jr. "Construction and Use of an
Astronomy Test Item File." American Journal of Physics
46(9): 914-9 (1978).

2169.   Wareing, Carol. "Developing the WASP: Wareing Attitudes
Toward Science Protocol." Journal of Research in Science
Teaching 19(8): 639-45 (1982).

2170.   White, Richard T. and Lindsay D. Mackay. Tests of
Perception of Scientists and Self. Paper presented at the
annual meeting of the National Association for Research
in Science Teaching, 1974. ED 095 011 (Arlington, VA:
ERIC, 1974).

BIOLOGY

2171.   Benson, Bernard W. and Linda L. Young. "The Development
and Implementation of an Instrument to Assess Cognitive
Performance in High School Biology; Assessment of
Cognitive Transfer in Science Inventory." Journal of
Research in Science Teaching 8(3): 211-24 (1971).

2172.   Butler, Delbert Franklin. A Test for Measuring Selected
Life Science Concepts of Elementary School Children. ED
013 206 (Ann Arbor, MI: University Microfilms, Order No.
66-4412, 1965).

2173.   Hettick, Vergil and George C. Turner. An Evaluative Study
of Teacher Constructed Test Items for BSCS Biology. Final

Report. ED 018 371 (Arlington, VA: ERIC, 1967).

2174. Hounshell, Peter B. Seafarers Knowledge Inventory. ED 222
        330 (Arlington, VA: ERIC, 1982).

2175. Hounshell, Peter B. and Carolyn Hampton. Marine Attitude
        Survey. ED 222 331 (Arlington, VA: ERIC, 1982).

2176. _____. Marine Education Knowledge Inventory. ED 222 329
        (Arlington, VA: ERIC, 1982).

2177. Koos, Eugenia M. and James Y. Chan. Criterion-referenced
        Tests in Biology. Paper presented at the annual meeting
        of the American Educational Research Association, 1972.
        ED 062 399 (Arlington, VA: ERIC, 1972).

2178. Nelson, Clarence H. Testing and Evaluation in the
        Biological Sciences. ED 015 876 (Washington, D. C.:
        Commission on Undergraduate Education in the Biological
        Sciences, 1967).

2179. Palmer, D. G. Bank of Items for H.S.C. Biology Level III
        and Division 1 with Computerised Self-moderation and
        Error Analysis Procedures Using the Items From the Bank.
        ED 137 053 (Arlington, VA: ERIC, 1972).

2180. Ramsay, Helen P. "Designing Self-tests for Biology."
        Journal of Biological Education 11(2): 95-102 (1977).

2181. Reese, Charles Dennis. "The Construction of a Pictorial
        Classroom Test in Biology and an Evaluation of
        Administering the Test by Four Different Procedures."
        Ph.D. diss., University of Maryland, 1973. ED 089 966.
        Available from University Microfilms, Ann Arbor, MI.

2182. Tamir, P. "An Alternative Approach to the Construction of
        Multiple Choice Test Items." Journal of Biological
        Education 5(6): 305-7 (1971).

CHEMISTRY

2183. Delorenzo, Ronald A. Computer Assisted Instruction and
        Computer Test Construction in Chemistry at Middle Georgia
        College. Paper presented at the Two Year College
        Chemistry Conference, 1977. ED 139 644 (Arlington, VA:
        ERIC, 1976).

2184. Denny, Rita T. "The Mathematics Skill Test (MAST) for
        Chemistry." Journal of Chemical Education 48(12): 845-46
        (1971).

2185. Johnson, K. J. "Pitt's Computer-generated Chemistry
        Exam." In Proceedings of the Conference on Computers in
        Undergraduate Curricula, pp. 199-204 (1973).

2186. Johnson, K. Jeffrey and others. "Computer Series, 14:
        Computer-assisted Test Construction in Chemistry."
        Journal of Chemical Education 58(2): 177-81 (1981).

2187. Marks, Ronald L. Differences in Learning Outcomes Between a New and a Traditional Chemistry Course. ED 016 620 (Arlington, VA: ERIC, 1966).

MISCELLANEOUS

2188. Tilford, M. P. "Toward the Development of an Instrument to Measure the Attitude Toward Science of Negro Students: A Research Report." School Science and Mathematics 73: 367-72 (1973).

2189. Tobin, Kenneth G. and William Capie. "Development and Validation of a Group Test of Integrated Science Processes." Journal of Research in Science Teaching 19(2): 133-41 (1982).

2190. Torrence, David. Measurement of Science Processes in Intermediate Grades Through Instructional Television. Paper presented at the National Convention of the National Science Teacher's Association, 1977. ED 143 328 (Arlington, VA: ERIC, 1977).

2191. Torrence, David R. The Television Test of Science Processes. ED 138 466 (Arlington, VA: ERIC, 1976).

2192. Trembath, Richard J. and James P. Barufaldi. The Frequencies & Origins of Scientific Misconceptions. Paper presented at the annual meeting of the National Association for Research in Science Teaching, 1981. ED 207 846 (Arlington, VA: ERIC, 1981).

PHYSICS

2193. Chelu, C. J. and L. R. B. Elton. "An Item Bank for Multiple-choice Questions." Physics Education 12(4): 263-7 (1977).

2194. Coulter, Byron L. "Improving Tests in Basic Physics." American Journal of Physics 43(6): 499-501 (1975).

2195. De Jong, Marvin L. "Relevant Physics Examinations." Physics Teacher 9(8): 463-64 (1971).

2196. Eichenberger, Rudolph J. "Creativity Measurement Through Use of Judgment Criteria in Physics." Educational and Psychological Measurement 38(2): 421-27 (1978).

2197. _____. "The Development and Validation of a Judging Instrument to Evaluate Creative Products in Physics." Ed.D. diss., Univ. of Northern Colorado, 1972. ED 111 606. Available from University Microfilms, Ann Arbor, Michigan.

2198. Enger, Rolf C. "The USAF Academy Basic Physics Exam File." Journal of College Science Teaching 10(4): 240-43 (1981).

2199. Feldker, Paul F. "Computer-generated Physics Tests." Physics Teacher 11(5): 304-5 (1973).

2200. Ganiel, Uri and Avi Hofstein. <u>Objective and Continuous Assessment of Student Performance in the Physics Laboratory</u>. Paper presented at the annual meeting of the National Association for Research in Science Teaching, 1981. ED 206 509 (Arlington, VA: ERIC, 1981).

2201. Lunde, Barbara K. and James Jones. "Let the Students Write the Exam." <u>Physics Teacher</u> 10(5): 270-72 (1972).

2202. Nelson, James. "AAPT/NSTA High School Physics Examination." <u>Physics Teacher</u> 21(2): 100-3 (1983).

Sensory-Motor

2203. Garvey, Reba and Thomas R. Kimball. Development of a Perceptual-motor Rating Scale for Classroom Teachers to Record Child Behavior. Paper presented at the annual meeting of the American Educational Research Association, 1978. ED 152 856 (Arlington, VA: ERIC, 1978).

2204. Gotz, K. O., R. Lynn, A. R. Borisy and H. J. Eysenck. "New Visual Aesthetic Sensitivity Test. 1. Construction and Psychometric Properties." Perceptual and Motor Skills 49(3): 795-802 (1979).

2205. Grundvig, John L. The Expanded Sensory-perceptual Examination as a Diagnostic Screening Instrument for Organic Brain Damage. ED 077 978 (Arlington, VA: ERIC, 1973).

2206. Kojima, Hideo. "Assessment of Field Dependence in Young Children." Perceptual and Motor Skills 46(2): 479-92 (1978).

2207. Lockheed, Marlaine E. and others. "Validation of a Children's Group Embedded Figures Test." Perceptual and Motor Skills 44(3): 1259-63 (1977).

2208. Orpet, Russel E. The Development of an Experimental Sensory-motor and Movement Skills Test Battery. Paper presented at the annual meeting of the American Educational Research Association, 1972. ED 062 365 (Arlington, VA: ERIC, 1972).

2209. Turaids, Dainis and others. "A Perceptual Test Battery: Development and Standardization." Elementary School Journal 72(7): 351-61 (1972).

2210. Tyler, Nancy B. "A Stereognostic Test for Screening Tactile Sensation." American Journal of Occupational Therapy 26(5): 256-60 (1972).

MOTOR

2211.   Adair, Jane D. "Construction and Validation of an Instrument Designed to Assess States of Consciousness During Movement Activity." Dissertation Abstracts International 43(3-A): 719-20 (1982).

2212.   Adams, Arthur R. Jr. "A Test Construction Study of Sport-type Motor Educability for College Men." Ph.D. diss., Louisiana State University and Agricultural and Mechanical College, 1954.

2213.   Arnett, Chappelle and Margaret M. Thompson. Perceptual-motor and Motor Performance Test Batteries Developed for Pre-school Through Grade Six Children. ED 049 303 (Arlington, VA: ERIC, 1970).

2214.   Briggs, Peter F. and Auke Tellegen. "Development of the Manual Accuracy and Speed Test (MAST)." Perceptual and Motor Skills 32(3): 923-43 (1971).

2215.   Charlop, Marjorie and Constance W. Atwell. "The Charlop-Atwell Scale of Motor Coordination: A Quick and Easy Assessment of Young Children." Perceptual and Motor Skills 50(3, pt. 2): 1291-1308 (1980).

2216.   Dinucci, James M. and Elois B. Pelton. The Construction of a Muscular Strength Test Battery for Girls in the Primary Grades. Paper presented at the National Convention of the American Alliance for Health, Physical Education and Recreation, 1974. ED 098 242 (Arlington, VA: ERIC, 1974).

2217.   Dinucci, James M. and John Roger Shore. The Construction of a Motor Fitness Test Battery for Boys in the Lower Elementary Grades. Paper presented at the convention of the American Association for Health, Physical Education and Recreation, 1973. ED 081 737 (Arlington, VA: ERIC, 1973).

VISION

2218.   Kephart, N. C. The Relationship of Measured Perceptual Processes to School Learning. Paper presented at the annual meeting of the American Educational Research Association, 1971. ED 054 859. (Arlington, VA: ERIC, 1971).

2219.   McDaniel, Ernest. New Film Tests of Visual Perception. Paper presented at the annual meeting of the American Educational Research Association, 1971. ED 054 201 (Arlington, VA: ERIC, 1971).

Social Studies

2220. Brown, L. B., ed. "Testing in the Social Studies: Symposium." Social Education 40: 503-41 (1976).

2221. Diederich, Paul B. and Marvin Maskovsky. "Measuring the Effects of Newspapers in the Classroom." Social Education 34(2): 173-84 (1970).

2222. Evaluation and Social Studies: Practical Ideas for Classroom Teachers. ED 148 713 (Arlington, VA: ERIC, 1976).

2223. Fox, Karen and others. An Analysis of the Relationship Between NCSS Curriculum Guidelines and Social Studies Achievement Tests. ED 173 199 (Arlington, VA: ERIC, 1978).

2224. _____. "Graduation Competency Testing in the Social Studies: A Position Statement of the National Council for Social Studies." Social Education 43(5): 367-69 (1979).

2225. Gaines, W. George. Measuring Social Studies Achievement: Criterion-referenced Versus Norm-referenced Tests for the Classroom Teacher. Paper presented at the annual meeting of the Mid-South Educational Research Association, 1972. ED 078 072 (Arlington, VA: ERIC, 1972).

2226. Hardy, Helen. "A Knowledge Test for Georgia Studies." Georgia Social Science Journal 12(4): 5-11 (1981).

2227. Harris, Margaret L. and B. Robert Tabachnick. Measuring Social Studies Concept Attainment: Boys and Girls. Report from the Project on a Structure of Concept Attainment Abilities. ED 075 273 (Arlington, VA: ERIC, 1971).

2228. Hunkins, Francis P. "Rationales for Testing in the Social Studies." Social Education 40(7): 504-8 (1976).

2229. Koen, Frank. Specifications for the Design of a Test of Knowledge of Foreign Cultural Patterns. Final Report. ED 049 463 (Arlington, VA: ERIC, 1971).

2230. Lopatka, R. Development of Models for Assessing Affective
Objectives in the Social Studies. A Report to the
Minister's Advisory Committee on Student Achievement. ED
179 574 (Arlington, VA: ERIC, 1980).

2231. _____. Report on the Development and Administration of
the High School Social Studies Achievement Tests. Fall,
1978. ED 179 572 (Arlington, VA: ERIC, 1978).

2232. Madden, John R. and others. Rose Tree Media Social
Studies Curriculum Evaluation. Final Report. ED 065 425
(Arlington, VA: ERIC, 1971).

2233. Muir, Sharon Pray. A Test for Inquiry Social Studies,
Grades 5 and 6 (and) Administrator's Guide. ED 160 514
(Arlington, VA: ERIC, 1976).

2234. Payette, Roland Francis. Development and Analysis of a
Cognitive Preference Test in the Social Sciences. Final
Report. ED 066 376 (Arlington, VA: ERIC, 1967).

2235. Smith, Ruth Cowen. "Objective Examinations in Social
Studies (Making Them More Relevant)." Clearing House
51(1): 10-14 (1978).

2236. Tabachnick, B. Robert and others. Selection and Analysis
of Social Studies Concepts for Inclusion in Tests of
Concept Attainment. ED 051 310 (Arlington, VA: ERIC,
1970).

ECONOMICS

2237. Helburn, Suzanne Wiggins. "How to Develop Your Own Social
Studies Tests in Economics." Social Education 40(7):
533-7 (1976).

2238. Primary Test of Economic Understanding. Examiner's
Manual. Revised Edition. ED 080 396 (Iowa City:
University of Iowa, Bureau of Business and Economic
Research, 1971).

GEOGRAPHY

2239. Bettis, Norman C. Geographic Literacy Among Intermediate
Level Students in the United States: Fact or Fiction
(and) National Council for Geographic Education:
Intermediate Level Geography Test, Draft No. 3, Fall
1979. Parts I, II, & III. Prepared for the annual meeting
of the National Council for Geographic Education, 1979.
ED 183 459 (Arlington, VA: ERIC, 1979).

2240. Burrill, Robert M. "Modified Objective Questions for
Tests in Introductory Geography." Journal of Geography
75(6): 338-42 (1976).

2241. The Certificate of Secondary Education: Experimental
Examinations: Geography. ED 049 962 (New York: British
Information Services, 1966).

2242. Martorella, Peter H. Evaluating Geographic Concept Learning: A Model for Classroom and Research Applications. Paper presented at the annual meeting of the National Council for Geographic Education, 1972. ED 106 178 (Arlington, VA: ERIC, 1972).

2243. Monk, Janice J. "Preparing Tests to Measure Course Objectives." Journal of Geography 70(3): 157-62 (1971).

2244. Senathirajah, Nallamma and Joel Weiss. Evaluation in Geography: A Resource Book for Teachers. ED 055 121 (Toronto: OISE, 1971).

HISTORY

2245. Alpern, Mildred. "Develop Your Own Tests in World History." Social Education 40(7): 517-23 (1976).

2246. Blackey, Robert. "A Guide to the Skill of Essay Construction in History." Social Education 45(3): 178-82 (1981).

2247. Briggs, Peter F. and others. "Seven Scales for the Minnesota-Briggs History Record with Reference Group Data." Journal of Clinical Psychology 28(4): 431-48 (1972).

2248. Kishler, Thomas C. "A Self-contained Examination." Exercise Exchange 18(1): 8-11 (1973).

2249. Kurfman, Dana. Teacher-made Test Items in American History: Emphasis Junior High School. Bulletin Number 40. ED 118 495 (Arlington, VA: ERIC, 1968).

2250. Lewy, Arieh and Shlomo Shavit. "Types of Examinations in History Studies." Journal of Educational Measurement 11(1): 35-42 (1974).

POLITICAL SCIENCE

2251. Peters, Eileen. "Develop Your Own Tests in Political Science." Social Education 40(7): 528-32 (1976).

Speech and Hearing

2252. Brown, Kenneth L. and others. Assessment of Basic
Speaking and Listening Skills: State of the Art and
Recommendations for Instrument Development. Volume I. ED
178 969 (Arlington, VA: ERIC, 1979).

2253. _____. Assessment of Basic Speaking and Listening Skills:
State of the Art and Recommendations for Instrument
Development. Volume II. ED 178 970 (Arlington, VA: ERIC,
1979).

2254. Plattor, Emma and others. Test Development for Assessing
Achievement in Listening and Speaking. ED 179 576
(Arlington, VA: ERIC, 1979).

HEARING

2255. Cooper, Robert L. and Jonathan D. Kaye. The Development
of a Test of Deaf Children's Linguistic Competence. Final
Report. ED 014 827 (Arlington, VA: ERIC, 1967).

2256. Decaro, James J. An Instrument and Research Design for
Assessing the Attitudes of Parents and Teachers Toward
Occupational Opportunities for Deaf People. Paper
presented at the annual meeting of the American
Educational Research Association, 1981. ED 204 393
(Arlington, VA: ERIC, 1981).

2257. Elkins, Earleen and others. Development of the Speech
Reception Test. Vital and Health Statistics, Data
Evaluation and Methods Research: Series 2-Number 71. ED
155 201 (Arlington, VA: ERIC, 1977).

2258. McKee, Barbara G. and Michael A. Hausknecht. Classroom
Assessment Techniques for Hearing Impaired Students: A
Literature Review. Paper presented at the annual meeting
of the American Educational Research Association, 1978.
ED 161 937 (Arlington, VA: ERIC, 1978).

2259. Meadow, Kathryn P. and others. Meadow/Kendall Social-
emotional Assessment Inventory for Deaf Students: Manual.

ED 225 330 (Arlington, VA: ERIC, 1980).

2260. Morrison, James A. and William B. Michael. "The Development and Validation of an Auditory Perception Test in Spanish for Hispanic Children Receiving Reading Instruction in Spanish." Educational and Psychological Measurement 42(2): 657-69 (1982).

2261. Quigley, Stephen P. and Cynthia M. King. "Syntactic Performance of Hearing Impaired and Normal Hearing Individuals." Applied Psycholinguistics 1(4): 329-56 (1980).

2262. Report of Construction of a Picture Interest Inventory for the Deaf, 1959-1961. ED 017 083 (Arlington, VA: ERIC, 1961).

2263. Restaino, Lillian C. R. and Penny A. Socher. Psycho-educational Assessment of Young Deaf Children. ED 060 603 (Arlington, VA: ERIC, 1969).

2264. Rudner, Lawrence M. The Development and Evaluation of a Quasi Non Verbal Cognitive Skills Test. ED 119 427 (Arlington, VA: ERIC, 1976).

2265. Sabatino, David A. "The Construction and Assessment of an Experimental Test of Auditory Perception." Exceptional Children 35(9): 729-37 (1969).

2266. Withrow, Frank B. The Development of a Receptive Communication Scale for Deaf Children. Final Report. ED 015 574 (Arlington, VA: ERIC, 1966).

SPEECH

2267. Belme, Jillian and Anne Gray. An Analysis of Preschool Teachers' Classroom Language. Mt. Druitt Early Childhood Project: Project Evaluation Report Number 3. ED 198 832 (Arlington, VA: ERIC, 1980).

2268. Bowen, Mack L. Some Procedures for Evaluating Language Development in Young Retarded Children. ED 059 565 (Arlington, VA: ERIC, 1971).

2269. Byers, Burton H. "Testing Proficiency in Interpersonal Communication." Speech and Drama 22(2): 2-7 (1973).

2270. Fluharty, Nancy Buono. "The Design and Standardization of a Speech and Language Screening Test For Use With Preschool Children." Journal of Speech and Hearing Disorders 39(1): 75-88 (1974).

2271. Grether, Craig Blaine. Psychoacoustic Assessment of Speech Communication Systems. The Diagnostic Discrimination Test. ED 048 588 (Springfield, VA: NTIS, 1970).

2272. Jones, Barry W. and Joe Grygar. "The Test of Syntactic Abilities and Microcomputers." American Annals of the Deaf 127(5): 638-44 (1982).

2273. Koike, K. J. M. and C. W. Asp. "Tennessee Test of Rhythm and Intonation Patterns." Journal of Speech and Hearing Disorders 46: 81-7 (1981).

2274. Lamb, D. H. "Speech Anxiety: Towards a Theoretical Conceptualization and Preliminary Scale Development." Speech Monographs 39: 62-7 (1972).

2275. Linares, Thomas A. Articulation Skills in Spanish-speaking Children. ED 212 156 (Ypsilanti, MI: Eastern Michigan University, Bilingual Programs, 1981).

2276. Margolis, Robert H. and Joseph P. Millin. "An Item-difficulty Based Speech Discrimination Test." Journal of Speech and Hearing Research 14(4): 865-73 (1971).

2277. Merklein, Richard A. "A Short Speech Perception Test for Severely and Profoundly Deaf Children." Volta Review 83(1): 36-45 (1981).

2278. Mulac, A. and A. R. Sherman. "Behavioral Assessment of Speech Anxiety." Quarterly Journal of Speech 60: 134-43 (April 1974).

2279. Ross, Mark and Jay Lerman. Word Intelligibility by Picture Identification. (Pittsburgh: Stanwix House, 1971).

2280. Rudegeair, Robert E. Linguistic Factors in the Assessment of Speech Sound Discrimination. Report No. 52. ED 125 004 (Arlington, VA: ERIC, 1975).

2281. _____. A New Approach to Assessing Speech Sound Perception in Children. Professional Paper No. 31. (Arlington, VA: ERIC, 1975).

2282. Scafe, Marla and Ina C. Siler. The Development of a Communication Competency Test at the University of Oklahoma. Paper presented at the annual meeting of the Central States Speech Association, 1979. ED 178 986 (Arlington, VA: ERIC, 1979).

2283. Scafe, Marla Gail. Putting Communication Competencies to Test: A Case in Point at the University of Oklahoma. Paper presented at the annual meeting of the Central States Speech Association, 1978. ED 155 738 (Arlington, VA: ERIC, 1978).

2284. Schwartz, A. H. and R. Goldman. "Variables Influencing Performance on Speech-sound Discrimination Tests." Journal of Speech and Hearing Research 17: 25-32 (1974).

2285. Tyrer, J. H. and J. M. Jordan. "Rationale and Short Description of the Queensland University Aphasia Test." British Journal of Disorders of Communication 6(2): 164-72 (1971).

2286. Van Riper, Charles. A Predictive Screening Test for Children with Articulatory Speech Defects. ED 010 165 (Arlington, VA: ERIC, 1966).

2287.   Wright, Revilla and Barbara Levin. _A Preschool Articulation and Language Screening for the Identification of Speech Disorders. Final Report_. ED 051 889 (Arlington, VA: ERIC, 1971).

Vocations

2288. Ammerman, Harry L. Performance Content for Job Training. Volume 3. Identifying Relevant Job Performance. Research and Development Series No. 123. ED 146 371 (Arlington, VA: ERIC, 1977).

2289. Arkava, Morton L. and Earl C. Brennen. "Toward a Competency Examination for the Baccalaureate Social Worker." Journal of Education for Social Work 11(3): 22-9 (1975).

2290. Atkins, Richard and others. Continuation of a Project to Develop a Vocational Classroom Teacher's "Hands-on" Instrument to Measure Entry and Exit Skills of the Special Education Student for Specific Occupations. Final Report. ED 147 550 (Arlington, VA: ERIC, 1977).

2291. Baldwin, Thomas S. The Development of Achievement Measures for Trade and Technical Education. Final Report. ED 044 526 (Arlington, VA: ERIC, 1970).

2292. _____. The Development of Achievement Measures for Trade and Technical Education. Progress Report Number Five. ED 018 669 (Arlington, VA: ERIC, 1967).

2293. _____. The Development of Achievement Measures for Trade and Technical Education. Progress Report Number Four. ED 018 613 (Arlington, VA: ERIC, 1967).

2294. _____. The Development of Achievement Measures for Trade and Technical Education. Progress Report Number One. ED 018 668 (Arlington, VA: ERIC, 1966).

2295. _____. The Development of Achievement Measures for Trade and Technical Education. Progress Report Number Three. ED 015 278 (Arlington, VA: ERIC, 1966).

2296. Beach, David P. Modification of the Affective Work Competencies Inventory for Use With Vocational Students. Paper presented at the annual conference of the Eastern Educational Research Association, 1981. ED 203 045 (Arlington, VA: ERIC, 1981).

2297.   Blai, Boris Jr. Career Education and Predicting Job
        Satisfaction. ED 215 113 (Arlington, VA: ERIC, 1982).

2298.   Bolton, Brian and Katie Brown. "The Development of an
        Instrument to Assess Work Attitudes of Deaf
        Rehabilitation Clients." Journal of Rehabilitation of the
        Deaf 4(4): 18-29 (1971).

2299.   Burke, D. A. and D. F. Sellin. "Measuring the Self
        Concept of Ability as a Worker." Exceptional Children 39:
        126-32, 145-51 (1972).

2300.   Camp, William G. Development of an Attitude Scale for
        Vocational Research: A Systematic Approach. ED 178 582
        (Arlington, VA: ERIC, 1976).

2301.   Carroll, J. C. and W. E. Scotchford. "The Design and
        Marking of Practical Tests for Craft Trainees." Training
        Officer 5(1): 14-19 (1969).

2302.   Casey, T. J. "Development of a Leadership Orientation
        Scale on the SVIB for Women; Strong Vocational Interest
        Blank." Measurement and Evaluation Guidance 8: 96-100
        (July 1975).

2303.   Corder, Reginald and Richard W. Watkins. Search for and
        Development of Instruments Measuring Student Outcomes of
        Experience-based Career Education Programs. External
        Evaluator's Final Report on the Experience-based Career
        Education Programs. Volume VII. ED 155 176 (Arlington,
        VA: ERIC, 1976).

2304.   Crawford, Patricia. Development of a Student Needs
        Assessment Inventory for Secondary School Guidance
        Departments. ED 198 469 (Arlington, VA: ERIC, 1979).

2305.   Crites, John O. "Career Maturity." NCME Measurement in
        Education 4(2): (1973). See ED 077 976 for related
        information.

2306.   _____. "Problems in the Measurement of Vocational
        Maturity." Journal of Vocational Behavior 4(1): 25-30
        (1974).

2307.   _____. "Testing for Career Adjustment and Development."
        Training and Development Journal 36(2): 20, 22-8 (1982).

2308.   _____. Vocational Development and Vocational Education in
        Adolescence. Final Report. ED 058 451 (Arlington, VA:
        ERIC, 1969).

2309.   Cromack, Theodore R. Characteristics of a Locally
        Developed Licensure Examination. Paper presented at the
        annual meeting of the National Council on Measurement in
        Education, 1979. ED 173 430 (Arlington, VA: ERIC, 1979).

2310.   Cunningham, J. W. and others. The Development of Activity
        Preference Scales Based on Systematically Derived Work
        Dimensions: An Ergometric Approach to Interest
        Measurement. Ergometric Research and Development Series
        Report No. 15. ED 149 039 (Arlington, VA: ERIC, 1975).

2311. Denton, William T. Student Evaluation in Vocational and
       Technical Education. ED 089 098 (Arlington, VA: ERIC,
       1973).

2312. The Development of Achievement Measures for Trade and
       Technical Education. Progress Report Number Two. ED 018
       629 (Arlington, VA: ERIC, 1966).

2313. Dunnette, Marvin D. and Stephan J. Motowidlo. Police
       Selection and Career Assessment. ED 130 042 (Arlington,
       VA: ERIC, 1976).

2314. Elzey, Freeman F. and Samuel Levine. Personal-social and
       Vocational Scale for the Mentally Retarded. ED 010 594
       (Arlington, VA: ERIC, 1966).

2315. Erickson, Richard C. and Tim L. Wentling. Measuring
       Student Growth: Techniques and Procedures for
       Occupational Educational. ED 126 364 (Boston: Allyn and
       Bacon, 1976).

2316. Falk, Dennis S. and others. Perspectives on Health
       Occupational Credentialing. A Report of the National
       Commission for Health Certifying Agencies. ED 201 820
       (Arlington, VA: ERIC, 1979).

2317. Fantaci, Anthony and others. "The U.S. Employment Service
       Occupational Test-development Program." Journal of
       Employment Counseling 14(2): 59-64 (1977).

2318. Fernandes, Kathleen and Andrew M. Rose. An Information
       Processing Approach to Performance Assessment: II. An
       Investigation of Encoding and Retrieval Processes in
       Memory. Technical Report No. 2, November 16, 1977 Through
       November 30, 1978. ED 171 761 (Arlington, VA: ERIC,
       1978).

2319. Fiks, A. I. and others. Public Assistance Worker Job
       Trial. Final Technical Report. ED 133 463 (Arlington, VA:
       ERIC, 1976).

2320. Finch, Curtis R. and Joseph T. Impellitteri. "The
       Development of Valid Work Performance Measures." Journal
       of Industrial Teacher Education 9(1): 36-49, 71 (1971).

2321. Foley, John P. Jr. Criterion Referenced Measures of
       Technical Proficiency in Maintenance Activities. Final
       Report. Paper presented at the annual meeting of the
       Human Factors Society, 1975. ED 114 640 (Arlington, VA:
       ERIC, 1975).

2322. Frederickson, Edward W. and others. Assessment
       Alternatives for a High Skill MOS. Volume I. Problem
       Procedures and Results. Volume II. Appendices. ED 131 107
       (Arlington, VA: ERIC, 1975).

2323. Freeberg, Norman E. Development of Evaluation Measures
       for Use with Neighborhood Youth Corps Enrollees. Final
       Report. ED 051 288 (Arlington, VA: ERIC, 1968).

2324. Freijo, T. D. and A. W. Ward. "Case Study of the

Development of a Career Education Achievement Test."
Measurement and Evaluation in Guidance 9: 51-9 (July
1976).

2325. Fruchter, Dorothy A. and Malcolm James Ree. *Development
of the Armed Services Vocational Aptitude Battery: Forms
8, 9, and 10. Final Report 19 December 1975-31 January
1977.* ED 145 000 (Arlington, VA: ERIC, 1977).

2326. Gael, Sidney. *Development of Job Task Inventories and
Their Use in Job Analysis Research.* ED 143 984
(Washington, D. C.: American Psychological Association,
JSAS MS 1445, 1976).

2327. Gandy, Gerald L. "The Development of a Psychological-
vocational Evaluation Referral Instrument." *Psychology: A
Quarterly Journal of Human Behavior* 16(20: 47-50 (1979).

2328. Gavin, Anne T. *Guide to the Development of Written Tests
for Selection and Promotion: The Content Validity Model.
Technical Memorandum 77-6.* ED 152 853 (Arlington, VA:
ERIC, 1977).

2329. Goldstein, Harris K. *The Development of an Instrument to
Measure Casework Knowledge, the Tulane Assessment Scale
for Caseworkers.* ED 003 675 (Arlington, VA: ERIC, 1965).

2330. Gorth, William Phillip and Hariharan Swaminathan.
*Criterion-referenced Item Banking in Electronics:
Appendix G. Final Report.* ED 097 414 (Arlington, VA:
ERIC, 1972).

2331. Gould, R. Bruce. *Air Force Officer Qualifying Test Form
N: Development and Standardization. Final Report for
Period March 1974 - March 1978.* ED 166 241 (Arlington,
VA: ERIC, 1978).

2332. Gray, H. Dean and others. *Career Education Readiness
Test. Final Report.* ED 167 703 (Arlington, VA: ERIC,
1978).

2333. Hales, L. W. and B. Fenner. "Work Values of 5th, 8th, and
11th Grade Students: Ohio Work Values Test." *Vocational
Guidance Quarterly* 20: 199-203 (1972).

2334. Hartz, John and others. *The Systems Approach to
Assessment and Evaluation of Post Secondary Vocational
Education Programs. Employability Inventory: Findings and
Analyses.* ED 164 994 (Arlington, VA: ERIC, 1978). For
related information see ED 164 991.

2335. Hecht, James T. *The Development and Structure of
Professional Examinations Planned for National Use.* Paper
presented at the annual meeting of the National Council
on Measurement in Education, 1979. ED 171 799 (Arlington,
VA: ERIC, 1979).

2336. Hoots, William R. Jr. *The Development of an Evaluation
Scheme for Career Education in the Middle Grades. Final
Report.* ED 113 451 (Arlington, VA: ERIC, 1973).

2337.   Humphry, Betty. Development and Analysis of a Taped and
        Written Test for Guidance Counselors: A Pilot Study. ED
        081 782 (Arlington, VA: ERIC, 1973).

2338.   Jacobsen, Kaare and Harry N. Drier Jr. The Comprehensive
        Career Education Staff Development Questionnaire. A
        Multidimensional Attitude Scale. Attitudes Assessment
        Instrument. Attitudes Toward Career Education Series. ED
        115 992 (Columbus, OH: Center for Vocational Education,
        Ohio State University, 1974).

2339.   Kazanas, H. D. and L. D. Kieft. An Experimental Project
        to Determine More Effective Vocational Teacher
        Certification Procedures in Michigan by Competency
        Examinations. Final Report of Phase I. ED 013 884
        (Arlington, VA: ERIC, 1966).

2340.   Landman, Janet T. and others. "Measuring Life Skills of
        Adolescents: Tests for Everyday Living (TEL)."
        Measurement and Evaluation in Guidance 13(2): 95-106
        (1980).

2341.   Linehan, Jean D. A Chance to Get Ahead: Proficiency
        Examinations for Clinical Laboratory Personnel. Final
        Report. ED 097 381 (Arlington, VA: ERIC, 1974).

2342.   McFadden, Dennis. Development and Utilization of a
        National Vocational-technical School Achievement Testing
        Program Using the Printing Trades as a Pilot Area. Final
        Report. ED 016 850 (Arlington, VA: ERIC, 1967).

2343.   McKillip, Richard H. and others. The Professional and
        Administrative Career Examination: Research and
        Development. Personnel Research Report 77-1. ED 159 179
        (Arlington, VA: ERIC, 1977).

2344.   McLaurin, William A. and others. Rationale for and
        Development of a Battery of Performance Tests for
        Vocational Selection. ED 079 391 (Arlington, VA: ERIC,
        1973).

2345.   Maguire, Thomas O. and others. Development of Scales on
        Attitudes Towards the World of Work. ED 171 956
        (Arlington, VA: ERIC, 1979).

2346.   _____. Development of Scales on Attitudes Towards the
        World of Work. (Executive Summary.) ED 171 955
        (Arlington, VA: ERIC, 1979).

2347.   Maier, Milton H. and Edmund F. Fuchs. An Improved
        Differential Army Classification System. ED 070 933
        (Springfield, VA: National Technical Information Service,
        1972).

2348.   Maier, Milton H. and Stephen F. Hirshfeld. Criterion-
        referenced Job Proficiency Testing: A Large Scale
        Application. Research Report 1193. ED 161 953 (Arlington,
        VA: ERIC, 1978).

2349.   Malgady, Robert G. and Peter R. Barcher. "The Vocational
        Adaptation Rating Scales." Applied Research in Mental

Retardation 3(4): 335-44 (1982).

2350. Mannen, Howard A. and Richard C. Willing, ed. _Current Research Techniques in Military Personnel Assessment_. ED 049 445 (Springfield, VA: National Technical Information Service, 1970).

2351. _Manual for the USES Basic Occupational Literacy Test. Section 2: Development_. ED 170 343 (Arlington, VA: ERIC, 1972).

2352. _Measuring Student Achievement in Health Occupations Education_. ED 139 818 (Arlington, VA: ERIC, 1976).

2353. Mietus, Walter S. "The Development of an Instrument Measuring Values Associated with Work." _Journal of Industrial Teacher Education_ 14(4): 63-72 (1977).

2354. Mietus, Walter S. and Robert Gnidziejko. _A Comparison Work Values Held by Students, Parents and Teachers. Final Report_. Volume I. ED 133 506 (Arlington, VA: ERIC, 1975).

2355. Miller, Gary G. and Wayne S. Sellman. _Development of Psychometric Measures of Student Attitudes Toward Technical Training: Norm Group Report_. ED 099 420 (Arlington, VA: ERIC, 1973).

2356. Miller, Robert E. _Development and Standardization of the Air Force Officer Qualifying Test Form L_. ED 076 858 (Springfield, VA: National Technical Information Service, 1972).

2357. _____. _Development and Standardization of the Air Force Officer Qualifying Test Form M_. ED 109 203 (Arlington, VA: ERIC, 1974).

2358. Mitchell, Jimmy L. and Ernest J. McCormick. _Development of the PMPQ: A Structural Job Analysis Questionnaire for the Study of Professional and Managerial Positions. PMPQ Report No. 1_. ED 183 575 (Arlington, VA: ERIC, 1979).

2359. Moore, Earl and Frank Wellman. _Field Validation of the Career Education Curriculum Project Modules. Phase II. K-6 Validation. Final Report. Part I_. ED 177 282 (Arlington, VA: ERIC, 1978).

2360. _____. _Field Validation of the Career Education Curriculum Project Modules. Phase II. 7-12 Instrument Development. Final Report. Part II_. ED 177 283 (Arlington, VA: ERIC, 1978).

2361. Morrell, Dale L. _The Development of Vocational Modules and an Evaluative Instrument at Readability Levels Which are Comprehensible by all Students in the High School Vocational Program. Final Report_. ED 146 400 (Arlington, VA: ERIC, 1977).

2362. Muratti, Jose E. and others. _Developing Parallel Career and Occupational Development Objectives and Exercise (Test) Items in Spanish for Assessment and Evaluation_. ED 182 320 (Arlington, VA: ERIC, 1979).

2363. Norris, Dwight R. and James A. Buford Jr. "A Content Valid Writing Test: A Case Study." Personnel Administrator 25(1): 40-44 (1980).

2364. Occupational Competency Tests, Procedures and Instructions for Construction or Revision. ED 018 547 (Arlington, VA: ERIC, 1962).

2365. Oliver, J. Dale. "Measuring Outcomes in Performance-based Instruction." Performance and Instruction 19(10): 8-10 (1980).

2366. Osborn, William C. Developing Performance Tests for Training Evaluation. Paper presented at the U.S. Continental Army Command Training Workshop, 1971. ED 077 934 (Arlington, VA: ERIC, 1973).

2367. _____. "Framework for Performance Testing." Training in Business and Industry 11(5): 28-31 (1974).

2368. Osborn, William C. and J. Patrick Ford. Research on Methods of Synthetic Performance Testing. Final Report. ED 170 346 (Arlington, VA: ERIC, 1976).

2369. Panitz, Adolf and C. Thomas Olivo. National Occupational Competency Testing Project. A Consortium for Occupational Competency Testing of Trade and Industrial/Technical Teachers. Phase I: Planning--Organizing--Pilot Testing. Volume 3, Handbook for Developing and Administering Occupational Competency Tests. ED 057 217 (Arlington, VA: ERIC, 1971).

2370. _____. National Occupational Competency Testing Project. A Consortium for Occupational Competency Testing of Trade and Industrial/Technical Teachers. Phase II. Directions for: Area Test Center Coordination, Test Development, and Test Administration. ED 057 218 (Arlington, VA: ERIC, 1970).

2371. _____. The State of the Art of Occupational Competency Testing. National Occupational Competency Testing Project, Volume 2, Phase One. ED 051 378 (Arlington, VA: ERIC, 1970).

2372. Parry-Hill, J. W. Jr. The Initial Development and Validation of a Short Form Occupational Analysis Inventory Based on Systematically Derived Work Dimensions. Toward an Educational System Articulated with Adult Society. ED 149 136 (Arlington, VA: ERIC, 1975).

2373. Percival, Robert R. "A Competency-measurement Instrument for Evaluating School Counselors." Ed.D. diss., North Texas State University, 1974. ED 108 097. Available from University Microfilms, Ann Arbor, MI.

2374. Primoff, Ernest S. Application of Job Element (J-scale) Method to Job Analysis and Selection of Inspectors. Paper presented at the annual meeting of the American Psychological Association, 1958. ED 061 260 (Arlington, VA: ERIC, 1958).

2375. Reagles, Kenneth W. and others. "Development of a Scale of Client Satisfaction for Clients Receiving Vocational Rehabilitation Counseling Services." Rehabilitation Research and Practice Review 3(2): 15-22 (1972).

2376. Reardon, F. and others. "Development and Evaluation of an Occupational Inventory." Journal of Educational Measurement 9: 151-3 (1972).

2377. Remer, Rory. The Development of an Instrument to Provide Performance Predictive Information for Counselor Trainee Selection: Phase I. Paper presented at the annual meeting of the American Educational Research Association, 1974. ED 103 448 (Arlington, VA: ERIC, 1973).

2378. Remer, Rory and William Sease. "The Development of a Criterion Instrument for Counselor Selection." Measurement and Evaluation in Guidance 7(3): 181-7 (1974).

2379. Rice, Linda Maxwell and others. Student Assessment System. Domain Referenced Tests. Cosmetology. Volume I: Skills. Georgia Vocational Education Program Articulation. ED 197 133 (Arlington, VA: ERIC, 1980).

2380. Richardson, Bill K. and others. Development and Evaluation of Example-anchored Scales of Interpersonal Functioning for Rehabilitation Counseling Research. ED 094 286 (Arlington, VA: ERIC, 1972).

2381. Roberts, Robert C. and others. Development of an Instrument for Prescribing Compensatory Education for Vocational Trainees. Vocational Education Project. Final Report. ED 112 058 (Arlington, VA: ERIC, 1976).

2382. Roby, Wallace R. and William Juzwic. Developing and Testing an Instrument to Assess Performance Skills That are Important in a Variety of Occupations. Final Report. ED 177 329 (Arlington, VA: ERIC, 1978).

2383. Ross, Raymond J. Development of Examinations for Assessment of Occupational Competency. Final Report. ED 086 861 (Arlington, VA: ERIC, 1973).

2384. Seeley, Leonard C. and others. Development of the Armed Services Vocational Aptitude Battery (ASVAB) Forms 2 and 3. Technical Paper 289. ED 161 913 (Arlington, VA: ERIC, 1978).

2385. Shill, James F. and others. Development and Testing of Criteria for the Identification and Selection of Mentally Handicapped Students for Vocational Programs (and) a Review of Related Literature Concerning Components of Systems and Studies that Impact on Identification and Selection of EMRS and Slow Learners for Vocational Programs (and) VERT: Vocational Education Readiness Test. Final Report. ED 170 467 (Arlington, VA: ERIC, 1978).

2386. Skaff, L. B. "Development of a Shorthand Aptitude Test." Business Education Forum 27: 26-8 (October 1972).

2387. Spirer, Janet E., ed. Performance Testing: Issues Facing Vocational Education. Research and Development Series No. 190. ED 187 930 (Arlington, VA: ERIC, 1980).

2388. Stuit, Dewey. Personnel Research and Test Development. (Princeton: Princeton University Press, 1947).

2389. Super, D. E. and J. M. Kidd. "Vocational Maturity in Adulthood: Toward Turning a Model into a Measure." Journal of Vocational Behavior 14: 255-70 (June 1979).

2390. Swanson, Leonard and Bernard Rimland. A Preliminary Evaluation of Brief Navy Enlisted Classification Tests. ED 087 810. Available from NTIS. (1970).

2391. Tittle, Carol Kehr and Donald G. Zytowski, eds. Sex-fair Interest Measurement: Research and Implications. ED 166 416 (Arlington, VA: ERIC, 1978).

2392. U. S. Army Training Support Center, Individual Training and Evaluation Directorate. Guidelines for Development of Skill Qualification Tests. (Fort Eustis, VA: Author, 1977).

2393. Westbrook, Bert W. and Joseph W. Parry-Hill Jr. "The Measurement of Cognitive Vocational Maturity." Journal of Vocational Behavior 3(3): 239-51 (1973).

2394. Westbrook, Bert W. and Marjorie M. Mastie. "Three Measures of Vocational Maturity: A Beginning to Know About." Measurement and Evaluation in Guidance 6(1): 8-16 (1973).

2395. Westbrook, Bert W. and others. "The Development of a Measure of Vocational Maturity." Educational and Psychological Measurement 31(2): 541-43 (1971).

2396. _____. "An Instrument to Measure Vocational Maturity." Educational and Psychological Measurement 32(4): 1131-3 (1972). For related information see ED 101 145.

2397. Wilson, Clark L. and others. A Manual for Use in the Preparation and Administration of Practical Performance Tests. ED 069 713 (Arlington, VA: ERIC, 1971).

CAREERS AND INTERESTS

2398. Akamine, Toshio and Harold G. Heiner. Development of an Experimental Forced-choice Occupational Preference Inventory. Report No. 23. Final Report. ED 022 959 (Arlington, VA: ERIC, 1968).

2399. Alley, William E. and others. Development of Factor-referenced Subscales for the Vocational Interest-career Examination. Interim Report for Period January 1975-January 1976. ED 156 721 (Arlington, VA: ERIC, 1977).

2400. Athanasou, James A. Vocational Interest Survey--Six Scales for the Measurement of Holland's Vocational Typology. Research Report. ED 223 643 (Arlington, VA:

ERIC, 1982).

2401.   Becker, Ralph L. "Vocational Choice: An Inventory
        Approach." Education and Training of the Mentally
        Retarded 8(3): 128-36 (1973).

2402.   Begin, Luc. "The Canadian Occupational Interest
        Inventory." School Guidance Worker 32(4): 38-41 (1977).

2403.   Bernknopf, Stanley and others. "Developing a Needs-based
        Guidance System: A Psychometric Approach." Measurement
        and Evaluation in Guidance 8(3): 180-86 (1975).

2404.   Bledsoe, Joseph C. and Donald H. Dalton. "Construction
        and Validation of the Dalton Vocational Importance
        Questionnaire: A Test of Ginzberg's Theory of
        Occupational Choice." Perceptual and Motor Skills 51(10):
        215-19 (1980).

2405.   Butzow, John W. and Clarence M. Williams. "The Content
        and Construct Validation of the Academic-vocational
        Involvement Scale." Educational and Psychological
        Measurement 33(2): 495-8 (1973).

2406.   Campbell, David P. Some Desirable Characteristics of
        Interest Inventories. Paper presented at the American
        Personnel and Guidance Association Convention, 1969. ED
        033 417 (Arlington, VA: ERIC, 1969).

2407.   Campbell, David P. and others. "A New Edition of the
        SVIB: The Strong-Campbell Interest Inventory."
        Measurement and Evaluation in Guidance 7(2): 92-5 (1974).

2408.   A Career Planning Inventory for Adults. April 1, 1978-
        June 30, 1979. ED 178 707 (Arlington, VA: ERIC, 1979).

2409.   C.A.S.E.S. (Career Awareness for Secondary and Elementary
        Students) Testing Instrument: Final Report. ED 097 513
        (Arlington, VA: ERIC, 1973).

2410.   D'Costa, Ayres G. The Development of a Vocational
        Interest Survey Using the Data-People-Things Model of
        Work. Paper presented at the American Personnel and
        Guidance Association Convention, 1969. ED 033 385
        (Arlington, VA: ERIC, 1969).

2411.   Droege, Robert C. and John Hawk. "Development of a U.S.
        Employment Service Interest Inventory." Journal of
        Employment Counseling 14(2): 65-71 (1977).

2412.   Echternacht, Gary J. and others. Development and Validity
        of a Vocational and Occupational Interest Inventory. ED
        095 213 (Arlington, VA: ERIC, 1973).

2413.   _____. Stage I: Development of VOICE. ED 090 245
        (Arlington, VA: ERIC, 1973).

2414.   Elton, Charles F. and Harriet A. Rose. "A Vocational
        Interest Test Minus Sex Bias." Journal of Vocational
        Behavior 7(2): 204-14 (1975).

2415. Fadale, Laverna M. <u>Career Awareness of Elementary School Children</u>. Paper presented at the annual meeting of the American Educational Research Association, 1974. ED 109 210 (Arlington, VA: ERIC, 1974).

2416. _____. <u>An Instrument to Determine Career Awareness</u>. ED 082 061 (Arlington, VA: ERIC, 1973).

2417. Fadale, Laverna M. and others. <u>Career Education Concept Inventory</u>. ED 087 869 (Arlington, VA: ERIC, 1974).

2418. Figel, William J. <u>Developing an Academic Ability Scale for the Kuder Occupational Interest Survey</u>. Paper presented at the American Personnel and Guidance Association meeting, 1973. ED 078 000 (Arlington, VA: ERIC, 1973).

2419. Hansen, Jo-Ida C. "Exploring New Directions for Strong-Campbell Interest Inventory Occupational Scale Construction." <u>Journal of Vocational Behavior</u> 9(2): 147-60 (1976).

2420. Harmon, Lenore W. <u>Technical Aspects: Problems of Scale Development, Norms, Item Differences by Sex, and the Rate of Change in Occupational Group Characteristics</u>. ED 095 371 (Arlington, VA: ERIC, 1974).

2421. Holland, John L. <u>An Introductory Guide to the Community College Guidance Profile (CCGP)</u>. ED 032 573 (Iowa City, Iowa: American College Testing Program, 1968).

2422. Impellitteri, Joseph T. and Jerome T. Kapes. <u>The Measurement of Occupational Values</u>. ED 059 357 (Arlington, VA: ERIC, 1971).

2423. Jeffs, George A. <u>Occupational Aspiration Scale for Females</u>. ED 019 404 (Arlington, VA: ERIC, 1963).

2424. Jensen, Harald E. and others. <u>Armed Services Vocational Aptitude Battery Development (ASVAB Forms 5, 6, and 7). Final Report 1 July 1974-30 November 1976</u>. ED 146 212 (Arlington, VA: ERIC, 1976).

2425. Juni, S. and E. J. Kloenig. "Contingency Validity as a Requirement in Forced-choice Item Construction: A Critique of the Jackson Vocational Interest Survey." <u>Measurement and Evaluation in Guidance</u> 14: 202-7 (January 1982).

2426. Lokan, Janice J. <u>The Development and Preliminary Evaluation of an Instrument to Measure the Vocational Interests of Low-reading High School Students</u>. Paper presented at the annual conference of the National Council for Measurement in Education, 1973. ED 078 012 (Arlington, VA: ERIC, 1973).

2427. Lunneborg, Patricia W. "The Vocational Interest Inventory: Development and Validation." <u>Educational and Psychological Measurement</u> 39(2): 445-51 (1979).

2428. Meir, Elchanan I. and Azy Barak. "A Simple Instrument for

Measuring Vocational Interests Based on Roe's Classification of Occupations." _Journal of Vocational Behavior_ 4(1): 33-41 (1974).

2429. Meir, Elchanan I. and others. "Interest Inventories Based on Roe's Classification Modified for Negative Respondents." _Journal of Vocational Behavior_ 7(1): 127-33 (1975).

2430. Mitchell, Sandra K. and others. _A Vocational Interest Inventory Based on Roe's Interest Areas_. ED 054 209 (Arlington, VA: ERIC, 1971).

2431. _A New Counselee Assessment/Occupational Exploration System and Its Interest and Aptitude Dimensions_. ED 201 741 (Arlington, VA: ERIC, 1981).

2432. Reilly, Richard R. and Gary J. Echternacht. "Some Problems with the Criterion-keying Approach to Occupational Interest Scale Development." _Educational and Psychological Measurement_ 39(1): 85-94 (1979).

2433. _____. "Validation and Comparison of Homogeneous and Occupational Interest Scales." _Applied Psychological Measurement_ 3(2): 177-85 (1979).

2434. _Technical Report for the Unisex Edition of the ACT Interest Inventory (UNIACT)_. ED 224 814 (Arlington, VA: ERIC, 1981).

2435. Thomas, Hollie B. _A Measure of Career Development Responsibility_. Paper presented at the annual conference of the National Council on Measurement in Education, 1974. ED 093 935 (Arlington, VA: ERIC, 1974).

2436. Tuttle, Thomas C. and others. _Dimensions of Job Satisfaction: Initial Development of the Air Force Occupational Attitude Inventory. Interim Report, 1 July 1972-30 June 1974_. ED 112 146 (Arlington, VA: ERIC, 1975).

2437. Weis, Susan F. and Constance Hubbard. "The Vocational Commitment Index." _Home Economics Research Journal_ 2(2): 105-11 (1973). For related information see ED 090 292.

2438. Young, Darius Robert. "The Development of a Construction Industry Interest Inventory." Ph.D. diss., Ohio State University, 1968. ED 025 620. Available from University Microfilms, Ann Arbor, MI.

MECHANICAL ABILITY

2439. Ebbert, J. Marvin. "The Development of a Standardized Achievement Test for Small Gasoline Engine Instruction." Ph.D. diss., Purdue University, 1964. ED 020 367 (Ann Arbor: University Microfilms, 1964).

2440. Kaltsounis, George L. and others. _The National Aptitude Survey. Formal Report and Test Manual_. ED 018 835 (Arlington, VA: ERIC, 1968).

2441. McKnight, A. James and others. The Development of Job-oriented Examinations for Postal Equipment Maintenance Positions: Subtask Report. ED 113 533 (Arlington, VA: ERIC, 1969).

SELECTION AND RATING FORMS

2442. Abbatiello, Aurelius. "Technical Manual Editor Analysis Profile: Test Construction and Preliminary Standardization for Personnel Selection." Ph.D. diss., Loyola University of Chicago, 1958.

2443. Allen, Ted W. and others. An Information Processing Approach to Performance Assessment: III. An Elaboration and Refinement of an Information Processing Performance Battery. Technical Report No. 3, November 16, 1977 Through November 30, 1978. ED 171 736 (Arlington, VA: ERIC, 1978).

2444. Backman, Margaret E. The Development of Micro-tower: A Battery of Standardized Work Samples for Assessing Vocational Aptitudes. Paper presented at the Department of Rehabilitation Services Education Conference, 1977. ED 152 834 (Arlington, VA: ERIC, 1977).

2445. Beach, D. P. and others. "Development and Possible Uses of an Inventory of Affective Worker Competencies." Journal of Industrial Teacher Education 20: 27-40 (1982).

2446. Bemis, S. E. and others. "Development of a New Occupational Aptitude Pattern Structure for the GATB." Vocational Guidance Quarterly 22: 130-5, 189-94 (December 1973-March 1974).

2447. Brown, William R., John A. Dohme and Michael O. Sanders. "Changes in the U.S. Army Aviator Selection and Training Program." Aviation, Space, & Environmental Medicine 53(12): 1173-76 (1982).

2448. Daniels, L. K. "Experimental Edition of a Rating Scale of Vocational Adjustment for the Mentally Retarded." Training School Bulletin 69: 92-8 (August 1972).

2449. Daniels, Lloyd K. and James A. Stewart. "Development of a Vocational Adjustment Rating Scale for the Mentally Retarded." Training School Bulletin 68(1): 10-4 (1971).

2450. Gibson, Dennis L. and others. Manual for the Minnesota Satisfactoriness Scales. Minnesota Studies in Vocational Rehabilitation: XXVII. ED 048 497 (Minneapolis: Work Adjustment Project, University of Minnesota, 1970).

SPECIFIC VOCATIONS

Computer Programming

2451. Palormo, Jean M. Computer Programmer Aptitude Battery, Manual. ED 012 876 (Chicago: Science Research Associates,

1967).

Dentistry

2452.   Kastrinos, William and Samuel A. Livingston. The
        Development of a Proficiency Examination for Dental
        Auxiliaries. ED 186 440 (Arlington, VA: ERIC, 1979).

2453.   Lee, Mickey M. and Andrew L. Sonis. Dental Students'
        Attitudes Toward the Handicapped Scale (DSATHS): A
        Standardized Instrument for Assessing Dental Students'
        Attitudes Toward the Handicapped. Paper presented at the
        International Association of Dentistry for the
        Handicapped Conference, 1982. ED 221 552 (Arlington, VA:
        ERIC, 1982).

2454.   Mathews, John J. and Harald E. Jensen. Screening Test.
        Battery for Dental Laboratory Specialist Course:
        Development and Validation. Final Report for Period July
        1974-June 1977. ED 151 425 (Arlington, VA: ERIC, 1977).

Engineering

2455.   Dennien, R. T. and others. "Devising Evaluation
        Instruments for Technological Problem Solving." Journal
        of Curriculum Studies 5(2): 122-32 (1973).

2456.   Lebold, William K. and others. The Purdue Interest
        Questionnaire--An Interest Inventory to Assist
        Engineering Students in Their Career Planning. Paper
        presented at the Annual Frontiers in Education Conference
        of the Institute of Electrical and Electronics Engineers
        and the American Society for Engineering Education, 1977.
        ED 170 312 (Arlington, VA: ERIC, 1977).

2457.   Michael, William B. and Kenneth R. Colson. "The
        Development and Validation of a Life Experience Inventory
        for the Identification of Creative Electrical Engineers."
        Educational and Psychological Measurement 39(2): 463-70
        (1979).

Law

2458.   Gunderson, D. F. and Robert Hopper. Screening Applicants
        for Employment in Law Enforcement. Paper presented at the
        annual meeting of the Communication Association, 1974. ED
        102 435 (Arlington, VA: ERIC, 1974).

Medicine

2459.   Alfici, C. and others. Test de Evaluacion de
        Conocimientos Medicos-CIIPME (Test of Evaluation of
        Medical Knowledge-CIIPME). Publication No. 42. ED 118 639
        (Arlington, VA: ERIC, 1975).

2460.   Andrew, Barbara J. A Methodology for the Development of
        Examinations to Assess the Proficiency of Health Care

Professionals. ED 084 280 (Arlington, VA: ERIC, 1974).

2461. Andrew, Barbara J. and others. National Program for the Evaluation of Primary Care. Physician's Assistants. Final Report. ED 134 678 (Arlington, VA: ERIC, 1976).

2462. An Audiovisual Teaching Module to Assist Examiners in the Administration of a Practical Performance Examination for the Emergency Medical Technician-Ambulance (EMT-A). Consisting of a 90-minute Audiovisual Presentation in Either 16MM Sound or 3/4" Video-cassette Plus a "User's Guide" Describing in Detail the Total Examination Procedure. Final Report. ED 161 948 (Arlington, VA: ERIC, 1977).

2463. Campbell, Gene and Bruce Simpson. Student Assessment System. Domain Referenced Tests. Allied Health Occupations/Practical Nursing. Volume II: Theory. ED 197 131 (Arlington, VA: ERIC, 1980).

2464. Crawford, William R. Assessing Performance When the Stakes are High. Paper presented at American Educational Research Association Convention, 1970. ED 037 785 (Arlington, VA: ERIC, 1970).

2465. Delineation of Roles and Functions of Diagnostic Radiologic Technology Personnel and Development of Proficiency Tests; Final Report. ED 123 242 (Arlington, VA: ERIC, 1974).

2466. Development of Occupational Therapy Proficiency Examinations, Therapist Level, Assistant Level. Final Report. ED 174 443 (Arlington, VA: ERIC, 1975).

2467. Development of Proficiency Examinations and Procedures for Two Levels of Respiratory Therapy Personnel. Final Report. ED 128 383 (Arlington, VA: ERIC, 1974).

2468. Erviti, Vivian and others. The Development of Rating Scales to Assess the Performance of Medical Students in Clinical Settings. Paper presented at the annual meeting of the American Association of Medical Colleges, 1979. ED 186 458 (Arlington, VA: ERIC, 1979).

2469. Final Report of an Expansion of a Model for Development of Proficiency/Equivalency Tests for Clinical Laboratory Personnel, July 1, 1980-June 30, 1981. ED 206 880 (Arlington, VA: ERIC, 1981).

2470. Grussing, Paul G. and others. "Development of Behaviorally-anchored Rating Scales for Pharmacy Practice." American Journal of Pharmaceutical Education 43(2): 115-20 (1979).

2471. Holloway, Richard L. "The Development of a Domain-referenced Test of Pharmacy Competence." American Journal of Pharmaceutical Education 43(2): 112-14 (1979).

2472. Jouett, Michael L. The Internal Validation of Level II and Level III Respiratory Therapy Examinations. Final Report. ED 128 464 (Arlington, VA: ERIC, 1976).

2473. Meyer, Thomas. A Feasibility Study in Determining Individual Practice Profiles of Physicians as a Basis for Continuing Education of These Physicians Utilizing a Postgraduate Perceptor Technique. Final Report. ED 052 299 (Arlington, VA: ERIC, 1970).

2474. Newble, David I. "The Development and Assessment of a New Examination of the Clinical Competence of Medical Students." Assessment and Evaluation in Higher Education 7(3): 216-24 (1982).

2475. Pancorbo, Salvador and others. "Development of an Evaluative Procedure for Clinical Clerkships." American Journal of Pharmaceutical Education 44(1): 12-16 (1980).

2476. Pike, Lewis W. and others. Prediction of Job Performance for Negro and White Medical Technicians; Development of the Instrumentation. ED 035 013 (Arlington, VA: ERIC, 1969).

2477. Sivertson, Sigurd E. "Computerized Test Bank for Clinical Medicine." Educational Technology 13(3): 38-9 (1973).

2478. Smith, Harry A. and Edward Kifer. "Student Evaluation in an Externship Using the Rasch Model." American Journal of Pharmaceutical Education 44(1): 6-11 (1980).

2479. Smull, Ned W. and others. A Profile Examination System for Physician Extenders and a Method for Curricular Prescription. Final Report. ED 148 900 (Arlington, VA: ERIC, 1977).

2480. Sturges, Jack and Patricia Quina. An Instrument to Predict Job Performance of Home Health Aides--Testing the Reliability and Validity. ED 120 198 (Arlington, VA: ERIC, 1971).

2481. Synder, John R. and Jana C. Wilson. "Evaluation of Student Performance in the Clinical Setting Using the Process Skills Approach." Journal of Allied Health 9(2): 125-31 (1980).

Miscellaneous

2482. Brekke, Milo L. Instrumentation to Assess Readiness for Ministry. Paper presented at the Adult Education Research Conference, 1978. ED 152 798 (Arlington, VA: ERIC, 1976).

Nursing

2483. Baltz, Terry M. and Joseph G. Turner. "Development and Analysis of a Nursing Home Aide Screening Device." Gerontologist 17(1): 66-9 (1977).

2484. Gross, Linda C. and Catherine W. Bevil. "The Use of Testing to Modify Curricula for RNs." Nursing Outlook 29(9): 541-45 (1981).

2485. Student Performance Evaluation: The Hidden Agenda in

Nursing Education. Conference Proceedings. Paper
presented at the 2nd Regional Conference, 1978. ED 173
392 (Arlington, VA: ERIC, 1979).

Sales

2486.   Saxe, Robert and Barton A. Weitz. "The SOCO Scale: A
        Measure of the Customer Orientation of Salespeople."
        Journal of Marketing Research 19(3): 343-51 (1982).

Addendum

TEST CONSTRUCTION

2487. Arter, Judith A. Two Case Studies of Local Test Development. ED 266 169 (Arlington, VA: ERIC, 1985).

2488. Arter, Judith A. and Gary D. Estes. Item Banking for Local Test Development: Practitioner's Handbook. ED 266 166 (Arlington, VA: ERIC, 1985).

2489. Barman, Charles R. "The Development of Computer-based Piagetian Assessment Instruments." Journal of Research and Development in Education 19: 29-32 (summer 1986).

2490. Bowers, John J. Database Management for Item Banking and Test Development: An Application of dBase II for the Microcomputer. ED 246 088 (Arlington, VA: ERIC, 1984).

2491. Brightman, Harvey J. and others. "Constructing and Using Computer-based Formative Tests." Educational Technology 24(6): 36-38 (1984).

2492. Brzezinski, Evelyn J. "Microcomputers and Testing: Where Are We and How Did We Get There." Educational Measurement: Issues and Practice 3(2): 7-10 (1984).

2493. Burns, Joseph C., James R. Okey and Kevin C. Wise. "Development of an Integrated Process Skill Test: TIPS II." Journal of Research in Science Teaching 22(2): 169-77 (1985).

2494. Choppin, Bruce. "Item Banking Using Sample Free Calibration." Evaluation in Education: An International Review Series 9(1): 81-85 (1985).

2495. _____. "Principles of Item Banking." Evaluation in Education: An International Review Series 9(1): 87-90 (1985).

2496. Clark, Julia H. "Racial Test Bias: An Artifact of Test Development Methodology?" Dissertation Abstracts International 46(3-A): 652 (1985).

2497. Deck, Dennis and others. Reviews of Microcomputer Item

Banking Software. ED 266 167 (Arlington, VA: ERIC, 1985).

2498.   Doron, Rina. The "Average System" -- A New Technique for Equating Scores on Different Tests Constructed from an Item Bank. ED 264 288 (Arlington, VA: ERIC, 1984).

2499.   Driscoll, Marcy Perkins and Martin Tessmer. "The Rational Set Generator: A Method for Creating Concept Examples for Teaching and Testing." _Educational Technology_ 25: 29-32 (1985).

2500.   Estes, Gary D. and Judith A. Arter. Item Banking for State and Local Test Development and Use: Specific Guidelines for Local Practitioners. ED 242 763 (Arlington, VA: ERIC, 1984).

2501.   Estes, Gary D., ed. Examples of Item Banks to Support Local Test Development: Two Case Studies With Reactions. ED 266 168 (Arlington, VA: ERIC, 1985).

2502.   Fleming, Margaret and Barbara Chambers. "Teacher-made Tests: Windows on the Classroom." _New Directions for Testing and Measurement_ 19: 29-38 (1983).

2503.   Frechtling, Joy A. and Margot A. Schenet. A Funny Thing Happened on the Way to the Printer: The Saga of Developing a Customized Test. ED 243 922 (Arlington, VA: ERIC, 1984).

2504.   Frederiksen, Norman. "Construct Validity and Construct Similarity: Methods for Use in Test Development and Test Validation. 20th International Congress of Applied Psychology (1982, Edinburgh, Scotland)." _Multivariate Behavioral Research_ 21(1): 3-28 (1986).

2505.   Fremer, John. "Using Microcomputers to Develop Tests: An Alternate Point of View." _Educational Measurement: Issues & Practice_ 3(2): 14-15 (1984).

2506.   Gable, Robert K. Instrument Development in the Affective Domain. (Boston: Kluwer-Nijhoff Publishing, 1986).

2507.   Garg, Rashmi and others. "A Comparison of Examinee Sampling and Multiple Matrix Sampling in Test Development." _Journal of Educational Measurement_ 23(2): 119-30 (1986).

2508.   Guliksen, Harold. Creating Better Classroom Tests. ED 268 149 (Arlington, VA: ERIC, 1985).

2509.   Haksar, Lucy. "Design and Usage of an Item Bank." _Programmed Learning and Educational Technology_ 20(4): 253-62 (1983).

2510.   Haladyna, Thomas M. and Gale H. Roid. "A Comparison of Two Approaches to Criterion-referenced Test Construction." _Journal of Educational Measurement_ 20(3): 271-82 (1983).

2511.   _____ . "Reviewing Criterion-Referenced Test Items." _Educational Technology_ 23(8): 35-38 (1983).

2512. Haladyna, Thomas M. and Steven M. Downing. A Quantitative Review of Research on Multiple-Choice Item Writing. ED 255 580 (Arlington, VA: ERIC, 1985).

2513. Hambleton, Ronald K. "Using Microcomputers to Develop Tests." Educational Measurement: Issues & Practice 3(2): 10-14 (1984).

2514. Hambleton, Ronald K. and others. "Applications of Microcomputers to Classroom Testing." New Directions for Testing and Measurement; (Testing in the Schools) 19: 65-77 (1983).

2515. Hammer, Carol. "Writing Better Essay Questions." Clearing House 59: 298 (March 1986).

2516. Hanson, Ralph A. and others. "Differences in Instructional Sensitivity Between Item Formats and Between Achievement Test Items." Journal of Educational Measurement 23(1): 1-12 (1986).

2517. Herman, Joan. Guidelines for Developing Diagnostic Tests. Methodology Project. ED 252 559 (Arlington, VA: ERIC, 1984).

2518. _____. A Practical Approach to Local Test Development. Resource Paper No. 6. Research Into Practice Project. ED 252 563 (Arlington, VA: ERIC, 1984).

2519. Herman, Joan and Lynn Winters. Test Design Manual: Guidelines for Developing Diagnostic Tests. Diagnostic Testing Project. ED 266 159 (Arlington, VA: ERIC, 1985).

2520. Kolen, Michael J. and David Jarjoura. "Item Profile Analysis for Tests Developed According to a Table of Specifications." Applied Psychological Measurement 8(3): 321-31 (1984).

2521. Kolstad, Rosemarie K. and Robert A. Kolstad. "A Common Misuse of Multiple Choice Test Items." Clearing House 58: 394 (May 1985).

2522. Kolstad, Rosemarie K., Donald R. Coker and R. Daniel Creider. "The Improvement of Testing Through Cooperation Between Teachers and Computer Personnel." Educational Technology 24: 36-8 (May 1984).

2523. Leary, Linda F. and Neil J. Dorans. "Implications for Altering the Context in Which Test Items Appear: A Historical Perspective on an Immediate Concern." Review of Educational Research 55: 387-413 (Fall 1985).

2524. McCallum, L. W. "CATGEN: A Computer Assisted Test Generator." Teaching of Psychology 12(1): 45-46 (1985).

2525. McMorris, Robert F. and others. "Effects of Incorporating Humor in Test Items." Journal of Educational Measurement 22(2): 147-55 (1985). See ED 230 588 for related information.

2526. Matter, M. Kevin and Glynn Ligon. Issues in Developing a

Local Minimum Competency Test: Our BEST Effort. ED 251 470 (Arlington, VA: ERIC, 1984).

2527. Miller, Patrick W. and Harley E. Erickson. Teacher-Written Student Tests: A Guide for Planning, Creating, Administering, and Assessing. (Washington, D.C.: National Education Association, 1985).

2528. Millman, Jason and Judith A. Arter. "Issues in Item Banking." Journal of Educational Measurement 21: 315-30 (winter 1984).

2529. Morrison, Perry R. "LIKERT: An Applesoft Program for the Construction, Administration, and Scoring of Likert Scales." Behavior Research Methods & Instrumentation 15(1): 97-98 (1983).

2530. Nitko, Anthony J. and Tse-Chi Hsu. "A Comprehensive Microcomputer System for Classroom Testing." Journal of Educational Measurement 21: 377-90 (winter 1984).

2531. O'Brien, Michael and John P. Hampilos. The Feasibility of Creating an Item Bank From a Teacher-made Test Using the Rasch Model. ED 259 005 (Arlington, VA: ERIC, 1984).

2532. Oosterhof, Albert C. and David F. Salisbury. "Some Measurement and Instruction Related Considerations Regarding Computer-assisted Testing." Educational Measurement: Issues and Practice 4(1): 19-23 (1985). See ED 247 258 for related information.

2533. Peiser, Carlos and Baruch Nevo. "Classic Versus Fixed Distractors in General Information Tests." Educational Technology 23: 30-2 (1983).

2534. Plake, Barbara S. and Renee M. Huntley. "Can Relevant Grammatical Cues Result in Invalid Test Items?" Educational & Psychological Measurement 44(3): 687-96 (1984).

2535. Plake, Barbara S., ed. Social and Technical Issues in Testing: Implications for Test Construction and Usage. (Hillsdale, N.J.: L. Erlbaum Associates, 1984).

2536. Quellmalz, Edys S. "Designing Writing Assessments: Balancing Fairness, Utility, and Cost." Educational Evaluation & Policy Analysis 6: 63-72 (spring 1984).

2537. Roeber, Edward D. "Using Microcomputers to Assess Achievement and Instruction." Educational Measurement: Issues and Practice 3(2): 27-28 (1984).

2538. Roid, Gale H. New Technologies in the Writing of Test Items. ED 255 566 (Arlington, VA: ERIC, 1984).

2539. Rose, Janet S. and others. Instructional Validity: Merging Curricular, Instructional and Test Development Issues. ED 247 306 (Arlington, VA: ERIC, 1984).

2540. Schott, Franz and others. "A General Procedure for the Construction of Content-valid Items for Goal-oriented

Teaching and Testing." Studies in Educational Evaluation 10(2): 179-89 (1984).

2541. Schuh, Allen J. "A Simplified Method of Test Construction From Traditional Methods of Item Analysis." Bulletin of the Psychonomic Society 22(6): 566-67 (1984).

2542. Schurr, K. Terry and L. W. Henriksen. "Effects of Item Sequencing and Grouping in Low-inference Type Questionnaires." Journal of Educational Measurement 20(4): 379-91 (1983).

2543. Silva, Sharron J. A Comparison of Traditional Approaches and Item Selection for Criterion-referenced Measurement. ED 261 076 (Arlington, VA: ERIC, 1985).

2544. Siskind, Teri G. and Janet S. Rose. CRT Development: An Overview of Why and How--One District's Perspective. ED 269 477 (Arlington, VA: ERIC, 1986).

2545. Teplitz, Charles. "Computer-assisted Test Construction for the Decision Sciences." Simulation & Games 14(3): 297-308 (1983).

2546. Theunissen, T. J. "Binary Programming and Test Design." Psychometrika 50(4): 411-20 (1985).

2547. Vittitoe, Ted W. and James V. Bradley. "A Teacher's Dream Come True -- A Simple Program for Writing Tests." American Biology Teacher 46(3): 178-82 (1984).

2548. Weiten, Wayne. "Violation of Selected Item Construction Principles in Educational Measurement." Journal of Experimental Education 52(3): 174-78 (1984).

2549. Willson, Victor L. and Cecil R. Reynolds. "Constructing Short Forms From Composite Tests: Reliability and Validity." Educational and Psychological Measurement 45: 469-75 (1985).

2550. Wright, Benjamin D. and Susan R. Bell. "Item Banks: What, Why, How." Journal of Educational Measurement 21: 331-45 (winter 1984).

2551. Written Test Construction. Vocational Instructor Teaching Skills Project. ED 262 232 (Arlington, VA: ERIC, 1985).

FINE ARTS

2552. Brand, Manny. "Development and Validation of the Home Musical Environment Scale for Use at the Early Elementary Level." Psychology of Music 13(1): 40-48 (1985).

2553. King, Alison. The Art Self-concept Inventory: Development and Validation of a Scale to Measure Self-concept in Art. ED 241 567 (Arlington, VA: ERIC, 1983).

2554. Nierman, Glenn E. "The Development of a Test of Verbal Descriptors in Music." Bulletin of the Council for

Research in Music Education 84: 20-33 (fall 1985).

2555. Olson, Ivan. "Measurement of Musical Awareness (Test)."
Bulletin of the Council for Research in Music Education
77: 31-42 (winter 1984).

2556. Sutton, Kenneth. "The Development and Implementation of a
Music Therapy Physiological Measures Test." The Journal
of Music Therapy 21: 160-9 (winter 1984).

FOREIGN LANGUAGES

2557. Cziko, Gary A. and Nien-Hsuan Jennifer Lin. The
Construction and Analysis of Short Scales of Language
Proficiency: Classical Psychometric, Latent Trait, and
Nonparametric Approaches. ED 243 949 (Arlington, VA:
ERIC, 1984).

2558. Ravid, Ruth. "Presentation of Procedures for Development
of a Second Language Achievement Test." Foreign Language
Annals 16(3): 201-5 (1983).

2559. Raymond, Mark R. and Dennis M. Roberts. "Development and
Validation of a Foreign Language Attitude Scale."
Educational & Psychological Measurement 43(4): 1239-46
(1983).

MATHEMATICS

2560. Blitch, Judith Y. "Development of an Instrument to
Measure Mathematics Attitude of Elementary Children."
Dissertation Abstracts International 46(4-A): 918 (1985).

2561. Collis, Kevin F. "Development of a Group Test of
Mathematical Understanding Using Superitem/SOLO
Technique." Journal of Science and Mathematics Education
in Southeast Asia 6(1): 5-14 (1983).

2562. Greenan, James P. "The Development and Validation of
Generalizable Mathematics Skills Assessment Instruments."
Journal of Vocational Education Research 9(3): 14-30
(1984). See ED 248 323 for related information.

2563. Wilmot, Barbara A. "The Design, Administration, and
Analysis of an Instrument Which Identifies Mathematically
Gifted Students in Grades Four, Five and Six."
Dissertation Abstracts International 44(6-A): 1718
(1983).

MISCELLANEOUS

Courtship and Marriage

2564. Alley, Patricia M. "The Family Responsibility Index: A
Behavioral Measure of Marital Work Allocation." Journal
of Personality Assessment 48(1): 3-5 (1984).

2565. Amruthraj, Brunda and Indira J. Prakash. "Development of
       a Marital Satisfaction Scale." Psychological Studies
       30(2): 124-26 (1985).

2566. Atkinson, Brent J. and Paul N. McKenzie. "The
       Personalized Spouse Observation Checklist: A Computer-
       generated Assessment of Marital Interaction." Journal of
       Marital and Family Therapy 10(4): 427-29 (1984).

2567. Bentivegna, Santo W. "Development of the Pre-marital Role
       Expectation Inventory II and Its Relationship to Marital
       Satisfaction." Dissertation Abstracts International
       43(8-B): 2700 (1983).

2568. Booth, Alan and others. "Measuring Marital Instability."
       Journal of Marriage and the Family 45(2): 387-93 (1983).

2569. King, Charles E. and Andrew Christensen. "The
       Relationship Events Scale: A Guttman Scaling of Progress
       in Courtship." Journal of Marriage and the Family 45(3):
       671-78 (1983).

2570. Miller, Philip C., Herbert M. Lefcourt and Edward E.
       Ware. "The Construction and Development of the Miller
       Marital Locus of Control Scale." Canadian Journal of
       Behavioral Science 15(3): 266-79 (1983).

2571. Pinto, Rodger P. and James G. Hollandsworth. "A Measure
       of Possessiveness in Intimate Relationships." Journal of
       Social & Clinical Psychology 2(3): 273-79 (1984).

2572. Waring, E. M. "The Measurement of Marital Intimacy."
       Journal of Marital and Family Therapy 10(2): 185-92
       (1984).

Education

2573. Adams, Gary L. "Using Empirical Item Sequencing in
       Developing the Comprehensive Test of Adaptive Behavior."
       Education (Chula Vista, Calif.) 106: 197-201 (winter
       1985).

2574. Blocher, Donald and others. "Development and Preliminary
       Validation of an Instrument to Measure Cognitive Growth."
       Counselor Education & Supervision 25(1): 21-30 (1985).

2575. Block, Barbara A. "The Development and Validation of an
       Instrument to Observe and Record Sexist Classroom
       Behavior of Home Economics Teachers." Dissertation
       Abstracts International 44(11-A): 3305-6 (1984).

2576. Blunt, Adrian. "Development of a Thurstone Scale for
       Measuring Attitudes Toward Adult Education." Adult
       Education Quarterly 34(1): 16-28 (1983).

2577. Bridges, K. Robert. "The Parent Education Design Scale:
       Development and Factor Structure." Educational and
       Psychological Measurement 45: 729-35 (winter 1985).

2578. Cassel, Russell N. and Susie L. Cassel. "Cassel Computer

Literacy Test (CMLRTC)." Journal of Instructional Psychology 11(1): 3-9 (1984).

2579. Clinton, Barbara Jeanne and others. "The Development and Validation of an Instrument to Assess Problem Identification Skills of Instructional Supervisors." Educational and Psychological Measurement 43(2): 581-86 (1983).

2580. Cohen, Allan S. Developing and Administering a State-wide Speech Placement Testing Program. ED 265 585 (Arlington, VA: ERIC, 1985).

2581. Conyers, John G. and others. Developing District Made Criterion Referenced Tests: A Standard of Excellence for Effective Schools. ED 256 039 (Arlington, VA: ERIC, 1984).

2582. Fraser, Barry J. and others. "Development of an Instrument for Assessing Classroom Psychosocial Environment at Universities and Colleges." Studies in Higher Education 11(1): 43-54 (1986).

2583. Hall, Eleanor G. and Landa L. Trentham. "The Development and Validation of a Gifted Student Screening Scale." Diagnostique 9(3): 161-71 (1984).

2584. Kamphaus, Randy W. and Cecil R. Reynolds. "Development and Structure of the Kaufman Assessment Battery for Children." Journal of Special Education 18(3): 213-28 (1984).

2585. Kane, Stephen M. "The Development and Utilization of an Instrument Designed to Measure Employer Satisfaction and Receptivity Towards the Concept of Cooperative Education." Journal of Cooperative Education 22(1): 11-20 (1985).

2586. Kumar, Dileep and S. P. Ahluwalia. "Development of Attitude Towards Educational Innovations Scale (AEIS)." Asian Journal of Psychology & Education 11(1): 28-31 (1983).

2587. Lam, Y. L. Jack. "Toward the Construction of a School Environment Instrument: A Conceptual Framework." Canadian Journal of Education 10: 362-82 (fall 1985).

2588. Matthews, Doris B. and Jim Frank Casteel. The Development of a Parent Attitudinal Questionnaire As a Measure of School Success. ED 230 587 (Arlington, VA: ERIC, 1983).

2589. Norris, Stephen P. and Ruth King. The Design of a Critical Thinking Test on Appraising Observations. Studies in Critical Thinking, Research Report No. 1. ED 260 083 (Arlington, VA: ERIC, 1984).

2590. Oddi, Lorys F. "Development and Validation of an Instrument to Identify Self-directed Continuing Learners." Adult Education Quarterly 36(2): 97-107 (1986).

2591.   Padilla, Michael J. and others. The Development and
        Validation of a Test of Basic Process Skills. ED 256 628
        (Arlington, VA: ERIC, 1985).

2592.   Pascale, Pietro J. and others. "The Development and
        Validation of an Elementary School Substitute Teacher
        Questionnaire." Educational and Psychological Measurement
        44(2): 507-11 (1984).

2593.   Peterson, Donovan and others. "Measurement of Teacher
        Performance: A Study in Instrument Development." Teaching
        and Teacher Education 1(1): 63-77 (1985).

2594.   Phelps, Joanne, Lynn Stempel and Gail Speck. "The
        Children's Handwriting Scale: A Diagnostic Tool." The
        Journal of Educational Research (Washington, D.C.) 79:
        46-50 (September/October 1985).

2595.   Prater, Doris. "The Development of a Criterion-referenced
        Test of Basic Writing Skills." Journal of Research &
        Development in Education 18(1): 12-16 (1984).

2596.   Reed, Jeffrey G. and others. The College Descriptive
        Index (C.D.I.): Development and Background Information.
        Technical Manual. ED 236 206 (Arlington, VA: ERIC, 1983).

2597.   _____. "Development of the College Descriptive Index: A
        Measure of Student Satisfaction." Measurement and
        Evaluation in Counseling and Development 17(2): 67-82
        (1984).

2598.   Rose, Janet S. and W. James Popham. Developing a
        Defensible Language Skills Test for Teachers. ED 247 292
        (Arlington, VA: ERIC, 1984).

2599.   Saracho, Olivia N. "Construction and Validation of the
        Play Rating Scale." Early Child Development & Care 17(2-
        3): 119-230 (1984).

2600.   Saur, Rosemary E. and others. "A Measure of the Classroom
        Environment for Hearing-impaired Learners: The
        Development and Pilot of the Learning Environment Scale."
        American Annals of the Deaf 129(4): 355-61 (1984).

2601.   Schrader, William B. The Graduate Management Admission
        Test: Technical Report on Test Development and Score
        Interpretation for GMAT Users. ED 251 483 (Arlington, VA:
        ERIC, 1984).

2602.   Scott, Judith and John C. Brantley. "Development of an
        Inventory of Teachers' Attitudes Towards Sex-role
        Stereotyping and Knowledge of Sex Differences." Sex Roles
        9(3): 341-53 (1983).

2603.   Torardi, Mary Montag. The Development of a Computer
        Literacy Assessment Instrument. ED 256 342 (Arlington,
        VA: ERIC, 1985).

2604.   Treagust, David F. and Barry J. Fraser. Validity and Use
        of a Classroom Environment Instrument for Higher
        Education. ED 269 228 (Arlington, VA: ERIC, 1986).

2605. Waldman, David A. "Development of a Modified University Residence Environment Scale." Journal of College Student Personnel 26(1): 70-72 (1985).

2606. Wedman, John F. and Gregory P. Stefanich. "Guidelines for Computer-based Testing of Student Learning of Concepts, Principles, and Procedures." Educational Technology 24: 23-8 (June 1984).

2607. Wells, Kathleen M. The Development of a Critical Thinking Skills Performance Assessment: An Interdisciplinary Approach to Validating Achievement of School Goals. ED 229 424 (Arlington, VA: ERIC, 1983).

2608. Wolfgang, Charles H. and Pamela Phelps. "Preschool Play Materials Preference Inventory." Early Child Development and Care 12(2): 127-41 (1983).

Health and Physical Education

2609. Albert, Werner G. and Robert I. Simpson. "Test Construction Procedures for Evaluating Alcohol Education: The 'Decisions and Drinking' Program." International Journal of the Addictions 18(7): 1019-27 (1983).

2610. Brown, Idalyn S. "Development of a Scale to Measure Attitude Toward the Condom as a Method of Birth Control." Journal of Sex Research 20(3): 255-63 (1984).

2611. Colgan, Sharon M. "The Athletic Success Scale: A Theoretical Analysis, Construction, and Validation of a Measuring Instrument." Dissertation Abstracts International 46(7-B): 2445-46 (1986).

2612. Fabian, Lou and Marilyn Ross. "The Development of the Sports Competition Trait Inventory." Journal of Sport Behavior 7(1): 13-27 (1984).

2613. Grussing, Paul G. and others. "The Federal Drug Law Examination: Development, Performance, and Curricular Effects." American Journal of Pharmaceutical Education 47(1): 1-10 (1983).

2614. Olsen, Larry K., Ronald K. Hambleton and Robert Simon. "Development and Application of the Student Test Used in the School Health Education Evaluation." Journal of School Health 55: 309-15 (October 1985).

2615. Ruderman, Audrey J. and David J. McKirnan. "The Development of a Restrained Drinking Scale: A Test of the Abstinence Violation Effect Among Alcohol Users." Addictive Behaviors 9(4): 365-71 (1984).

2616. Smith, Marcia C. and Mark H. Thelen. "Development and Validation of a Test for Bulimia." Journal of Consulting & Clinical Psychology 52(5): 863-72 (1984).

2617. Torabi, Mohammad R. and John R. Seffrin. "A Three Component Cancer Attitude Scale." Journal of School Health 56: 170-4 (May 1986).

2618.   Veenker, C. H. and Mohammad R. Torabi. "A Three Component
        Alcohol Attitude Scale." Journal of School Health 54(5):
        204-7 (1984).

        Learning Disabilities

2619.   Abelseth-Lillienstein, Janet L. "The Development and
        Validation of a Scale to Measure the Social Competence of
        Mentally Retarded Persons." Dissertation Abstracts
        International 44(2-A): 430 (1983).

2620.   Das, J. P., Kar-La Schokman-Gates, and Deirdre Murphy.
        "Development of a Measure of Extraversion and Neuroticism
        for Mentally Retarded Persons." American Journal of
        Mental Deficiency 90(5): 540-49 (1986).

2621.   Dunlap, William C. "The Development and Validation of an
        Assessment Instrument for Use with the Deaf Blind: The
        Severely Handicapped Progress Inventory." Educational and
        Psychological Measurement 44(4): 1067-71 (1984).

2622.   Honan, Rita. "The Development of an Instrument to Assess
        Learned Helplessness in the Mentally Retarded."
        Dissertation Abstracts International 46(7-B): 2498
        (1986).

        Psychology

2623.   Abidin, Richard R. Parenting Stress Index: Manual,
        Administration Booklet (and) Research Update. ED 238 896
        (Arlington, VA: ERIC, 1983).

2624.   Adams, Russell L. and others. "Development of a Satz-
        Mogel Short Form of the WAIS-R." Journal of Consulting
        and Clinical Psychology 52(5): 908 (1984).

2625.   Aman, Michael G. and others. "The Aberrant Behavior
        Checklist: A Behavior Rating Scale for the Assessment of
        Treatment Effects." American Journal of Mental Deficiency
        89(5): 485-91 (1985).

2626.   Avison, William R. and others. "Screening for Problem
        Parenting: Preliminary Evidence on a Promising
        Instrument." Child Abuse and Neglect: The International
        Journal 10(2): 157-70 (1986).

2627.   Barratt, William R. "Interpersonal Power in Psychological
        Environments: The Development of an Instrument to Assess
        Five Bases of Interpersonal Power." Dissertation
        Abstracts International 44(8-A): 2356 (1984).

2628.   Beaber, Rex J., Albert Marston, Joe Michelli and Mark J.
        Mills. "A Brief Test for Measuring Malingering in
        Schizophrenic Individuals." American Journal of
        Psychiatry 142(12): 1478-81 (1985).

2629.   Beck, Niels C. and others. "Development and Cross-
        validation of a Short Form for the WAIS-R." Journal of
        Consulting and Clinical Psychology 51(6): 864-69 (1983).

2630. Beckham, Ernest E. and Russell L. Adams. "Coping Behavior in Depression: Report on a New Scale." Behaviour Research & Therapy 22(1): 71-75 (1984).

2631. Beitchman, Joseph H. and others. "The Development and Validation of the Children's Self-report Psychiatric Rating Scale." Journal of the American Academy of Child Psychiatry 24(4): 413-28 (1985).

2632. Bray, James H., Donald S. Williamson and Paul E. Malone. "Personal Authority in the Family System: Development of a Questionnaire to Measure Personal Authority in Intergenerational Family Processes." Journal of Marital & Family Therapy 10(2): 167-78 (1984).

2633. Breunlin, Douglas C. and others. "Evaluating Family Therapy Training: The Development of an Instrument." Journal of Marital and Family Therapy 9(1): 37-47 (1983).

2634. Brown, Steven D. and Dee A. Reimer. "Assessing Attachment Following Divorce: Development and Psychometric Evaluation of the Divorce Reaction Inventory." Journal of Counseling Psychology 31(4): 521-32 (1984).

2635. Carey, Michael P., Mary L. Kelley, Ray R. Buss and W. Owen Scott. "Relationship of Activity to Depression in Adolescents: Development of the Adolescent Activities Checklist." Journal of Consulting & Clinical Psychology 54(3): 320-22 (1986).

2636. Chambless, Dianne L. and others. "Assessment of Fear in Agoraphobics: The Body Sensations Questionnaire and the Agoraphobic Cognitions Questionnaire." Journal of Consulting and Clinical Psychology 52(6): 1090-97 (1984).

2637. Clarke, Margaret and Joseph Hornick. "The Development of the Nurturance Inventory: An Instrument for Assessing Parenting Practices." Child Psychiatry and Human Development 15: 49-63 (fall 1984).

2638. Cone, John D., David D. Delawyer and Vicky V. Wolfe. "Assessing Parent Participation: The Parent/Family Involvement Index." Exceptional Children 51: 417-24 (fall 1985).

2639. Dixon, Roger A. and David F. Hultsch. "The Metamemory in Adulthood (MIA) Instrument." Psychological Documents 14(1): 3; MS 2605 (1984).

2640. _____. "Structure and Development of Metamemory in Adulthood." Journal of Gerontology 38(6): 682-88 (1983).

2641. Fry, P. S. "Development of a Geriatric Scale of Hopelessness: Implications for Counseling and Intervention With the Depressed Elderly." Journal of Counseling Psychology 31(3): 322-31 (1984).

2642. Ishiyama, F. Ishu and David J. Chabassol. "Fear of Success Consequence Scale: Measurement of Fear of Social Consequences of Academic Success." Psychological Reports 54(2): 499-504 (1984).

2643. Keane, Terence M. and others. "Empirical Development of an MMPI Subscale for the Assessment of Combat-related Posttraumatic Stress Disorder." Journal of Consulting and Clinical Psychology 52(5): 888-91 (1984).

2644. Lerner, Phillip S. "The Development of a Self-report Inventory to Assess Obsessive Compulsive Behavior." Dissertation Abstracts International 43(9-B): 3034 (1983).

2645. Lewis, Bonnie Yegidis. "The Wife Abuse Inventory: A Screening Device for the Identification of Abused Women." Social Work 30(1): 32-5 (1985).

2646. Linehan, Marsha M. and others. "Reasons for Staying Alive When You Are Thinking of Killing Yourself: The Reasons for Living Inventory." Journal of Consulting and Clinical Psychology 51(2): 276-86 (1983).

2647. Lustman, Patrick J. and others. "Factors Influencing College Student Health: Development of the Psychological Distress Inventory." Journal of Counseling Psychology 31(1): 28-35 (1984).

2648. McCutcheon, Lynn E. "Development of the Psychological Facts on Aging Quiz." Community/Junior College Quarterly of Research and Practice 10(2): 123-29 (1986).

2649. Malgady, Robert G., Giuseppe Costantino and Lloyd H. Rogler. "Development of a Thematic Apperception Test (TEMAS) for Urban Hispanic Children." Journal of Consulting & Clinical Psychology 52(6): 986-96 (1984).

2650. Malouff, John. "Development and Validation of a Behavioral Peer-rating Measure of Depression." Journal of Consulting & Clinical Psychology 52(6): 1108-9 (1984).

2651. Mashal, Meeda M. "The Development and Validation of an Interrole Strain Questionnaire for Dual-worker Couples." Dissertation Abstracts International 46(1-B): 347 (1985).

2652. Matson, Johnny L., Anthony F. Rotatori and William J. Helsel. "Development of a Rating Scale to Measure Social Skills in Children: The Matson Evaluation of Social Skills With Youngsters (MESSY)." Behaviour Research & Therapy 21(4): 335-40 (1983).

2653. Motto, Jerome A., David C. Heilbron and Richard P. Juster. "Development of a Clinical Instrument to Estimate Suicide Risk." American Journal of Psychiatry 142(6): 680-86 (1985).

2654. O'Malley, Stephanie S. and others. "The Vanderbilt Psychotherapy Process Scale: A Report on the Scale Development and a Process-outcome Study." Journal of Consulting and Clinical Psychology 51(4): 581-86 (1983).

2655. Ownby, Raymond L. Development of a Scale to Assess Attention Deficit Disorder in Children. ED 236 881 (Arlington, VA: ERIC, 1983).

2656. Raulin, Michael L. and Jennifer L. Wee. "The Development
       and Initial Validation of a Scale to Measure Social
       Fear." Journal of Clinical Psychology 40(3): 780-84
       (1984).

2657. Singer, Sandra and others. "Development and Validation of
       a Test Battery to Measure Differentiated Cognitive
       Abilities in Three-Year-Old Children." Educational and
       Psychological Measurement 44(3): 703-13 (1984).

2658. Smith, Pauline. "Application of the Information
       Processing Approach to the Design of a Non-verbal
       Reasoning Test." The British Journal of Educational
       Psychology 56: 119-37 (1986).

2659. Stiffman, Arlene R. and others. "A Brief Measure of
       Children's Behavior Problems: The Behavior Rating Index
       for Children." Measurement & Evaluation in Counseling &
       Development 17(2): 83-90 (1984).

2660. Wagner, Mark S. "Construction and Validation of the ABC
       Parenting Self Perception Scale." Dissertation Abstracts
       International 45(1-A): 158 (1984).

2661. Wasserman, Theodore H. "Development of the Children's
       Dysfunctional Cognition Scale." Child and Family Behavior
       Therapy 5(4): 17-24 (1983).

2662. Work, William C. "The Development and Validation of a
       Scale for Measuring Social Competence in Young Children."
       Dissertation Abstracts International 45(5-B): 1604
       (1984).

2663. Zemore, Robert. "Development of a Self-report Measure of
       Depression-proneness." Psychological Reports 52(1): 211-
       16 (1983).

PERSONALITY

2664. Baker, Earl H. "The Development and Validation of the
       Student Personality Assessment Form." Dissertation
       Abstracts International 45(11-B): 3638 (1985).

2665. Barbery, Madeline. "The Development and Initial Construct
       Validation of the Women's Attitudes Toward Careers
       Scale." Dissertation Abstracts International 43(12-A):
       3883 (1983).

2666. Beere, Carole A., Daniel W. King, Donald B. Beere and
       Lynda A. King. "The Sex-role Egalitarianism Scale: A
       Measure of Attitudes Toward Equality Between the Sexes."
       Sex Roles 10(7-8): 563-76 (1984).

2667. Berrenberg, Joy L. "Development of a Multidimensional
       Measure of Belief in Personal Control." Dissertation
       Abstracts International 43(7-B): 2386 (1983).

2668. Bowd, Alan D. "Development and Validation of a Scale of
       Attitudes Toward the Treatment of Animals." Educational &
       Psychological Measurement 44(2): 513-15 (1984).

2669. Boyle, Gregory J. "Critical Review of State-trait
       Curiosity Test Development." Motivation & Emotion 7(4):
       377-97 (1983).

2670. Broughton, Ross. "A Prototype Strategy for Construction
       of Personality Scales." Journal of Personality & Social
       Psychology 47(6): 1334-46 (1984).

2671. Brown, George S. "Development of an Objectively Scorable
       Nonverbal Personality Measure." Dissertation Abstracts
       International 45(11-A): 3331 (1985).

2672. Carey, John C., Dinah L. Hamilton and Garth Shanklin.
       "Development of an Instrument to Measure Rapport Between
       College Roommates." Journal of College Student Personnel
       27: 269-73 (May 1986).

2673. Carp, Frances M. and Abraham Carp. "Structural Stability
       of Well-being Factors Across Age and Gender, and
       Development of Scales of Well-being Unbiased for Age and
       Gender." Journal of Gerontology 38(5): 572-81 (1983).

2674. Collins, Clare E. "The Development of an Instrument to
       Measure Coping Responses in Working Mothers."
       Dissertation Abstracts International 44(2-A): 385 (1983).

2675. Connell, James P. "A New Multidimensional Measure of
       Children's Perceptions of Control." Child Development
       56(4): 1018-41 (1985).

2676. DeJong-Gierveld, Jenny and Frans Kamphuis. "The
       Development of a Rasch-type Loneliness Scale." Applied
       Psychological Measurement 9(3): 289-99 (1985).

2677. Deutsch, Diane K. "The Development, Reliability, and
       Validity of an Instrument Designed to Measure Grief."
       Dissertation Abstracts International 43(12-A): 3844
       (1983).

2678. Dise-Lewis, Jeanne E. "The Assessment of Stress in
       Children: Development of the Life Events and Coping
       Inventory." Dissertation Abstracts International 45(2-B):
       667 (1984).

2679. Duttweiler, Patricia C. "The Internal Control Index: A
       Newly Developed Measure of Locus of Control." Educational
       & Psychological Measurement 44(2): 209-21 (1984).

2680. Falbo, Toni and Sharyn S. Belk. An Instrument to Measure
       Self-righteousness. ED 237 872 (Arlington, VA: ERIC,
       1983).

2681. Farmer, Helen S. "Development of a Measure of Home-career
       Conflict Related to Career Motivation in College Women."
       Sex Roles 10(9-10): 663-75 (1984).

2682. Farmer, Richard and Norman D. Sundberg. "Boredom
       Proneness: The Development and Correlates of a New
       Scale." Journal of Personality Assessment 50(1): 4-17
       (1986).

2683. Friedman, Barry R. "Development and Validation of a Multidimensional Scale for the Assessment of the Need for Power." Dissertation Abstracts International 45(2-A): 498-99 (1984).

2684. Gaffney, Lisa R. "A Multiple-choice Test to Measure Social Skills in Delinquent and Nondelinquent Adolescent Girls." Journal of Consulting & Clinical Psychology 52(5): 911-12 (1984).

2685. Gapinski, Marianne P. "The Construction of Internally Consistent Content Subscales for the Minnesota Multiphasic Personality Inventory." Dissertation Abstracts International 44(6-B): 1959 (1983).

2686. Gibbs, John C. and others. "Construction and Validation of a Multiple-choice Measure of Moral Reasoning." Child Development 55(2): 527-36 (1984).

2687. Goldfarb, Lori A., Elisabeth M. Dykens and Meg Gerrard. "The Goldfarb Fear of Fat Scale." Journal of Personality Assessment 49(3): 329-32 (1985).

2688. Halpern, Harris S. "Development and Construct Validation of a Multidimensional Scale of Attitudes Toward Homosexuality." Dissertation Abstracts International 45(8-B): 2732 (1985).

2689. Hasenstab, Kathleen M. "Development of Activities and an Instrument to Measure Attitudes of Respect in Elementary Students." Dissertation Abstracts International 43(7-A): 2231 (1983).

2690. Heerboth, Joel R. "Development and Validation of an Irrational Beliefs Inventory." Dissertation Abstracts International 45(8-B): 2688 (1985).

2691. Herzberger, Sharon D., Esther Chan and Judith Katz. "The Development of an Assertiveness Self-report Inventory." Journal of Personality Assessment 48(3): 317-23 (1984).

2692. Ho, Robert and Jacqueline I. Lloyd. "Development of an Australian Work Ethic Scale." Australian Psychologist 19(3): 321-32 (1984).

2693. Iazzo, Anthony N. "The Construction and Validation of Attitudes Toward Men Scale." Psychological Record 33(3): 371-78 (1983).

2694. Jensen, Mary A. "Development of a Preschool Self-concept Scale." Early Child Development and Care 22(2-3): 89-107 (1985).

2695. Juhasz, Anne M. "Measuring Self-esteem in Early Adolescents." Adolescence 20(80): 877-87 (1985).

2696. Kurtines, William and June B. Pimm. "The Moral Development Scale: A Piagetian Measure of Moral Judgment." Educational & Psychological Measurement 43(1): 89-105 (1983).

2697. Larsen, Knud S. "Attitudes Toward Nuclear Disarmament and Their Correlates." Journal of Social Psychology 125(1): 17-21 (1985).

2698. Lewis, Bonnie Y. "The Development and Initial Validation of the Wife Abuse Inventory." Dissertation Abstracts International 44(9-A): 2742 (1984).

2699. Mathews, Walter M. and Abraham W. Wolf. Measuring Attitude Toward Computers: The Computer Appreciator-critic Attitude Scales. ED 231 886 (Arlington, VA: ERIC, 1983).

2700. Maurer, Matthew M. and Michael R. Simonson. Development and Validation of a Measure of Computer Anxiety. ED 243 428 (Arlington, VA: ERIC, 1984).

2701. Ollendick, Thomas H. "Development and Validation of the Children's Assertiveness Inventory." Child & Family Behavior Therapy 5(3): 1-15 (1983).

2702. Paludi, Michele A., Debra Geschke and Melanie Smith. "The Development of a Measure of Preschoolers' Knowledge of Sex-determined Role Standards." Child Study Journal 14(3): 171-83 (1984).

2703. Plotkin, Lori S. "A Study of Personality and the Parent-adolescent Relationship: The Development of the Parent-adolescent Relationship Survey." Dissertation Abstracts International 46(9-B): 3255-56 (1986).

2704. Plunkett, James W., Barbara Riemer, Neil Kalter and Dana Alpern. "Parents' Beliefs About Children's Reactions to Divorce: The Development of an Assessment Instrument." Journal of the American Academy of Child Psychiatry 24(3): 334-37 (1985).

2705. Powell, Jack L. and Alice G. Brand. The Development of an Emotions Scale for Writers. ED 268 152 (Arlington, VA: ERIC, 1986).

2706. Raulin, Michael L. "Development of a Scale to Measure Intense Ambivalence." Journal of Consulting & Clinical Psychology 52(1): 63-72 (1984).

2707. Ray, John J. "A Scale to Measure Conservatism of American Public Opinion." Journal of Social Psychology 119(2): 293-94 (1983).

2708. Reker, Gary T. and Paul T. P. Wong. "Psychological and Physical Well-being in the Elderly: The Perceived Well-being Scale (PWB)." Canadian Journal on Aging 3(1): 23-32 (1984).

2709. Robison, Floyd F. "Construction of an Instrument to Measure Risk Taking Inclination Among Elderly Men and Women." Dissertation Abstracts International 43(8-A): 2610 (1983).

2710. Schatz, Eleanor M. and Lynn R. Buckmaster. "Development of an Instrument to Measure Self-actualizing Growth in

Preadolescents." The Journal of Creative Behavior 18(4): 263-72 (1984).

2711. Scheier, Michael F. and Charles S. Carver. "The Self-consciousness Scale: A Revised Version for Use With General Populations." Journal of Applied Social Psychology 15(8): 687-99 (1985).

2712. Schmidt, Nancy and Vello Sermat. "Measuring Loneliness in Different Relationships." Journal of Personality & Social Psychology 44(5): 1038-47 (1983).

2713. Schroeder, Mary A. "Development and Testing of a Scale to Measure Locus of Control Prior to and Following Childbirth." Maternal-Child Nursing Journal 14(2): 111-21 (1985).

2714. Seyfarth, Leonard H. and others. "Attitude Toward Evangelism: Scale Development and Validity." Journal of Social Psychology 123(1): 55-61 (1984).

2715. Snyder, Gary R. "The Development of an Assertiveness Measure." Dissertation Abstracts International 46(6-B): 2119 (1985).

2716. Steele, Cam Monroe and N. L. Reinsch Jr. Measuring Telephone Apprehension. ED 233 407 (Arlington, VA: ERIC, 1983).

2717. Stolberg, Arnold L. and Ann J. Ullman. "Assessing Dimensions of Single Parenting: The Single Parenting Questionnaire." Journal of Divorce 8(2): 31-45 (1984).

2718. Streiner, David L. and Harold R. Miller. "Can a Good Short Form of the MMPI Ever Be Developed?" Journal of Clinical Psychology 42(1): 109-13 (1986).

2719. Thomas, Immanuel and H. Sam Raj. "Measurement of Self-esteem: An Inventory for Secondary School Pupils." Psychological Studies 29(1): 29-33 (1984).

2720. Tobacyk, Jerome and Gary Milford. "Belief in Paranormal Phenomena: Assessment Instrument Development and Implications for Personality Functioning." Journal of Personality & Social Psychology 44(5): 1029-37 (1983).

2721. Toris, Carol. Suggested Approaches to the Measurement of Computer Anxiety. ED 254 540 (Arlington, VA: ERIC, 1984).

2722. Wise, Steven L. "The Development and Validation of a Scale Measuring Attitudes Toward Statistics." Educational & Psychological Measurement 45(2): 401-5 (1985).

2723. Yamauchi, Kent T. "The Construction and Validation of a Money Attitude Scale." Dissertation Abstracts International 45(3-B): 1035 (1984).

READING

2724. Baldasare, John, Gale R. Watson and Stephen G. Whittaker.

"The Development and Evaluation of a Reading Test for Low Vision Individuals With Macular Loss (Pepper Visual Skills for Reading Test)." <u>Journal of Visual Impairment & Blindness</u> 80: 785-9 (June 1986).

2725.   Dole, Janice A., Steven A. Harvey and Virginia S. Feldman. "The Development and Validation of a Listening Comprehension Test as a Predictor of Reading Comprehension: Preliminary Results." <u>Educational Research Quarterly</u> 9(4): 40-46 (1984-85).

2726.   Kirsch, Irwin S. and John T. Guthrie. "Adult Reading Practices for Work and Leisure (Development of Reading Activity Inventory)." <u>Adult Education Quarterly</u> 34: 213-32 (summer 1984).

2727.   Lyman, Barbara Gallow. <u>The Construction of a Criterion-referenced Test of Reading for College Freshmen: An Overview of Theoretical Considerations</u>. ED 251 804 (Arlington, VA: ERIC, 1983).

2728.   Rose, Janet S. and William C. Gustin. <u>Elementary/Middle School Reading Comprehension vs. High School Mathematics: Two Different Approaches to CRT Development</u>. ED 269 479 (Arlington, VA: ERIC, 1986).

2729.   Wixson, Staton E. "The Test of Early Reading Ability (TERA)." <u>Reading Teacher</u> 38(6): 544-47 (1985).

SCIENCE

2730.   Bunting, Trudi E. and Lawrence R. Cousins. "Environmental Personality in School-age Children: Development and Application of the 'Children's Environmental Response Inventory.'" <u>Journal of Environmental Education</u> 15(1): 3-10 (1983).

2731.   Chin, Jack. <u>The Development of an Instrument for Evaluating the Effects of an Environmental Education Program on Young Children's Environmental Attitudes: A Pilot Study</u>. ED 257 683 (Arlington, VA: ERIC, 1985).

2732.   Donovan, Edward P. and others. "A New Science and Engineering Career Interest Survey for Middle School Students." <u>Journal of Research in Science Teaching</u> 22(1): 19-30 (1985).

2733.   Ellis, James D. and Paul J. Kuerbis. <u>The Development of a Test of Computer Literacy for Science Teachers in Grades K-12</u>. ED 266 952 (Arlington, VA: ERIC, 1986).

2734.   Hale, Michael E. and others. "Using Computer Animation in Science Testing." <u>Computers in the Schools</u> 2(1): 83-90 (1985). See ED 248 111 for related information.

2735.   Harty, Harold and Dwight Beall. "Toward the Development of a Children's Science Curiosity Measure." <u>Journal of Research in Science Teaching</u> 21(4): 425-36 (1984).

2736.   Hassan, Abdel Moneim Ahmed and Robert L. Shrigley.

"Designing a Likert Scale to Measure Chemistry Attitudes." School Science and Mathematics 84: 659-69 (December 1984).

2737. Hodson, Derek. "The Effect of Changes in Item Sequence on Student Performance in a Multiple-choice Chemistry Test." Journal of Research in Science Teaching 21: 489-95 (May 1984).

2738. Koballa, Thomas R. "Designing a Likert-type Scale To Assess Attitude Toward Energy Conservation: A Nine Step Process." Journal of Research in Science Teaching 21(7): 709-23 (1984).

2739. McInerney, Joseph D. and Barbara Schulz. "The Biology Test is Coming (Developed by the National Science Teachers Association and the National Association of Biology Teachers)." The Science Teacher 53: 44-5 (March 1986).

2740. Rideng, I. Made and R. A. Schibeci. "The Development and Validation of a Test of Biology-related Attitudes." Research in Science & Technological Education 2(1): 21-29 (1984).

2741. Texley, Juliana T. and John Norman. "The Development of a Group Test of Formal Operational Logic in the Content Area of Environmental Science." Journal of Research in Science Teaching 21: 589-97 (September 1984).

SOCIAL STUDIES

   Economics

2742. O'Brien, Mary Utne and Steven J. Ingels. The Development of the Economics Values Inventory. Report to the Foundation for Teaching Economics. ED 250 243 (Arlington, VA: ERIC, 1984).

2743. Whitehead, David J. The Development and Testing of an Economics Attitude Scale. Research Papers in Economics Education. ED 257 769 (Arlington, VA: ERIC, 1985).

VOCATIONS

2744. Archer, Edith L. and Harry Leverette. Development and Administration of an Employee Competence Test. ED 262 058 (Arlington, VA: ERIC, 1985).

2745. Berger, Peter M. "Occupational Needs Questionnaire: An Instrument to Measure Job Satisfaction." Dissertation Abstracts International 45(4-B): 1310-11 (1984).

2746. Butcke, Pamela and others. "Measuring Occupational Stress Among Counselors: A Multidimensional Concept." Measurement and Evaluation in Guidance 17(1): 24-31 (1984).

2747. Cantor, Jeffrey A. and Edward N. Hobson. The Development of a Model for Construction of Criterion Referenced System Achievement Tests for the Strategic Weapon System Training Program. ED 268 178 (Arlington, VA: ERIC, 1986).

2748. Clark, Diane J. "A Model and Example of the Construction of Criterion-referenced Employee Selection Tests." Dissertation Abstracts International 46(5-B): 1726 (1985).

2749. Coscarelli, William C. "Development of a Decision-making Inventory to Assess Johnson's Decision-making Styles." Measurement & Evaluation in Guidance 16(3): 149-60 (1983).

2750. Fimian, Michael J. "The Development of an Instrument to Measure Occupational Stress in Teachers of Exceptional Students." Techniques 1(4): 270-85 (1985).

2751. _____. "The Development of an Instrument to Measure Occupational Stress in Teachers: The Teacher Stress Inventory." Journal of Occupational Psychology 57(4): 277-93 (1984).

2752. Friedlander, Myrna L. and Linda G. Ward. "Development and Validation of the Supervisory Styles Inventory." Journal of Counseling Psychology 31(4): 542-58 (1984).

2753. Grussing, Paul G. and others. "Development of Pharmacy's First Specialty Certification Examination: Nuclear Pharmacy." American Journal of Pharmaceutical Education 47(1): 11-18 (1983).

2754. Johnson, Kenneth A. Designing and Implementing an Ergonomics Inventory to Improve Management of Human Factors Programs. ED 247 400 (Arlington, VA: ERIC, 1984).

2755. Komaki, Judith L., Stacey Zlotnick and Marjane Jensen. "Development of an Operant-based Taxonomy and Observational Index of Supervisory Behavior." Journal of Applied Psychology 71(2): 260-69 (1986).

2756. Lanning, Wayne. "Development of the Supervisor Emphasis Rating Form." Counselor Education and Supervision 25(3): 191-96 (1986).

2757. Manuele, Caroline A. "The Development of a Measure to Assess Vocational Maturity in Adults with Delayed Career Development." Journal of Vocational Behavior 23(1): 45-63 (1983).

2758. Pray, W. Stephen and Nicholas G. Popovich. "The Development of a Standardized Competency Examination for Doctor of Pharmacy Students." American Journal of Pharmaceutical Education 49(1): 1-9 (1985).

2759. Stanton, Marietta P. Huben. "Objective Test Construction -- A Must for Nursing Educators." Journal of Nursing Education 22: 338-9 (October 1983).

Author Index

Aaron, Robert L., 1977
Abbatiello, Aurelius, 2442
Abbott, Robert D., 1174
Abeles, Harold F., 1, 872
Abelseth-Lillienstein, Janet L., 2619
Abidin, Richard R., 2623
Abraham, Eugene C., 2152
Abrahamson, R. E., 1716
Abramson, Theodore, 2
Achenback, Thomas N., 1520
Acker, S. R., 2065
Adair, Jane D., 2211
Adams, Arthur R. Jr., 2212
Adams, Gary L., 2573
Adams, Russell L., 2624, 2630
Adkins, Arthur, 3
Adkins, Dorothy C., 716, 1717, 1718
Agrawal, K. C., 896
Ahluwalia, S. P., 2586
Ahmann, J. S., 4
Aiken, Lewis R., 5, 717
Aikenhead, Glen S., 6, 7, 8, 9, 10
Aitken, Kenneth G., 897, 898, 899
Akamine, Toshio, 2398
Alban-Metcalfe, Robert J., 1719
Albert, Werner G., 2609
Albrecht, James E., 11
Aleamoni, Lawrence M., 12, 13
Alfici, C., 2459
Ali-Haik, Antoine R., 928
Allen, Dwight W., 14, 15
Allen, Jon G., 1720
Allen, R. R., 1001

Allen, Russell, 1653
Allen, Ted W., 2443
Alley, Patricia M., 2564
Alley, William E., 2399
Allison, Howard K., 16
Almgren, Eva, 1721
Al-Nassri, Sabah, 1300
Aloia, G. F., 1444
Aloia, S. D., 1444
Alper, T. G., 1722
Alpern, Dana, 2704
Alpern, Gerald D., 1038
Alpern, Mildred, 2245
Als, Heidelise, 1495
Alspaugh, John W., 1645
Altekruse, Michael K., 1498
Althoff, Michael E., 1374
Alvidres, Maria D., 718
Alvir, Howard P., 17, 18, 19
Aman, Michael G., 2625
Amend, J. R., 20
American Psychological Association, 21
Ames, Russell, 1723
Ammerman, Harry L., 2288
Amruthraj, Brunda, 2565
Anastasi, Anne, 22
Anastasio, Ernest J., 23, 264
Andersen, H. O., 2159
Anderson, Barbara J., 1375
Anderson, Carolyn C., 2083
Anderson, Elaine J., 2099
Anderson, Jo Craig, 1042
Anderson, Jonathan, 2033
Anderson, L. W., 1724
Anderson, Lorin W., 1042
Anderson, Norman H., 24
Anderson, Ora S., 1725
Anderson, Richard C., 719

Gaudia, Gil, 1013
Gavin, Anne T., 2328
Geis, Lynna, 796, 797, 806
Geisinger, Kurt F., 270
Gellman, Estelle, 1369
Gentry, Larry A., 851
George, Archie A., 1809, 1826
George, Carolyn S., 1810
George, K. D., 2146
Geppert, William J., 1081
Gerberich, J. Raymond, 752
Gerrard, Meg, 2687
Gerst, Marvin S., 1110
Geschke, Debra, 2702
Gesten, Ellis L., 1393
Gewirtz, Agatha, 961
Ghatala, Elizabeth S., 271
Gheoreghiu, V. A., 1531
Gibbs, J. C., 1811
Gibbs, John C., 1532, 2686
Gibson, Dennis L., 2450
Gibson, James L., 1812
Gibson, Susanne K., 852
Gies, Frederick John, 1645
Gifford, Janice A., 272
Giguere, Constance L., 1813
Gilbert, Lucia A., 1646
Gillan, Robert E., 1254
Gillmore, Gerald M., 273
Gioe, Adrienne, 1533
Gipps, Caroline, 962
Gitomer, Nancy L., 1379
Gitter, A. George, 1534
Glaser, Robert, 753
Glasnapp, Douglas R., 498, 516
Gleser, G., 1535
Gliksman, L., 1394
Glock, M. D., 4
Glover, Michael, 2010
Gnidziejko, Robert, 2354
Godfrey, Richard R., 687
Goehring, Harvey J. Jr., 1255
Goh, David S., 1014
Goheen, Howard W., 274
Goldberg, Carlos, 1814
Golden, Charles J., 1815
Goldenberg, D. S., 1466
Goldfarb, Lori A., 2687
Goldman, R., 2284
Goldstein, Harris K., 2329
Golmon, Melton E., 1256
Golub, Lester S., 807
Gonda, Judith, 1015
Goodman, John O., 1448
Goodman, Marvin, 1457
Goodwin, Coleen Rawson, 808
Goolsby, Thomas M. Jr., 1257
Gorder, Wayne Douglas, 878

Gordon, Belita, 2011
Gordon, Leonard V., 1816
Gordon, S. E., 1258
Gorth, W., 275
Gorth, William Phillip, 15, 276, 312, 598, 1667, 1668, 2330
Gotz, K. O., 2204
Gough, Harrison G., 1395
Gould, R. Bruce, 277, 2331
Gourgey, Annette F., 1052
Graham, Darol L., 278
Graham, Glenn T., 740
Graham, Norman, 809
Graham, P. J., 1605
Grasha, Anthony F., 1606
Grass, Stephen, 2
Grate, John H., 1697
Graw, P., 1553
Gray, Anne, 2267
Gray, David B., 1817
Gray, H. Dean, 2332
Gray, William M., 279, 280, 281, 282
Grayson, A., 275
Greaney, Vincent, 1669
Greco, Victor T., 1474
Green, Bert F., 283
Green, Donald Ross, 284, 285, 286, 582, 583
Green, Margaret E., 1259
Green, Molly A., 1169, 1170, 1171
Green, Russel F., 1016
Green, Samuel B., 287
Greenan, James P., 2562
Greenberg, H. M., 1818
Greenberg, Lydia, 1670
Greenberger, Ellen 1819, 1853
Greene, John F., 1820, 1976
Greene, Michael B., 1260
Greenwald, Anthony G., 1753
Greeson, Richard J., 1536
Grether, Craig Blaine, 2271
Gribbin, Kathy, 1030
Grice, H. H., 1821
Griffin, Peg, 2012
Griggs, Mildred Barnes, 634
Grisay, A., 2090
Grise, Philip, 1458
Grissom, Stephen, 1763
Gristle, M., 1822
Griswold, George H., 288
Grohsmeyer, Frederick, 1111
Gronlund, Norman E., 289, 290, 754, 755
Grosek, Robert J., 1537
Gross, Linda C., 2484
Gross, Ruth B., 1538
Grossman, Jack H., 1261

Subject Index

About the Compiler

NANCY PATRICIA O'BRIEN is Associate Professor of Library Administration at the University of Illinois at Urbana-Champaign.